The Last Pretty Lake in New Jersey: Cedar Lake

By John Stibravy, Ph.D.

Edited by Tony Smith, Ph.D. and Becky Gingras, D.P.A.

A picture of Cedar Lake (located 35 miles west of Manhattan), where geese still fly and bass still nibble.

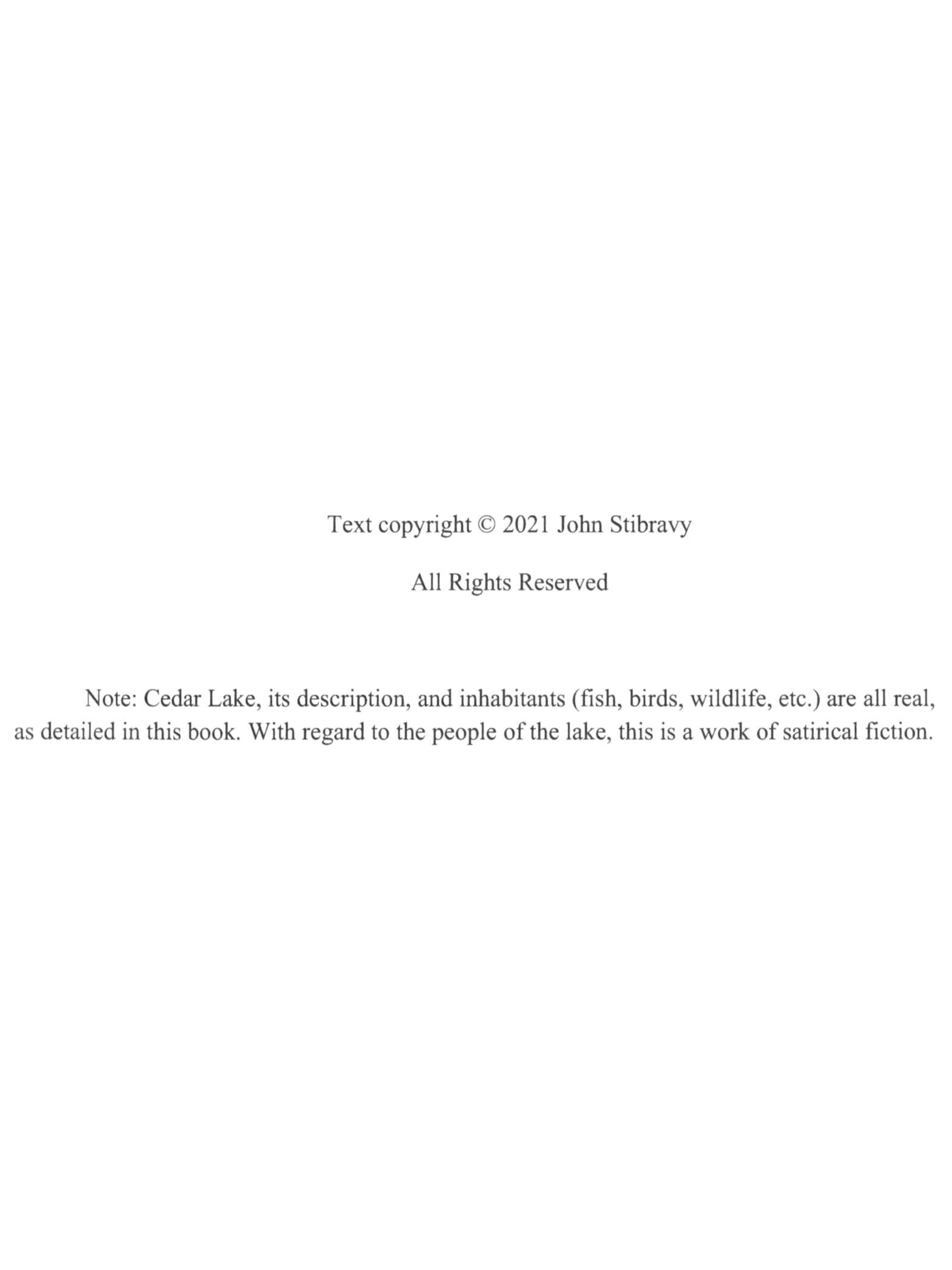

Note: Cedar Lake, its description, and inhabitants (fish, birds, wildlife, etc.) are all real, as detailed in this book. With regard to the people of the lake, this is a work of satirical fiction.

Table of Contents

Acknowledgements

The history of the lake was generally composed from the writings of Charles M. Toelaer, specifically *Bridging the Years In Denville* and *Reflections of Denville*. Charles' sources consisted of The Denville Public Library, The Morris County Public Library, and the Denville Historical Society. Product names are trademarks of respective companies.

Original manuscript transcribed by Hady Wolfe Transcription and Typing of Redlands, California.

Thanks to everyone for their help!

Preface

When I was at Mass in June 1993, an angel whispered to me to write a book about the lake that I lived on. So, here it is. Perhaps this book is why I survived sudden cardiac arrest in 2017 after being dead for 40 minutes. I started this book in 1994 and set it aside awaiting improvement. After 26 years, it has improved.

When I was young, life on the lake was very, very different from life there today. You may be appalled at some of the actions from back then, but that's how life was. The only heat in our lakeside cabin was a granite rock fireplace, an old hot water heater that vented into the kitchen, and a green, rusty propane stove. Replacement propane tanks were $20. Eventually, we had modern electric blankets. Laundry was done using a plunger and a scrub board in the bathtub with a single paned glass window above it. Clothes were hung on a rope line held up by pole supports, a pole with a "V" in the end, using round-headed clothes pins. The front porch was screens only, tilted so the rain water would run away from the house. Big four-feet-long roll up wooden blinds with guide ropes fastened to the floors were designed to keep rain out, but in a thunderstorm the rain squirted through the spaces between the blind slates. Milk came from the Alderney Dairy on Route 10 at 202. The glass bottles of milk with cream on top under a paper tab were delivered to the cabin by the milkman driving a brown delivery truck with a rounded front and cursive white lettering. The milk was left inside a wood and wire open-top box by the kitchen door.

The town was different too. Gone in addition to the dairy are the Hub bar, the Dairy Queen, the post office on Bloomfield Ave, and the uptown library. The biggest loss of all was the Denville Shack on Route 46. Missing is the aluminum post in the center of Morris Ave. at Diamond Spring Rd. that indicated cars should stop. I remember Pocono Road when that barn with stores in it really was a barn, and the medical building did not exist. The mall out on I-80 used to be a small strip mall surrounded by fields. I remember the original owner at the Denville Hardware, and the old couple at Peer's Store back when it was a store, though mostly empty inside.

The people in this book whom I knew in 1954 have mostly gone somewhere away across the water, vanishing into the morning fog. A few people are still around, in their 80s as of 2021, and they may remember what life was like back then.

Up until 2000, I used Dallas's old wooden rowboat from which he caught the huge pickerel in 1959. It was laid up on flower pots on the shore in 2000, and then dry rotted by 2010. The final time it was on the water was in October 1999, before the big Y2K scare. The trees have since grown up between the boat and the water, as shown in the pic below. The mounted fish now hangs over the clubhouse bar.

A Note for Students and Aspiring Writers

People often wish to know where an author's style came from. What is his audience and what are its expectations? How was the novel created? For those interested, I will tell you how this book came to be.

The first draft was written in 1994 on a MAC 512, the second word processor I owned. Its forerunner was a MAC 125 that I wrote on in 1985. The printer was a dot matrix. Connected paper came out of a box and around the roller using a tractor feed system. Individual sheets had to be torn apart to separate the pages. The sides of each sheet where the feed holes were had to be torn off also. Considering that I typed my graduate work on an IBM Selectric typewriter in 1984, the MAC was a fantastic improvement. Those early MACs had a huge following of devotees and were all the rage. The first word processor at my office was a CPT unit which used an eight-inch black floppy disk that really was floppy. Anyone remember those disks?

In drafting the novel, I was not particularly happy with the character sketches. Many of them were not only ironic or satirical, but bitter. I wasn't sure about the usefulness of the lake's history, or whether readers would enjoy the details of the fish and wildlife. I contemplated a two volume set but as the novel developed, the better choice for unity was one novel. The novel sat in a box in a closet for 26 years. I restarted it early in 2020. I was influenced by people to let it gather strength for a while, and also to return to it in order to finish it. To those people I say, "Thank you for your wisdom."

I had faith that the angel who told me to write about the lake where I had grown up spoke the truth. It was a place to which I had always come home. The details in the book about life on the lake could only be written by someone who had lived those experiences such as fishing at 5 a.m., or cleaning fish at 10 p.m. outside by a living room floor lamp with bugs everywhere. There had been no book about the lake that I knew about since the death of Charles M. Toelaer, who wrote the history of the area's lakes. I also knew that many of the lake details about life there in the 1950s and 1960s would never be written unless I persevered. I was sure that people living in the area would be interested in reading about a style of living now mostly gone due to technology. I remember that we had a TV antenna on top of the cabin for New York City and northeastern New Jersey station reception. Our channels were 2, 4, 5, 7, 9, 11, and 13. There was no cable. A sign nailed to the garage offered a reward of $25 for the identity of anyone damaging private property. Laundry was hand-washed and hung on a line to dry.

As far as writings which influenced my style, the list is varied. *Under Milkwood*, *Walden*, *The Loved One*, *Bleak House*, *The Wind in the Willows*, *Time and Again*, and *Rabbit Hill* were the primary influences. Two which stand out as especially influential are *Time and Again* about going back to the late 1800s in New York City, and *Rabbit Hill* about the animals. As a writing student, I was repeatedly told to show the details. Exactly how was a pickerel cleaned? How did one catch a crayfish or frog? How could one catch pickerel in shallow water? These details bring a locale to life. Fortunately, I've either seen or done the activities discussed in this book.

Of the character sketches, the final one, "Beth," I found to be the most moving, and it has had numerous revisions. Each word was reviewed. On one hand, Beth, a modern commuter, travels between the lake and Washington, DC. She hates her condo there and the flight. In contrast, Beth comes alive when back on the lake, which is her natural habitat. There, she joins with nature to find peace while floating along in the canoe during rain.

I am sure students will discover more substance in this book about writing, style, and meaning. A good writer chooses every word with care. But for now, I believe I will go watch the lake move in the moonlight, and wish you success in your endeavors. If some task is worth the sacrifice, then make those sacrifices willingly. Put more directly, I urge you to finish the degree for which you enrolled. Don't ever surrender your goals without strong justification. When I was in graduate school, I commuted to classes 140 miles round trip on I-25 two nights a week, and every weekend was spent on assignments. I did that pace for three years. Most goals can be achieved if one is willing to devote the time and effort needed to succeed. So don't give up too easily.

Why did I finish this novel after 25 years? With no warning, I had sudden cardiac arrest in December 2017 and was dead for 40 minutes. It took two years to fully find my brain again. That incident persuaded me that the time had arrived to finish this novel. So, here it is.

--John Stibravy, 11/1/2020

Chapter 1: We Meet the Lake

There were those lake people who grew up and left the lake, and there were those who graduated from high school and stayed behind. I was one who stayed behind. For almost 70 years, I watched people of my generation move away to new careers, families, military life, warm sand, and hot breezes. But memories of them did not leave. I and a few others kept those memories alive and remained where we were raised.

The houses and places on the lake are still identified by their former owners. The Haire mansion, Mellissa's cabin, Ann and Demilt's house. Margaret and Dallas' house, the Ruppel house, Wayne's place, Oakers' boat. The Koester place, the Schulan house, the Girard house, the Kloepher estate, the house in which Susan lived. Greenview, the Leonard house, Grace's home, the Taminsky house, Foley's home. Many of the homes had the owners' names forged into an iron sign which still hung on a post by the water long after that owner was gone.

The past can be replayed over and over with no fear of change. The people and pets stored in one's memory will never age. Their lives and loves are frozen into a portrait and displayed on a portrait wall which can be looked at whenever one wishes to feel a sense of continuity and permanence. It's very reassuring. A happy memory will be forever static. People never leave, never break up, never age. The past is a safe place in which one's mind can survive. One can let the good times roll over and over for the rest of one's life. Carry on imaginary conversations, make a pretend rendezvous, imagine a happy future.

There was a time in the summer evenings when, after supper, the lake was crowded with fishing rowboats. Children learning to fish, serious elders fishing in the lily pads, couples chatting, with the bait in the water beneath a red and white bobber. Now, there are only one or two fishing boats on the water after supper. In the 1950s, the docks used to be crowded with neighbors watching the sunset over the mountain. Now, the docks are empty after supper. Everyone is inside, playing video games or watching TV.

When I was young, serious fishers cast into dark waters before sunrise. Each boat had usually one fisherman in it, but the boats formed a community out there in the morning fog. Old men – their children moved away – who fished as they had with their grandfathers because they had always fished. Now, often I am in the last remaining boat, fishing along the big island at the north end, a thermos of lukewarm coffee and a cheese sandwich for breakfast, the crumbs falling into the wet spider webs in the corners of the boat.

When I go to town, I see it as it was in 1955. I see the one screen theater playing an Elvis movie, the Texaco station where the gas jockey would check the oil and tires, the coal yard past the railroad tracks, the Phoebe Snow thundering past the station that forty years later burnt down. I see the people I used to know. The owner of the hardware store, the old barber with the razor strop on the chair, two bits for a haircut. The Italian couple at the fruit stand on Route 53. The man in the donut bus, dusted in flour, who gave free donuts to the kids. The Denville Shack, the Hub bar, the library in town, the post office on Bloomfield Ave. It's all there, just as it was.

At midnight in winter, by the fire in the granite fireplace, oil lamps lit, all is quiet as the snow falls. I picture all of the lake people I knew in their homes, asleep in their beds. It's very possible to live in the past, where there are no nightmares.

I started this book in 1994. *Decades* ago. So why finish it now? It's simple. Think of these terms: sudden cardiac arrest, artificial heart valve, pacemaker, defibrillator. Heart failure. Each term is a bit of motivation to pick up the ball point pen and write. The reader will find that even during the brief time from 1994 to 2020 that things are much different than portrayed in this book. So enjoy things as they were.

History of the Lake

The lake wasn't always. Unlike many of the mythological lakes which have apparently always been and always will be, there are no such delusions about the prettiest lake left in New Jersey. It's just that today, the lake is at its zenith of beauty – a mature, well-developed lake which welcomes wild swans and Canadian geese to its curvy shores. But there are no illusions that it was always that way, nor that it will remain that way. In fact, the lake today is slowly dying. Runoff from fertilizers results in much weed growth, and the constant falling of leaves into the lake results in a choking of the natural feeder springs and a reduction in the water depth. My grandfather told me that many years ago the depth at the center was 60 feet. Today, it's estimated to be about 15 feet. It's important to enjoy the lake while it still exists.

Before the lake, there was the Revolutionary War. General Washington sent scout parties to the top of Bald Hill along what would be the west shore of the lake to watch for movements of the British. The view from Bald Hill was the best in the area, as the hill is 908 feet above New York harbor and 350 feet above the lake. New York City is visible 35 miles to the east and the green mountains of Pennsylvania are visible 38 miles to the west. The hill was one of the most strategic lookouts in North New Jersey, and even today people can drive up the single lane dirt road to the top of the mountain where the road ends in a little dirt turn around loop. This road is difficult to find, as the entrance is not from the lake. As a result, the few people who live high above the lake are rarely disturbed by tourists. Perhaps that will change in the future.

The development of Bald Hill paralleled that of the lake. Around 1910, Dr. George Donaldson built Cedar Crest on the highest point of Bald Hill, soon to be followed by six more cabins. These cabins were about halfway up the side of the hill, rather than on top. Living on Bald Hill in the early 1900's was rough work. There was no electricity, little water except rain, but plenty of firewood to chop. These early neighbors were always shouting to each other that firewood warmed the user twice: once when it was cut, and once when it was burned. In 1915, four more houses were added, followed by eleven more in 1918. Water was pumped from a natural spring at the north end of the hill into a reservoir, and then pumped up the side of the hill. A couple of workmen were hired by the Bald Hill Association which was started in December 1935, and the water company was called "The Diamond Spring Water Company." Today, a main road from the nearby town is still called Diamond Spring Road. In 1930, electricity arrived on the mountain, and except during thunderstorms, the era of oil lamps was over.

Besides Bald Hill, there is only one notable natural eye-catcher. On the north end of the lake is a rock formation, probably left by a glacier, called the Hog Pen. It's not as romantic a name as the battle scenes at Gettysburg, which is about 200 miles southwest of the lake, but the people who live on the lake like to remember their Hog Pen in the context of the war. Whenever the British soldiers would come near, the local people would drive their hogs into the stone ravine, throw brush across the entrance, and thus protect their hogs from becoming dinner. The lake as it exists today did not exist then, but its small ancestor did exist. It was called Cranberry Pond, and was only one-sixth of a mile long, hardly big enough to shelter a decent-sized bass. It ran north-south along the east side of Bald Hill, and was often more of a bog than a pond during the summer. In these early days, the 35 miles to New York City just as well could have been 350 miles. The roads were muddy, the whole area swampy and aguish, the soil rocky and shaded – not the best area in which to grow crops, but the hunting and fishing in the Rockaway Valley were excellent.

Around Cranberry Pond were a few houses along the bottom of Bald Hill, and a couple of cabins on the flatter land on the east side of the pond. There was nothing built on the swampy land to the south. Yet many of the ancestors of today were there in the late 1780s. These were the Canadian geese and the white swans, the bullfrogs, the blue cranes, the peepers, crickets, beaver, muskrats, ducks, and foxes. They were all there, and in 200 years, their descendants would still be there, having moved no further than two miles in eight generations.

The lake as it is today was started by men in 1890. Charles Selvage of Newark bought several hundred acres around Cranberry Pond from Walter Clark, who owned a large house at the base of Bald Hill. Selvage then flooded the tract of land, added a retaining wall and outlet to the east, and renamed the area Silver Lake for the silver moss which grew along the cranberry bogs and on the islands. There is no more silver moss at the lake today. The size of the lake at the time was 25 acres.

Around 1900, a new dam was built on the east side at what would be known as "The Cove," and the lake area enlarged to 99 acres. Charles D. Clark rented fishing boats to the public, and a fishing club, with its members from New York (usually called "The City"), built a small fishing lodge on the southeast corner of the lake. In 1906, the area of 320 acres was sold to M.W. Raynes and renamed Cedar Lake, and the modern era of sales to people from the City started.

Land for fishing cottages was sold to people from the City at two cents a square foot. They had to take the Delaware, Lackawanna, and Western Railroad through New Jersey, as the roads in the area were not good. At the lake in 1920, there was no city water, electricity, indoor water, nor hard roads. It was a place for hunting and fishing. None of the cottages were for winter use and the roads weren't even plowed during the winter.

Plots of land were advertised as "The Adirondacks of New Jersey," and posters showing men wearing derby hats while they fished, and women in long dresses standing among the cedar trees looking at the bug-infested water, were hung in all of the DL&W railroad stations. On June 2, 1925, the original real estate plan was declared bankrupt. Two days later, the landowners and real estate seller reorganized and kept selling plots of land to people from the City. A clubhouse was planned, and finally built in 1931 by the cove. Also built during the 1930's was the Rambler Inn on the west side, which was also called Mrs. Hummel's store.

Current Geography

The lake as it is today is much the same as it was by 1930, with the exception that several islands at the south end of the lake have disappeared. The lake is approximately 1½ miles long, north to south on the east side of Bald Hill, and three-quarters of a mile wide at the widest, which is east from Bald Hill to the cove. The lake is 38 feet at its deepest point, whereas I was told when young that it was once much deeper when first allowed to flood behind the man-made dam at the cove. There are several interesting features which attract fishermen.

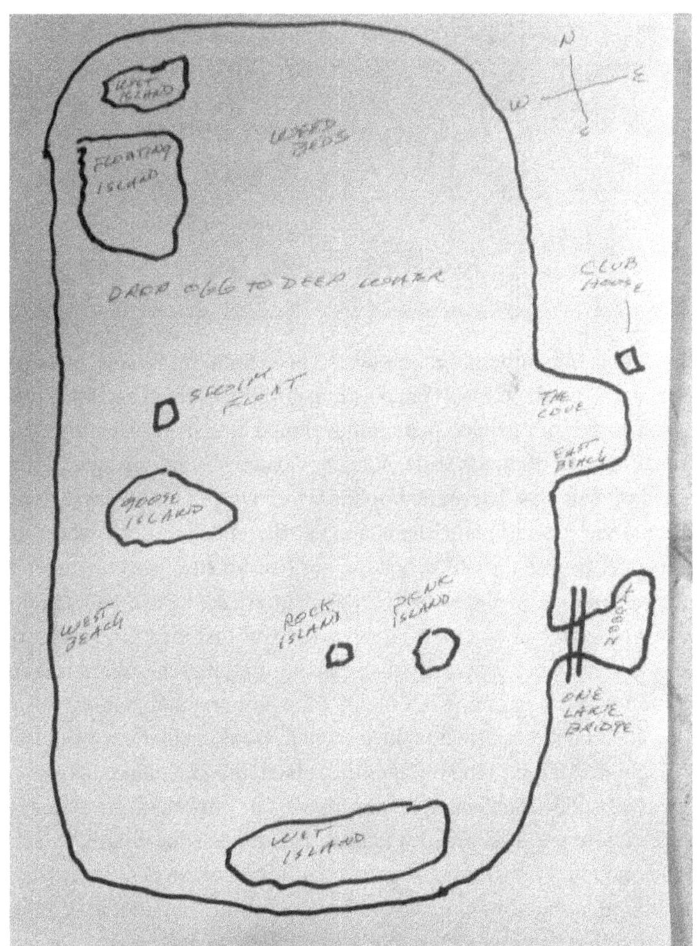

Since the lake was man-made, most of the original terrain that was once above water, and is now under water, is known. During the winter, when the water is drained down every third year by opening the dam to allow people to work on their docks, much of the underwater contours can be seen. This knowledge is very useful during the summer fishing season.

First, let's look at the north end of the lake. The swimming float is anchored in the middle of the lake, so the north end is defined as being to the north of the swimming float. Along the northwest corner of the lake, in an undeveloped area, is the floating island. This island, being some 50 yards long by 30 yards wide, actually floated around the lake during the 1930's to 1950's. Its direction of drift was determined by the wind. During the summer, when the thunderstorms rolled over the mountain, the island usually ended up somewhere on the east shore, often in the cove. During the fall, when the northeaster storms came, the island usually floated over to the west shore. As the island was of a significant size, owners of docks were very unhappy to go down to the water one morning and discover that the island had arrived during the night. The property owners were especially distressed to find that the island had arrived just when a birthday or July 4th celebration with plenty of swimming and boating was planned. As the island could be towed, sometimes affected dock owners would gather a rowboat flotilla, sling lines to the island, and tow it out to the middle of the lake, then let nature take over, and send the island to someone else's dock. The island was composed of brush and water trees, but there was no firm land on which to walk. The island was thus a great nuisance with little value. By 1954, the owners had had enough. Fred Helmer organized a flotilla of canoes and rowboats to go after the island and put a stop to the nonsense. After all, who would want to live at a lake on which an island could come floating along whenever it felt like it?

The flotilla, composed of serious-looking men in brown fishing hats, and their energetic sons, appeared out of the Saturday morning mist in June 1954. They flailed at the island with ropes, anchors, and cement blocks. Some of the boaters had to abandon their anchors when they later discovered they couldn't get them unhooked from the island. Once all of the boats were hooked on, Fred blew a whistle and everyone started to row and paddle. It was tough going, but while the women stood on the docks and waved, and the younger folks rowed shuttle boats back and forth, carrying coffee and beer to the rowers, the island moved northward. The event was photographed for the Morristown and Newark newspapers. After several hours of rowing, the men, the boats, and the island arrived at the northwest corner of the lake. One inch cables were strung around the island with great difficulty from the stable rowboats, while the canoes were used to place buoys and floats. Concrete blocks were dropped to the bottom with half-inch cables attached to the main one-inch cable, and the island left to its fate. In the evening, all of the men in the boats rowed and paddled over to the cove, beached their boats, and went up to the clubhouse for a beer or two. The photos of the towing were published in the two newspapers, and picked up by the *New York Times* as a human interest article. After a few beers in the clubhouse with the creaky floors, the men went home to wash up for supper, the island put down roots and made itself at home, and the lake quieted down. In time, the island became home for frogs, cranes, blackbirds, and some very big bass who moved into the watery caves under the water tree roots.

Today, the explorer who gets up close to the island can still locate the tie down cables in places. Between the island and the shore there is enough room to send a boat around the island, but it's a tight squeeze. This area is a favorite among children searching for painted turtles to catch and take home as pets. About 40 yards to the north of the floating island is a much smaller island, 10 yards in diameter, with no firm ground. Between this island and the shore are shallows where a pickerel sometimes looks for frogs for dinner, and there are rocky shallows along the north shore. The little bay between the floating island and the smaller island to the north is deeper than surrounding water, and a good place for pickerel to wait. North of an east-west line from the southern end of the floating island and the east shore lie weed banks four feet beneath the water, and a few stumps which the new fishermen soon discover. These stumps enjoy collecting lures, and over the past 40 years have collected enough that a diver could open their own bait shop just by picking lures off the north stumps.

Directly on that east-west line from the southern end of the floating island to the east shore lies the drop off from the weed bank to deeper water. This is a prime location for pickerel to be waiting, as well as rock bass. At the east end of this navigation line is an old stone boathouse, one of those that the boat can be directly rowed into, but this one, unlike others, has a deck on top for sitting and sun tanning. Many fishermen spend their evening trolling back and forth between that stone boathouse and the west shore looking for big pickerel. About 20 yards in front of that stone boathouse lies the stump bed. This is an underwater group of large stumps that shelter some of the largest bass in the lake, and a favorite destination of night fishermen.

Halfway down the east shore lies the cove. It is near the clubhouse with the weeds growing outside. From the north shore of the cove to the east end of the cove, an old stone wall can be seen and walked upon if the lake is low enough. They may have been part of the original retaining wall when the lake was first expanded in 1890, before the present dam at the cove was built (in 1900). At the south side of the cove, a similar wall and rock pile can be seen. Teenagers like to snorkel along these walls in search of turtles, which sometimes nip the feet of unwary explorers walking along the underwater walls. In the 1960's, a beach and two swimming platforms with swimming lanes buoyed between them were built along the cove shore, replacing the sounds of nature with the sounds of screaming children, especially during the Sunday swimming races. The area where the men beached their boats after towing the island is still as it was, and is used as an area for property owners who do not have docks to moor their boats. Many small minnows can be found in this area.

Two-thirds of the way down the lake to the south and 50 yards from the west shore lies Goose Island. On this island, composed entirely of mud and goose droppings, the geese and ducks nest for the night. At dusk, flocks of Canadian geese and wild ducks fly over the cove and land by Goose Island to spend the night. In the dark during the summer, little goose murmurs and cries can be heard all night long. Just before dawn, about 5:30 AM in the summer, the geese lift off from the water around the island to fly in search of the day's free food from the tourists. A little later, about 6:30 AM, the duck flocks either take off on a mission similar to the geese's, or set sail along the shore looking for handouts of bread. The only humans to go on the island composed of goose droppings were some of the Property Owners Board, in hip boots, who set up a wire Christmas tree. During December each year they run an electric line from the shore to the tree's plug which is attached to a stake at the edge of the island, so that the multicolored tree is lit each year. That tree has now moved to a little rock pile west of Picnic Island.

At the south end of the lake lie three islands. One, in the center of the lake, is a rocky projection. It can be walked upon, but the approach is shallow and the island small. Nowadays, the Christmas tree is there, and people don't walk on the rocks. Fifty yards to the west of this island is the West Beach – built in 1900. This is a sand-filled beach with a few trees, and a roped off swimming area. There are no swimming lanes at this beach. Directly to the east of the small island, and about 30 yards away, lies Picnic Island. This is an improved island with a dock on the north side, a sandy swimming beach on the east, and a picnic area. The island is 10 yards across, but firm and treed. It is a favorite place for skinny dipping at night and holiday lunches.

Along the southern shore lies another island composed mostly of water, much like the floating island to the north. People who live at the southern end of the lake like to say that this island floated also, but there is no proof of this. This island is 50 yards across, and surrounded by shallow weeds.

To the east of Picnic Island, a one-car bridge carries the east road over the entrance to the lagoon. Today, the lagoon is a symbol of the future death of the lake. It is barely passable today in a canoe. The narrow canoes of the lake are best for going into the lagoon, which goes into the forest for a half mile. Rowboats tend to get their oars tangled in the lily pads, roots, and vines in the lagoon and become stuck. In the 1940's, the lagoon was easily navigated in a rowboat, and there were several small islands which could be landed upon. Today, the shallow lagoon is still home for snakes, frogs, and turtles, but the fish have left for deeper waters. The bottom of the feeding chain is no longer fish, but insects and small frogs. It is believed that the lagoon will become dry land in 20 years, and the small bridge will be removed and a two-lane fill installed for cars. The approach to the lagoon is shallow and rock-filled, and several canoes have been holed trying to find the channel to the lagoon.

Around the lake, lily pad beds provide a good home to frogs and bass. Other than the demise of the lagoon and the shallowing of the water, the lake is much as it was in 1900.

To be on the lake is to be doing something. But regardless of what one is doing, the lake has a character unique in New Jersey. First, there were never any motor boats or motors of any sort allowed on the lake. This means that not only is there no roar of racing boats, there is no water skiing. This decision has resulted in a lake only 35 miles from Manhattan which has remained in a technological stasis for over 100 years. The same basic canoes and rowboats and sailboats used in 1900 are still used today. There are some aluminum canoes and rowboats now, but there are still many, many wooden rowboats and canoes on the lake that were built before 1940. If anything has changed, it is the advent of the modern sailboats such as the Sailfish and Sunfish one-person sailboats. The quiet of the lake, even with hundreds of people living around it now, brings the wildlife to the lake. White swans, Canadian geese, ducks, cranes, owls…birds of all sorts nest along the shores and islands.

When one is on the lake during a wind, the waves never exceed 2 feet even on the roughest days. These waves are plenty big for a rowboat, and enough to roll a canoe over, but do not occur very often. During the summer, the wind blows from the southwest to the northeast, so that those people living at the cove always have a breeze. During the winter, the wind comes down over the mountain from the west, and rushes across the frozen lake. This is the time when people stay inside by their fireplaces.

But during the summer, the weather is moderate, with high temperatures in the 80s and lows in the 60s at night. On rainy days, the lake is speckled with raindrops, and people sit on their roof-covered docks and watch the water. Sunny days start with morning fog which burns off by 9 AM, followed by gentle sun-tanning breezes. The wind picks up during the afternoons, and the sailboats cruise the lake for several hours. From 6 to 9 p.m., the wind dies away, and this is the time that the fisherman row out from their docks in search of bass and pickerel. After 9 p.m., the arrival of the bats brings the night wind, and under a full moon, people can lie in their beds, with the window open, and listen to the night breeze in the evergreens – with the owls, bullfrogs, peepers, and an occasional dog calling happily to each other.

Rowboats are just small versions of battleships. That's the key to having a good time with one's rowboat rather than feeling that everything having to do with rowboats is a chore. They have a bow and a stern. On the lake, no one uses the terms "port" or "starboard," but instead people use the terms "right" and left." A rowboat is a most useful craft on a lake. It is stable for fishing, doesn't roll badly in waves, and large ones can hold five people. It is particularly useful for older people to use without too much danger, and provides a good way to visit the neighbors without driving. Such a craft needs care, however. There are two types of rowboats on the lake: wooden and aluminum.

The only real rowboat is wooden. Most people believe that adults row in wooden boats, and children play in aluminum boats. So the goal of every adult on the lake is to have a real wooden rowboat. Newcomers to the lake spend months reading area weekly newspapers in search of wooden rowboats for sale. As not too many wooden boats are made anymore, the price of one usually exceeds $1,000. It is difficult to move also, as each boat weighs about 250 to 300 pounds and is awkward to pick up.

The boating season starts in May, when the crocuses are blooming and a fire in the fireplace is only needed on rainy, cool days. On nice days, when the temperature is in the 70's, it is time to work on the boat to prepare it for the water. All wooden boats leak, so the second goal of boat preparation is to caulk the bottom so that the water seepage is not too bad. "Not too bad" is defined as the occupant of the boat only having to bail a few scoops every 30 minutes.

Everyone involved must make sure that there is no wildlife still living under the boat after the winter. The spring boat repairs must start early enough so that an animal does not have babies under the boat. Since the boat is always stored upside down for the winter, it is not at all unusual for an animal such as a skunk or raccoon to drag weeds and brush under the boat and have a nice home for the winter. Residents of the lake have learned to make a lot of noise, and beat on the bottom of the boat with a long tree limb before approaching the boat for the first time in the spring to make sure that there is no skunk underneath. People who forget to beat upon the bottom of their boat with a long tree limb to check for skunk only forget once, and are reminded all summer while sitting in their boat.

Next comes caulking. A putty knife or screwdriver is used to remove all of the old caulking in the bottom seams. Good caulking can be left alone, but most of it will have dried out over the winter. It is usually dug out rather than pushed through the bottom of the boat. As there is caulking in each seam, and a seam between each board that makes up the bottom of the boat, there will be a lot of caulking to remove. A paint scraping knife is then used to remove the outside and inside flaking paint. Sometimes the inside paint will winter well and can be left alone, but it is best to repaint each year, and the paint helps to set the caulking.

On a warm day, the boat is caulked bottom side up. This task requires the installation of new rope caulking. Rope caulk can be bought at the boat store or made by twisting rope as tightly as possible when installing it. There will be gaps in the seams, and this is where the caulking goes. A strong screwdriver is used to press the new caulking into the cracks between the wood planks in the bottom of the boat. Both sides of the keel are likewise caulked where the keel runs the length of the boat. The keel should be inspected for rot, and any bad areas dug out and well caulked. The new caulking should be allowed to set up and dry for a day. The inside of the boat will not need to be caulked, since the water pressure forces the caulking deeper into each crack in the bottom of the boat.

After the caulking is dry (which usually takes a day), the outside of the boat should be painted with a coat of oil-based battleship gray, with a heavy layer applied to the caulked seams to stop leaks. Some people like to paint some trim, usually red or yellow, along the very top of the sides, but this must be done after the boat is flipped upright. Once the boat is flipped, the inside can be painted, usually the same color as the outside. In addition, the oar lock screws should be checked, and the oar locks oiled to prevent squeaking when the boat is rowed. Seats should be inspected for rot before painting, and replaced if needed. New anchor ropes are installed, as well as tie-up rope, and the boat, after drying for another day, is carried to the water and launched. As wood will swell once it is wet, the boat should be allowed to sink from the many leaks which the caulking will not have completely stopped. After resting on the bottom of the lake with the water halfway up the inside of the boat for a couple of days, the boat is bailed out and anchored in the sunshine so that the inside will dry out. If all has gone well, the hot June sun will keep the inside dry, while the swelling of the wood on the bottom of the boat will seal the caulking tight, resulting in a leak-free boat for the summer. It rarely works out perfectly, but that's the theory. In practice, a little bailing, especially with a heavy load of passengers, is required.

Aluminum rowboats are easy to care for. They require little except new anchor and dock line each year. From time to time, banging into docks and rocks will loosen one of the rivets in the bottom of the boat, and it will fall out, causing a leak. On the lake, this is cured by placing one's toe over the empty rivet hole. Once ashore, a flat-head bolt almost matching the diameter of the hole is inserted from the bottom side up into the boat, with a rubber washer between the head of the bolt and the bottom of the outside of the boat. With the bolt sticking up into the boat, a metal washer is dropped down on the bolt and two nuts screwed on from the inside. The bolt is usually just allowed to stick up into the boat. Why isn't the bolt installed with the shaft sticking down into the water rather than up towards people's feet? It's because if the bolt shafts were sticking out of the bottom of the boat, it would catch on concrete retaining walls, grass, and the docks, ripping the bolt out through the bottom and widening the hole. With the bolt flat on the bottom, and in between the aluminum guide ridges on the bottom, there is no chance that it will be snagged on something and pulled through the bottom, doing more damage. Of course, people must not step on the bolt sticking up into the boat, or it will get bent over and loosen up. It may also damage feet and be quite painful.

In the fall, before the lake is lowered for dock repair work, the boats are removed and stored. Most people store their aluminum boats in their garages, sometimes in place of their cars. The decision is sometimes regretted during the winter when one wishes for the car to start. The wooden rowboats are pulled up onto the shore or docks with a great deal of effort, as they are heavy, and flipped upside down to keep the snows from the inside of the boats. Boats stored on docks can rest on the wooden plank docks without harm, as the docks have lengthwise gaps between the planks, but boats stored on the land must be set up on rocks or flower pots to prevent rot and improve air circulation.

The oars are stored in the top of the docks or in a garage. Most oars are unpainted, just rubbed down with linseed oil a couple times a year. Boaters carve their initials in the oars, as well as their address, in case of loss on the lake. All boat items, be they boats or oars, eventually drift in somewhere according to the wind, and eventually find their way home. It is not at all unusual to see some wandering boat being towed back to its dock by a small child practicing his or her rowing, without even bothering to notify the owner that their boat is back. It's simply tied to the end of its proper dock and left, like an offering, and the Good Samaritan goes back to practicing rowing, up and down the lake.

Chapter 3: Animals and Birds of the Lake

The Skunk

In a steamy summer night, the sleeper has only to awake and walk outside to know that one of the most numerous of the lake animals is near: the skunk. The North Jersey version of the skunk may look like all other skunks, but it really is very different. It is extremely smart and fearless. The old saying that a skunk cannot spray if it is being sprayed with a garden hose has been proven to be false over and over again by the "summer only" people at the lake. The North Jersey lake skunks don't bother anymore to eat anything from the wild. They chow down on the tons of wasted human food that is thrown into garbage cans with loose-fitting tops. The favorite food is fried chicken, followed by Chinese eggrolls, and roast beef. What were once animals of the forest have become animals of the porches, for they love to nest under the front porches of the cabins, and under the bathroom floors in the plumbing access spaces. The summertime lake dwellers have discovered that fact when it is time to turn on the cabin water in the spring. Skunks also like to bring their young into the world under the wooden rowboats stored upside down on the shore for the winter. Many an eager teen fisherman has flipped over the rowboat in May without first rapping on the bottom with a long tree limb, only to discover that lake skunks can spray even better when they are not themselves being sprayed with a garden hose. Sometimes, in an unlucky family, the porch, bathroom, and boat are all rendered aromatic for the summer season by the skunks.

The year-round people have the same troubles, but they have learned two tricks to get the skunks away. One is to make a lot of noise in the area suspected of being a skunk home just before dark. The skunks will move out during the night, being polite animals. If one keeps watch all night, sometimes the whole family can be seen in the moonlight, heading up the walk. The other trick is to throw meaty snacks, such as fried chicken, over by the neighbor's porch. The skunk, knowing soon where the grass is greener, will move under the neighbor's porch. One has to be careful, though, because any scraps can attract the bears.

At the lake, wise people always walk at night with a flashlight in operation. Skunk's eyes in North New Jersey always look red in a light beam. Whether their eyes look the same way in Colorado is unknown, but in Jersey they look red. This may be a mutation, but the glow of red eyes is always a good reason to stand very still and allow the skunks to move at their own pace. If they are not surprised, crowded or threatened by loud children shouting "Skunk, skunk," they will go along without spraying. Barking dogs close by, however, will almost always cause them to spray away with glee. Therefore, skunks should be treated politely.

The Raccoon

If anything, the raccoon is smarter than the skunk. Jersey raccoons don't bother to open garbage cans – they open the house. They remove screens from windows, pry windows open, open chimney caps, and slide happily down into the living room. Once inside, they head for the kitchen, sometimes in packs, where they open every cabinet they find, followed by the opening of every box and container. The products inside are then eaten. Once dinner is over, they will make their escape by forcing windows open from the inside after loosening the hook catches. This is their preferred method of operation.

However, they have not forgotten to eat in the wild, and especially around the lagoon they can be seen at night looking for crayfish, minnows, and other nightly tidbits. Their hands give them remarkable flexibility in catching and cleaning food, and if they want to open something, they have enough weight to have a powerful grasp.

Their favorite place to spend the winter is under the aluminum siding that has been put on an old fishing cabin. These old cabins often have lots of nooks and cavities that were covered over when the siding was installed. The raccoons have learned to detect these spaces, and they spend several hours loosening the siding by pulling it away from the house. Eventually, the siding nails will be pulled out enough so that the raccoon family can move into a nice snug space for the winter. If their entry is not detected in the spring, the mother is likely to have her young in this space behind the siding and stay all year long. Only a close inspection of the siding up under the eaves will detect a loose piece of siding and the possibility that the raccoons are living behind it. One should be careful when checking for raccoons, especially since one with young will bite, and many of the Jersey raccoons have rabies. The other possibility is that the raccoons have moved out, and a skunk has moved in. Excitement is added to one's life by being sprayed by a skunk while crouched under the eave at the top of the cabin looking for raccoon nests. A raccoon or skunk can be persuaded to move out the next night by the application of ammonia or mothballs near their nests, as they do not like the odor.

Like the skunks, raccoons should be dealt with cautiously if firmly. For sure, all windows and chimneys of summer cabins should be closed very securely before departing for the winter season, lest a visitor spend the winter inside, examining the family treasures.

The Muskrat

The muskrat mostly resembles a beaver, and can only be seen two times: First, late in the evening, after the sun is behind the hill, but it is not yet dark. The muskrat, who always travels alone, can be seen swimming across the lake, leaving behind a wide "V" wake. His head and back can be seen, but the tail is below the water while swimming. Second, the other time that he can be seen is early in the morning, about 4 a.m., when he is up on land around the docks, looking for scraps.

14

The rest of this animal's life is a mystery. It is not known whether he hunts the lagoon, but it is suspected that he lives on the firm interior land of the big islands. He appears to be most active at night, never having been seen swimming during the main part of the day.

He is brown, with a small head, and not at all sociable. He does not conduct visits while people are on their docks or swimming, nor will he come very close to boats while he is swimming. He is not seen at all during the off-season of winter, but no one at the lake knows where the muskrat goes when the lake is frozen and the lawns are buried under the snow. It is known that he does not enter houses as does the raccoon, nor does he live under the porches and under the bathrooms as does the skunk. He is not found in the flower beds or empty dog houses, and he does not hide under the eaves of empty cabins. He is one of the few animal inhabitants of the lake who has not bothered to improve his life through association with humans, except to eat the remains of dock snacks. His habitats are his own, and he keeps his life private, leaving a rapidly forming "V" in the water as he heads for an unknown destination. Should one try to row after him, to see where he goes, he will dive under the surface and be gone, later resurfacing far away, and then continuing on.

The lake people suspect that this animal is exceptionally smart and cunning – too smart to be troubled by the foolish lake people and their ways. The spotting of a muskrat in the water is regarded by the lake people as good luck, sort of like shaking hands with a chimney sweep. People in their fishing boats would exclaim loudly, "Look, a muskrat!" and so feel lucky, even though they may not catch any fish for the evening. The muskrat, of course, probably had a fish or two for dinner, as a thin muskrat is never to be found – they're all fat and well-fed.

The Squirrels

There are two types of squirrels at the lake: the gray and the red. They both act the same way, but are colored differently. Squirrels at the lake are regarded with dislike, as they do bad things. They love to jump onto the birdfeeders and eat all of the bird seed. They also love to get into the summer cabins during the winter and tear apart the furniture. They usually accomplish entry through the chimney, but once gaining entry, they do not have the smarts to find the food in the cabinets, as the raccoons do. So they eat whatever there is to eat, namely the furniture and candles. Many of them starve to death over the winter, stuck inside a cabin. But before they pass away, they can – and usually do – cause considerable damage to the cabin's interior.

The only ways to keep them out of the cabins is to place wire over the chimney top, or burn a sulfur candle when the cabin is shut up for the winter. In the spring, the cabin should be checked carefully for live squirrels before bedding down for the first night of the summer season. Failure to do this may result in terror in the night as a frantic squirrel decides it is time to get out of the cabin, and comes out from hiding after the lights have been turned off and the summer residents have gone to bed for the first time in May.

Outside, they are most often seen in the fall, gathering the traditional nuts, or eating bread that the old ladies have left out for them. They like to go high up in the oak trees, with the maple trees their second choice, and wave their tails about. Oddly enough, there are not a lot of them about in the forest, and people believe that the owls thin out the squirrel population's young, so that not too many grow up. The rear haunches of squirrels make good eating, and are often eaten in West Virginia, but the people of North Jersey regard them more as pets rather than food. As such, they put up with their antics and chewing of the furniture. Sometimes, it might be better to eat them.

The Chipmunk

Chipmunks are the sprite of the land. They appear in any weather from woodpiles, holes in old concrete walls, and holes in the ground, busily gathering nuts. The chipmunks at the lake are very friendly, and can almost be made tame. They love to be fed seeds and bread and crackers. Some of these tidbits left on top of a concrete wall or on top of the woodpile will be sure to attract them.

Chipmunks tend to take the same trails repeatedly from their home in search of food. This habit often proves their undoing if a neighbor has a cat, but makes it easy to leave treats out for them. Their brown stripped coat makes them one of the lake's colorful creatures, but also easy not only for the cat to spot, but also the owl. The chipmunk is a creature of faith, for it never knows where the next meal is coming from. Each morning, it comes out of its hiding place, and goes searching for food. Thanks to the constant munching of the lake people, there are usually sufficient crumbs about to satisfy the chipmunk's small appetite.

The chipmunk only stands still to eat. The rest of the time it is moving so as not to be caught, or moving in search of food. But when a crumb is found, the chipmunk halts, picks up the crumb in its front paws, and eats, cramming the food in so that its cheeks bulge out. Sometimes, if a chipmunk knows that a cat lives nearby, it will rarely stop at all. The only glimpse that a homeowner has of the little creature is a brown streak along a retaining wall, most often out of the corner of one's eye, so that one cannot be totally sure if anything has been seen at all. Speed is the chipmunk's only real defense, for although its coat will blend in with some leaves, its constant searching movements soon attract the eyes of larger eaters. In the spring, when the old woodpile is at the lowest point, a chipmunk nest is sometimes found among the logs. It will be lined with dead brown leaves, and often full of nut shells. By the time the nest is discovered, the chipmunk will be gone, having moved on to another less disturbed location. By nesting far down in the woodpile, the chipmunk is well protected from the weather, and not likely to have to move before spring when the woodpile gets low. Chipmunks seem to have an instinct about woodpiles, and they will move in the day after the wood has been stacked. If one wishes to befriend the chipmunk known to live in the woodpile somewhere, a little bread and seed left under an overhanging log will bring the chipmunk out in a couple of days, provided that the birds cannot see the bread and seed themselves. Some chipmunks even like a little peanut butter or cheese left out for them.

The Bats

The bats draw the pall of night over the lake. In the summer, this happens about 8:45 p.m. They are not rare, and indeed thrive on the lake bugs and insects, especially the mosquitoes which thrive in North Jersey. Sometimes as many as 10 can be seen at once over the water, with the stars starting to appear behind them. They avoid the fishermen easily, of course, but the thin fishing line is another matter, and the polite fisherman will keep the pole and line down near the water so as to not get in the bats' way.

They often fly a foot above the water, rising to just over the fisherman's head as they fly through clouds of insects, moving like a black streak through the dusk. The fishermen call them "bug vacuums," so efficient is their swath through the insects. They are the start of night, when the night fishermen begin to think about heading out onto the water, and the evening fishermen think about heading back into the docks and preparing for bed. They are the modern equivalent of the lamp lighters of the Victorian era, for their appearance brings on the house and dock lights. Sometimes at the lake, they fly in squadrons through the dusk, seven of them in a formation, zigging and zagging back and forth as if they were being attacked by ground fire in a war, their dark shapes absorbing the light rather than reflecting it. They are a time clock in motion, and the fishermen beneath them feel the transition from light to dark, and so they shiver a little, take their oars in old hands, and row for the warmth.

The Blue Heron

Of all the lake birds, the blue heron is the most mystical, and not seen too often. It nests up at the north end of the lake along the north shore of the floating island. Looking like most water cranes, with a long brown beak, long stick legs, and a tuft of blue feathers on its head, it keeps to itself so much that it is rarely ever seen in its island habitat. It is sometimes seen in the air, with its neck extended and its beak leading the charge, legs out behind, heading up out of the island brush and south along the west shore. It is even more reclusive than the muskrat, not showing off its young as the geese and ducks do, nor coming around humans for a visit.

It has never been seen returning from the south, but sometimes can be spotted diving out of the sky, apparently straight down, towards the floating island, to disappear in an apparently suicidal drop into the island brush. It will not be seen again for weeks, and may be one of the most endangered and rare birds in North Jersey.

17

The Ducks

The ducks live to eat bread which is thrown to them by the lake people from their docks. The lake ducks come in many colors, like Joseph's coat. The all-white ducks make a lot of quacks when there is bread about, and wiggle their large tails in ecstasy. The all-brown ducks bite the tails of the white ducks, and thus get more of the bread to eat. The ducks with the green heads (mallards) tend to float further out in the water than the other ducks, and thus get less bread to eat. The rows of little brown ducks – the babies – are always fearless, and they come right up to people, nipping at their hands if possible.

The ducks spend all day visiting various lakes and ponds in search of free food, and frequently finding it. They sleep over at Goose Island, sometimes leaving with the dawn, sometimes making the circuit of the lake looking for early risers to feed them a little handout before moving on to other lakes. In this way, the ducks are fat and happy, and when they sleep on Goose Island, they quack happily through the night, dreaming duck dreams.

The Swans

The swans are the big white swans of fairy tales, who lead a tragic life. Their babies are inevitably eaten by the large snapping turtles, who sometimes even take a grown swan. Since the swans mate for life, it is a common and sad sight to see a lone swan following another pair through the water. The swans will occasionally come to the docks for bread, but one must be careful if trying to feed the swans by hand, for they will inadvertently give one a serious nip when they take the bread. The way to avoid this is to offer the bread to them with the bread placed on a flat hand, rather than grasped within fingertips. The swans will take the bread off of a flat hand without nipping.

They are the majestic birds of the lake, sailing with their wing tips up a little. Often, they sail in formation in a single line, stopping now and then to dunk their heads and long necks under the water for a little snack of green weed. When taking off, they need a long distance to get airborne: at least 40 yards. They start their takeoff by stretching their necks and wings out, then beating their wings up and down against the water. The sounds of their wings slapping the water at takeoff will echo all across the lake. As they gain just a little altitude, they will use their feet to run a few steps on the water's surface, and then they will slowly climb into the sky, the sounds of their wings going "swish-swish" in the morning air. For some reason, the morning air gives them the best lift, and they fly between 8 and 11 a.m. After that, they are not seen again until dusk, when formations of four or five swans will come in over the cove on the east side of the lake, heading west. Halfway across the lake, with an altitude of about 30 feet, they will bank left toward Goose Island, flail their wings, and drop to the water with their feet extended, landing for the night. Once on the water, the swans make no noise. They are silent and majestic, ignoring the silly ducks and the biting geese as they sail around the lake.

The Geese

The geese are Canadian Geese, with black heads holding white patches on the sides. They never travel anywhere without all of them going, as if their intelligence only operates when they are all doing the same thing. The geese are ruled by the time of day. At dawn, after a noisy night on Goose Island, they all take to the sky, 20 or 30 together, heading upwards from the island after taking off across the water toward the north. Their day, like that of the ducks, is spent visiting other area lakes in search of free bread from the people along the shoreline. Their favorite place to find treats is over at Indian Lake or on Lake Hopatcong. The geese fidget from one lake to another, trying to avoid finding real lake food for themselves by swarming about people on the shore. They often bite the hand that feeds them, and children who trust a goose not to bite when being given a little snack will get a nasty surprise.

When they are not eating, they are making messes on people's docks and landings, scattering their feathers along the lake roads and eating people's tender plants and grass. Although pretty to observe, they are rude and pushy, and honk almost constantly.

Their young, if not eaten by the turtles, learn to be pushy from their parents, and to honk all of the time also. But if the geese are rude on the ground, they are awesome in airborne formation, flying in large Vs. They like to fly clockwise from lake to lake during the day, and so they always arrive back on our lake just before the sun sets behind Bald Hill, around 7 p.m. They always come into the lake from the cove, from the east, all of their sun-touched wings out wide and necks level, gliding toward the mountain. About 40 yards north of Goose Island, they will all bank left, towards the south, extend their feet and arch their wings, and land 20 yards from the island, still in formation, and still honking. When the flights are approaching the lake at dusk, they announce their approach by loud honking, so that the lake people can go out on the ends of their docks to watch the flights arrive. Rain or shine, all summer long, they take off at dawn and land at dusk. When the young can fly, they go, too.

19

In October, when the mountain is red and yellow, they will sometimes circle the lake hour after hour, skimming over the treetops, practicing their flying. Then one morning, around 7 a.m., when the schoolchildren are waiting for the bus and a little smoke drifts out of the chimneys, they will all fly out of the cold morning mist, necks out, formation after formation taking off eastward, then turning south over the cove. They will not return until April. The silence of that first dusk after they are gone tells all of the lake people that winter is soon to come, and the colored leaves on the mountain are soon to fall. People don't sit on their docks much after the geese are gone, and those dock ends that can be removed from the water are pulled up, along with the last boats, and the swim float in the middle of the lake is pulled to shore. Boating is over for the year. The evenings seem much more lonely after the geese have left, for soon after them go the ducks and the swans, for none of them stay to see the electric Christmas tree lit out on Goose Island.

With the birds departing, people tend to caulking their houses and chimneys, storing their boats and oars and fishing tackle, stacking their firewood and housing their coal, finding winter underwear and warm pajamas, locating their snow shovels and tire chains, for it is tradition that the first snowfall will brush down from the mountain within four weeks of the birds' leaving. A few young boys still play barefoot in the shallows, looking for crayfish after school, while their mothers say the water's too cold to be wading in. But the children play in the water without heart, bored with water play, knowing that Halloween will soon come. After a while, the geese are forgotten as the winter holidays begin. Their return in April will be a surprise.

Chapter 4: The Fish, Turtles, Snakes, and Frogs

For as long as mankind can remember, fish have been caught and sometimes, eaten. The catching of fish is regarded as a task that can be performed equally well by children using a wood stick and a string, to middle-class workers, to upper class ladies and gentlemen. From surf rod fishing, to fly fishing in a stream, to lake fishing, the art of catching a fish is regarded as a heroic task to be undertaken by males and females alike. While it is true that the Fishing Club at Cedar Lake was all male, there were many women at the lake who out-thought the fish – as well as the men. For many people, the art of fishing was equaled by the art of rowing so as not to scare away the fish. A later chapter discusses the art of fishing. This chapter discusses the objects of the fishing art: namely, the fish to be found in the lake.

Along with the fish, this chapter also discusses other Jersey wildlife: the turtles, snakes, and frogs. These can be eaten also, but one may find that the result on the table is hardly worth the effort to catch and clean the product.

The Largemouth Bass

This is one of the two big sport fish in the lake, and is identified by a mouth which can open to four times its apparent size – all the better to swallow a frog whole! A black stripe on each side of the fish, running from nose to tail, is another telltale sign that a bass is the fish that has one's lure. The tail is a wide fan shape, and the belly fat. They are friendly, and can be tamed to hang around docks in pairs in the summer and receive handouts of night crawlers. Their young hatch in schools of hundreds, each tiny fish with the distinctive long black stripe on the sides. These young make a good snack for the pickerel.

Their size at this lake runs up to about 8 pounds, and they are generally discussed at the Fishing Club in terms of weight rather than length, but a keeper for sure would be about 16" long and weigh 4 pounds. They are best prepared for the kitchen by scaling them, after removing the insides, tail, head, and fins. The best recipe calls for baking them in aluminum foil, stuffed with onions.

Bass are to be found in shallow to moderately deep water. They hit best after the evening wind dies away, or just before dawn, when the surface is calm. A surface plug dropped over a weed bed growing a foot below the surface, or dropped next to the vertical edge of an island, or dropped over stumps or under overhanging trees is sure to produce a big result. When a bass locates a surface target, it will open its jaws wide and come up from underneath the lure. The water will explode upwards several feet as the bass hits the lure, and the fisherman knows that dinner or breakfast is at hand. Bass also like underwater fake worms and real night crawlers about two hours before sunset or just after sunrise, although one is likely to catch other unwanted fish such as bluegills. Of the sportfish, the bass is the best, for it provides lots of action, is easy to unhook, and does not have a slimy coating that some other fish have. They are fun to catch and let go and catch again and again. These bass don't seem to get much wiser.

There is one other place to find bass, and that is over old stumps at midnight. Much as Huck and Tom thought that warts could be cured by the water in an old stump at midnight, fishermen know that bass over old stumps can cure boredom at midnight. There may be nothing more exciting in life than to drop a night crawler into a dark lake at midnight under a full moon and feel the rod tip bend suddenly into the water. These bass of the midnight stumps are not like the bass of the weed beds or the islands. They are smart. Hook one of these smart, big ones and it will dive for the stump, wrapping the line around the old black, sunken tree remains. The line inevitably will break. Or, they will dive under the boat, surface on the other side while the fisherman waves the flashlight about in a panic, jump over the oar in a burst of water, tangle the line, and be gone. The night bass are as mysterious as the Asrai fairies, which are small and beautiful female fairies with green seductive eyes who melt away into pools of water when captured or exposed to sun. The night bass hang over the stumps of trees flooded decades ago, their gills and fins moving slowly, waiting for the fishermen to come so they can have some fun. Some of the older bass have even leapt into the boat when the fisherman drops a worm down to them, scaring the fisherman almost to death. The bottom around the stump bed is littered with lost poles dropped when a night bass came arching out of the water toward the fisherman's head. They are not to be trifled with, and only the brave go after the night bass out on the lake, under the full moon when the night is calm and the crickets noisy.

The Pickerel

The pickerel is a nasty fish that bites. Catch one of these and you'll find the fish will try to bite the hand that caught it. They look like a small barracuda, have rows of sharp, pointed teeth, and are the smaller sisters of the pike. Their heads are flat between mean eyes, like a crocodile's head, their tails more pointed towards the rear than a bass, and they look like a torpedo in the water, and move just as fast. Underwater, their skin is sometimes covered with a black chain pattern. Wise fishermen carry surgical tongs to reach into the pickerel's throat to remove swallowed hooks, and pliers to remove hooks in the jaw. At the lake, a big one would be 30 inches or more, and a good one to eat 22 inches or more. They are referred to by length, not weight.

Kitchen preparation includes removal of the head, insides, fins, tail, and skin. Removal of the skin is required since the fish is covered in slime. This slime will get all over the boat, net, clothing, and pliers. The fish is skinned because the slime will make the meat taste unhealthy unless the skin is removed. Just removing the scales will not do the job. Skinning is a mess. It is the last cleaning step, when the edge of the skin is held with pliers and the fingernail of the right thumbnail (for right-handed people) is used to separate the skin from the meat while pulling the skin with the pliers. The process is begun by slicing, with a very sharp knife, between the skin and the meat at the head end of the fish, all around it. The whole skin is removed as one piece, but care must be taken to prevent pulling hunks of meat off with the skin. Whenever this threatens to happen, the sharp knife must be used to separate the skin from the meat while the left thumbnail holds the skin flap instead of the pliers. If all goes well (which usually doesn't happen), the entire skin can be stripped from the fish in one smooth pulling motion. Usually what happens is that the separation cannot be started smoothly, and once that problem is solved – usually with a few slices of one's thumb – the pulling of the skin away from the meat takes hunks of meat along. Between being bitten by the bad-tempered fish and being cut by the cleaning knife, one would think that eating the pickerel would be a great reward. Unfortunately, it is bony. There are bones everywhere in the meat, so dinner is reduced to picking at one's food, lest the fish have the final triumph by choking its captor to death. This fish is a true believer in the saying that a fighter returns from the field of battle either with one's shield or on it. They are fighters to the end, as many an unwary fisherman has discovered as the pickerel's teeth close on a finger. The resulting panicky flip of the arm towards the water has freed many a large pickerel.

If a pickerel does make it to the kitchen, it is best cooked in the oven in aluminum foil, wrapped in bacon and onion rings, and stuffed with oysters. A good bottle of wine will go well with the pickerel. One should have a plentiful snack before dining, as one should not eat the fish in haste. Remember the bones! A little china plate for bones is a helpful gesture for guests, who should always be warned.

The pickerel, with its flat head between the eyes, lives in weed beds where it eats the bass young, and in deeper water where it eats all the other fish. In the 1950's, the lake had smallmouth bass, but they are all gone, eaten out of existence by the pickerel, who also ate all of the Chinese gold carp that were stocked in 1988 to control the weed beds. The carp didn't even last a year, but the pickerel got larger. Pickerel are best caught on spoons and spinners, usually in the late afternoon where weed beds drop off to deeper water, or in the deepest water. Sometimes, an aggressive pickerel can be found in rocky shallows and caught on a surface plug pulled rapidly through the water to resemble a frightened frog. In this case, the tail of the pickerel can be seen rising from the water as the fish rushes after the lure. Once hooked, they will tend to run and dive, tangling the line in the weeds. They will often turn and bite the line in two, so that most fishermen use steel leader when fishing for them. They are all mean and fast, and will bite about anything if hungry. (Then again, who among us wouldn't?) Much as Little Red Riding Hood walked into the forest at her peril, a fisherman casts a spinner into deep water at his peril, for below waits a set of jaws equaled only by the snapping turtles, powered by a cunning and dark mind.

The Perch

The perch is a sportsman in the lake, sort of like the afternoon tennis player over by the clubhouse. It's sort of the Boomer fish of the lake, an up-and-coming fish regarded by small children as a great catch, and by adults as a fun challenger. It yanks on the line as a far bigger fish would, exciting the fisherman with dreams of the big one. It is always caught on an underwater lure, usually a spinner or spoon, and is often mistaken for the bite of a pickerel.

This fish is identified by an orange tummy, yellow sides, and vertical black stripes, about five per fish. They are often too small to eat, growing about 12 inches long or smaller. If one does eat them, they can be scaled just as the bass can be.

They are found in moderately deep water, hanging halfway between the surface and the bottom, or in the shallower coves well away from shore. By avoiding the shore, they avoid being caught by small children. They also avoid the dark, deep haunts of the pickerel, as well as the weed beds where the bass wait.

Of all the fish in the lake, their life may be the best. People rarely bother to eat them, and perch have learned to avoid the larger game fish. They eat smaller fish, insects, and worms washed into the water by the rains. They are most active during the afternoon, playing underwater games with each other in the heat of a July day. If caught, they have an active defense system that one must avoid. The fin on the back is full of sharp spines, and the unwary fisherman holding a perch to remove a hook will find a spine going into his hand unless the spines are smoothed down and the fish held securely with the hand wrapped around the fish while the hook is removed. Their teeth are not a danger, being small, and they make an excellent prop in a photo before being thrown back to play some more. They are not in the lake in great numbers, but their spiny fin makes them rather inedible to larger fish, and so they play the day away in shafts of sunlight. They sulk on cloudy days and cannot be caught then.

The Rock Bass

The rock bass is getting rare, perhaps being eaten more and more by the pickerel. This fish looks like a fat bluegill, but larger. It lacks the stripe of the largemouth bass, has a dark black and green speckled side, and is flat, similar to a flounder. Like the perch, there is so little meat that it is rarely eaten and comes in a range of one to three pounds. It is most often caught at the lake on underwater lures, either worms or a spoon.

If eaten, it is scaled after the usual preparation, and then sliced in half along the spine, coated in cornmeal and pan fried. These fish hang in shallow water in the perch depth, feeding on insects and worms. Although they feed on surface insects at dusk, they will not hit a surface lure, although they might take a fly. It has been several years since one was caught, and they may be all gone now.

24

The Catfish

The lake catfish, like the rock bass, has not been seen for a while. They can be caught on cheese or worms fished right on the bottom, especially on mud. Dropping this bait onto a weed bed means that something else will eat it – perhaps a snapping turtle – and so people really do not fish for catfish at the lake. Sometimes their young could be seen along the shore, next to rocks, but the large ones stay on the bottom in the deepest part of the lake.

If caught, they also, like the pickerel, must be skinned, and of course, one must not be touched by the long whiskers coming out from the sides of the mouth, as they sting. The catfish can live forever out of water, and the usual method of killing them, unlike the knife through the spine at the rear of the fish head, involves the application of a hammer to the head. The catfish is then nailed to a tree with a nail through the head, and the skin stripped off, after which the insides and fins are removed. Sometimes they can be filleted, with the meat coated in cornmeal or flour and then pan fried. The catfish is the bottom feeder of the lake, and rarely caught for sport. The last one that anyone in the Fishing Club remembers being caught was in 1974. If there are any left today, they have gone to the deep.

The Sunny and the Bluegill

These are called pan fish in some parts of the country, but in New Jersey, they are called "Sunnys" or "Bluegills." At the most, they grow to be three pounds. They live along the shores and under the docks, living on ants, tree worms that fall into the water, and bread from the young children. These are the fish that children and older people feed. The fish enjoy striking bread pieces floating on the surface.

They nest close to shore, with their nests being easy to spot as round, sandy depressions about two feet in diameter. These sand craters are made by the mother fish using her tail fin to clean out the nest down to the firm sandy bottom. Walk out on any dock at the lake, and one can see 10 or 12 sunny nests around the dock. The terms "sunny" and "bluegill" are used interchangeably, but actually the sunny has a bright orange tummy. It is different from the perch in that it has no vertical stripe on its side. The bluegill lacks the orange tummy, but has dark blue tips at the edge of its gills on each side of its head.

These fish stay near shore for protection. Since they are small, they are rarely eaten by people, although children love to catch them by using bread balls as bait. The children drop their lines into the water from the docks. The larger bluegills are sometimes caught on worms when fishing for bass, but are rarely kept for food.

These fish are the easiest to tame of all the lake fish. A person lies on the end of the dock, holding a piece of bread in their hand. As the bread becomes wet, the person shreds the bread so that pieces sink toward the bottom. This attracts the sunnys, which begin to feed. When they have eaten all of the bread floating downward, they will begin to carefully eat the bread from one's hand, as long as the hand remains still. Eventually, the tamed fish will congregate at the end of the dock as soon as the person walks onto the dock. They learn to recognize the tread of the feeder, especially if they are fed the bread at the same time of day. This same feeding technique can be done while standing still or kneeling in the water, but is liable to result in inadvertent nips on tender body parts. Eventually, these fish can be tamed to the point that they can be held underwater.

The Turtles

There are several types of turtles at the lake, including snapping turtles, painted turtles, mud turtles, and the land version, known as the box turtle.

The snapping turtles are dangerous. They are equipped with a black-green armored back with pointy ridges up the center. They infest the whole lake, and can be seen on the surface on a calm evening, sticking their snouts up for air, with their backs just breaking water. They cannot be approached, and any rowing in their direction results in their diving for the bottom. They range in size up to the very large ones, with a back shell two feet in diameter. These very large snappers are rarely spotted out away from cover. They inhabit the weed beds around the floating island, even burrowing under the edge of the island to invade swans' nests. They are a threat to scuba divers, and several unwary fishermen and swimmers have been injured by encountering them. Smart fishermen carry a belt knife to cut their fishing line, with much shouting, if they see that they have hooked a snapping turtle. No one swims near the floating island at the north end of the lake for fear of the turtles.

In the 1960's, there were periodic scuba efforts to eradicate the big turtles by using spears, but the lake dwellers have given up the battle now, and there are many snapping turtles about. About 2/3 of the baby duck and swan population is lost to them each year. It is sad to see the pair of parent swans leading six little ones one day, and the next day leading only two, and none at all the next day. This sad slaughter happens year after year, but as the swan's nest is well hidden from people, the turtles feast well. There is, among the lake people, a suspicion that the turtles are responsible for the eradication of the gold carp and the catfish, but nothing has been proven. If a smaller one is caught, it is dispatched by applying a lighter flame to the tail end, and when the head is stuck out, applying a hatchet to the neck. One should be careful of the severed head, as the jaw will still snap for a few minutes.

The painted turtles look painted in swirls of red, orange, and yellow. They are the most attractive turtle at the lake, and can sometimes be seen along inhabited shores. They make fine summer pets in an aquarium, eating garden worms, and survive well if released back into the lake in September. Even their necks are painted, with a stripe of red and yellow over their base coat of black. They are friendly and fun and harmless, and old ladies talk about them showing the glory of nature. Most people don't think about the glory of nature, just the fact that they look nice.

The mud turtles are the lowest of the low. They are often covered in mud, grow to a foot across the shell, and have pointed noses. They eat mostly weeds and plants growing in the shallows, with a few minnows thrown in for satisfaction. They don't bite and aren't pretty, being dark green all over, and are often decorated with weeds and mud. The small children do not keep them as pets. They are rarely found around the docks, but rather inhabit the lagoon in the south and mud flats to the north of the floating island. In water of a moderate depth, they sometimes rise to the surface to take air and have a gentle look around. They are not particularly friendly and are alien to both the violent world of the snappers and the mystic world of the painted turtles.

The box turtles live on land, usually in shadowy, damp places in the forest around the lake, and in beds of myrtle and pachysandra. These turtles are pretty, with subdued yellows, reds, and browns. They have a high shell, and they often crane their neck upward to see above the ground cover they are traversing. Their heads are square-shaped, with a flat place between the eyes. The shells are usually around eight inches in diameter. Insects, flies, and worms compose their diet as they plod along. Their shell is quite tough, and should they encounter a dog, they can play dead inside their shell until the dog tires and moves away. They are the calmest of the turtles.

The Snakes

There are three types of North Jersey snakes at the lake: the copperhead, the garter snake, and the water snake. The copperhead is so named because its head and body are a copper color. These snakes can be found during a hot, dry summer when they come down from Bald Hill to the lake in search of water. They are often found unexpectedly in dry leaves and weeds, and if they are asleep, it is easy to step on one of them in July when most people are walking around the lake barefoot. Children exploring very small streams caused by the overflow from the cove dam, and small creeks that feed the lagoon, are usually the loser in the hide-and-seek game they didn't know they were playing with the snake. These snakes can be several feet long and ill-tempered due to the dry conditions and heat. They rarely swim, preferring the land to water. Their bite can be fatal, especially to a child. They can be found early in the morning, sunning themselves on concrete retaining walls by the water, or on the granite rocks in the early sunlight. They should be avoided if seen, as they tend to have a bad disposition.

The garter snakes are the harmless green snakes found in old rose beds, and sometimes under rotting birch logs used to set the boundaries of the flower beds. They are about eight inches long, and make playful pets, but are difficult to feed in captivity. They are useful players in nature, eating bugs that humans do not like. Unfortunately, they may also eat bugs humans do like, as they are not too discriminating. They will tend to avoid human contact. The larger ones like to eat the garden toad that is useful in limiting the bug population. Garter snakes should be removed to a forest area, where they will not eat the garden toads.

The water snake is black and long. It swims and swims and swims. If it swims along beneath the docks, it terrifies the human swimmers and sun-tanners. Everyone knows when a water snake is passing on an August evening by the shrieks of the swimmers as the snake proceeds along the shoreline.

These snakes eat frogs, fish, and very small water birds. They avoid contact with people, preferring the waters of the lagoon to the open lake water. It is not unusual to find four feet of water snake on a log in the lagoon. They operate much like the mud turtle, a part of no world except their own.

The Frogs

There are three types of frogs at the lake: bullfrog, green frog, and peeper. The bullfrog, often portrayed in movies about the South, really does grunt and groan with a deep voice. They live in boathouses, swamps, lily pad areas, the floating island, and wet, lonely shores. The patient person can find them at night by flashlight eventually, for each time they sense movement, they cease to grunt. But, they will start again in a little while, and the hunt can resume slowly. They can be caught by net and eaten, but it is more fun to listen to them. They are a dark green and will eat anything that can fit in their mouth – including other frogs.

The green frogs are smaller than the mighty bullfrogs, and they croak in a higher tone. They live around lily pads and islands, and usually do not grow to be too large. Their greatest enemy is the bass, which lurks under the lily pads, waiting for the frog to jump into the water. As long as they do not move, the bass will not be able to locate them by song alone, but let the frog twitch after an insect, and the bass may come right up under the lily pad, knocking the frog into the water and into becoming dinner for the bass. A frog which jumps from a lily pad or rock into the water is an easy target for the bass, which is usually waiting. They can also be targets for a wayward pickerel up in the rocky shallows.

The peepers are small water and land frogs. They spend part of their time in the water and part of their time on the shore. They croak with a high-pitched peep. On a summer or early fall night, all three types of frogs set up a pattern of logical croaking and peeping which lulls the lake people to sleep, and accompanies the skunks and raccoons in their nightly travels. More than any other living creature at the lake, the night belongs to the frogs, and they sing from dark 'til dawn, giving away their locations to those who hunt them in the dark.

Activities at the lake are centered around the clubs and organizations, and holidays. This chapter reviews the various holidays and special activities that occur at the lake.

July 4th

The Fourth of July is the central holiday of the summer season on the lake, much as it is the central holiday of the summer in the rest of the nation. This is the holiday when not only does everyone wear his or her bathing suits and sunglasses all day (no, it never has rained on July 4th at the lake), but everyone cooks huge hunks of beef on charcoal grills. No one at the lake uses a gas grill, as that's considered wimpy. The popular health wave of eating chicken and fish has not affected the celebration of the major summer holiday at the lake. The rule is still lots and lots of beef from the A&P on Route 53 on the grill for the afternoon and evening. The eating of beef at the lake is not done just at one time during the day by a family. Rather, it is done from 11 a.m. to midnight, with steak after steak landing on the grill to be cooked to a turn by red-faced, overweight, earnest cooks.

Along with the eating of red meat comes the consumption of summer drinks. The favorite is beer, while other folks at the lake drink the most-favored mixed drink, a grasshopper. People at the lake still like to use those Kmart brightly colored glasses in red and yellow swirled hues, but they have abandoned the little umbrellas that were popular in the 1950's. When drinking the drinks, which are served all day along with steaks, the women of the lake wear large floppy pink straw hats or white cloth safari-type hats with cloth tie strips as prevention against the effects of the wind. The men wear fishing caps or floppy hats, according to their age. Everyone wears sunglasses bought in town at the hardware store, pharmacy, or five and dime stores. It's a great faux pas to not have one's sunglasses on one's face for the Fourth of July.

Along with the drinks and the steaks, the people of the lake eat corn on the cob, boiled for 20 minutes in large pots on kitchen stoves. Also eaten is potato salad, which is left out in the humid, warm air from 11 a.m. to midnight. Also left out for all-day munching is pasta salad from the Italian gourmet shop by the train station, and cheese pastries from the Viking store. At the family gatherings, assorted cakes and pastries are brought by the aunts and nieces eager to show off their cooking skills.

The family gatherings at the lake are huge on the Fourth of July, for this is the opportunity for all of those city-bound folks to experience the country and the water. No doubt the lake is almost as crowded as is the Jersey shore on the holiday, with the beaches packed, and no place to park. The lake water is crowded with sailboats skippered by people who have never sailed before. Cars of visitors prowl around the lake roads with the drivers looking at the numbers on the mailboxes while the rest of the family looks at the hand-drawn map mailed to them by their distant relatives who have lived at the lake for years, and have no concept of where the new highways in the area of the lake go to or come from. Often, these maps show little two-lane roads entering the area of the lake, where there are now interstates only. If, by luck and skill, the guests find the lake, they are apt to be confused by the numbers running differently on the east side from the west side. This was because originally the two sides of the lake were formed into different property owners' associations, and different numbering schemes were designed. When, eventually, the guests find the house of their distant relations, everyone in the car rushes into the house, uses the bathroom, and changes into swimsuits.

The young visitors will locate the inflatable rafts and inner tubes, and head for the water with much screaming, while the adults will say, "How nice to see you again! It's been a long time! How about a beer?" And the adults will settle down by the water in the lounge chairs with the plastic webbing, and begin 12 hours of drinking before driving back to the City. The visitors, having white legs, will begin to turn red shortly, and keep drinking to cool off. As the heat grows, the adults will take to their big inner tubes, floating along by the docks as a new can of beer is handed down to the men floating about aimlessly in the inner tubes. The eating of steaks requires getting back out of the water, but the food can be eaten informally while sitting on the end of the dock, with the sun shining down on everyone's shoulders. The children swim, producing large splashes and screams, and occasionally spraying the adults with water sprayed from plastic water guns and red plastic ketchup bottles.

The best part of the Fourth of July is the evening fireworks show. This is the one evening of the year when the fishermen come back from fishing before dark, for the fireworks are launched out into the water. There are several levels of fireworks. Some families launch sky rockets trailing reds and yellows out over the lake, into which they fall after exhausting their fuel. Other families launch the small handheld rockets and twisters, and throw cherry bombs out over the water by hand, where they scare the fish nearly to death when they explode a few feet over the water. Still other families stand on the end of their docks and light sparklers in the children's hands. The children wave the sparklers back and forth until the inferno gets close to the end of the stick, and then they throw the sparklers out over the water where the unlucky swimmer will find the thin metal rod with their feet the next week. The children at the lake take great pride in the fact that they try to time the throw of the sparkler so that the sparkler burns out just before it hits the water, thus not wasting any of the scenic effects by throwing it too early. The fathers throwing the cherry bombs try the same game, delaying the throwing of the bomb until the fuse has burnt short enough that the bomb will explode in the air, and not be put out by landing in the water before it explodes. This maneuver is dangerous. Thus, from dark until late in the evening, the whole lake is a symphony of bangs, booms, and bursts while everyone not engaged in fireworks believes it is his or her patriotic duty to keep eating large overdone steaks and drinking beer or mixed drinks. Some of the adults who have drunk too much to get out of their inner tube will float against the docks and walls while they watch the show with their toes and fingers wrinkling, rather than trying to get out of the lake. Out on the swim float in the middle of the lake, the teenagers will try setting off huge explosions concocted from balloons and hydrogen, or will try launching gasoline-filled rockets which will explode high over the lake in a fiery replication of the northern lights. Huge explosions are also dangerous.

The best part of the holiday happens at exactly midnight, when several trumpeters and drummers from the local high school will stand at the end of a central dock, maybe one near the cove, and play martial music designed to flay the lake people into a fever pitch of patriotic emotion, while on the end of every dock, at every landing, at every beach, and in every lakefront yard, a red road flare is lit. Over 500 red flares burn for 20 minutes, turning the lake into a lake from hell, while the teens on the float ignite their biggest blasts of hydrogen balloons and gasoline. A few brave and solid citizens of the lake shoot off small dynamite charges tied to deer hunting arrows. These charges make a very satisfactory noise. Even the old people of the lake, having retired to take a short nap from the activities earlier in the evening, have been roused from bed to watch the flares be lit. Each family flare is lit by the oldest tottering member of the family present, and the universal red glow reminds everyone that they all live together in one community in harmony on the fire-ringed hellish lake. Gasoline and hydrogen are more than dangerous – they can be lethal. Playing with them for the 4th of July should not be attempted.

After the flares burn out, the guests grab a final beer, locate the children who have been running through the neighbor's flower beds, and head out into the highways jam-packed with people returning from the shore, going back to the City. The moonlit lake is left covered with a thick atmosphere of sulfur and gunpowder smoke. The residents have a final gulp of cold steak, dump the glowing charcoal embers into the dry leaves under the trees, wash away the greasy smoky taste in their mouths with a warm beer, send their children to bed, and retire themselves, with a few comments that this was the best fireworks ever that they could remember, and didn't Uncle Pete get a whale of a sunburn today?

For weeks afterwards, swimmers yell when they step on the remains of sparklers, and fishermen grumble when they catch the burnt-out bodies of rockets – but it was a wonderful Fourth of July.

Halloween was often a time for enduring the rain or the frost, but in either case it was the first holiday of the cold weather season which called for a big fire in the smoky granite fireplaces. If the holiday were met by rain, then children had parties inside by the fire, with the rain dripping out of the gutters which were full of the fall maple leaves, and the wind blew through the pines by the door. If the weather were frost and a full moon, then the smoke from the chimneys wafted across the lake and all of the children went trick-or-treating. Since the lake roads are not well lit, all of the young ones carried flashlights, and the outside cabin lights would be lit.

The costumes which the children wore were lake-oriented. One of the most popular costumes was the big green frog costume, and the second most popular costume was the generic fish costume. Other popular costumes were the alligator, the old fisherman, the wilderness explorer, and the water snake. Most of the costumes were homemade, the easiest to make being the old fisherman costume, because all of the clothes and trappings could be found in the family closet.

The most difficult to make was the water snake, although one could be made from a large cardboard box forced into a round shape, with green cloth stapled to the box which would then cover the child, and a green snake hood made of cloth for the head. The real trouble with the water snake costume was that snakes have no arms, and so how was the child to carry the Halloween trick-or-treat bag? This problem was solved by having another family member carry the bag of treats. At every door at which the snake appeared, the door opener would say brightly, "Oh, a water snake. I'm scared! Who's carrying the treat bag?" The other family member would then appear out of the dark and say "I am," and the bag would receive some more homemade cookies.

Many homemade goodies were handed out instead of store-bought treats. These homemade goodies included fudge, cookies, pieces of cake, and candied apples. There was nothing very fancy about Halloween, and there wasn't much effort made to scare the children when they arrived at the front or back doors, but at every house the children were invited in to warm up by the fire, to pet or step on the dog lying on the hearth, and to maybe have a piece of cake just out of the oven.

In some years, the teens would have a teen dance over at the clubhouse which had lights that flickered on and off due to poor wiring. These dances were always conducted by the Junior League, and the band was from the local Catholic high school, conducted by Mr. Baark, the same conductor who conducted at the summer Junior League dances. However, for the Halloween Dance, Mr. Baark would lower his dignity enough to dress in costume, usually in the form of a famous composer. Of course, only Mr. Baark knew his composers well enough to know whom he dressed as, so he was forced to tell everyone who inquired whom he was impersonating. His favorite was Mozart, and Mr. Baark would appear at the dance in a pink and sequined outfit with a white wig. The pink outfit, which was supposed to resemble one worn in the courts of Europe, looked suspiciously like a rock and roll costume from the band at the "Fun and Party" bar out on Route 46. The wig was not too well in place on Mr. Baark's head, and tended to rotate as the evening went along. The music played at these dances was often of a scary nature, with "Monster Mash," "The Witch Doctor," "Theme from the *Munsters*," "Love Potion No. 9," and Dracula movie music being played a lot. The women wore tight black boots and costumes in the witchy fashions, and the men dressed mostly as Robin Hood and aliens with antennas. The punch bowl was always spiked with whiskey and vodka, and among the treats served to the innocent teens was a very potent rum cake made by a Mrs. Henry who lived up on the north end of the lake. The President of the Junior League would act as the master of ceremonies, and introduce the songs. The band was usually pretty fair at making loud noise, and Mr. Baark was pretty fair at waving and grasping his baton, and so music was produced in the finest American tradition. One year, all of the boys in the band wore white wigs to match that of Mr. Baark, and they all resembled the dancing toadstools in *Fantasia* while they twitched to the dance music.

The chaperones were recruited from among the young rather than from the stodgy parents, and supplied with liberal amounts of the dance punch. As the dancers became increasingly thirsty from dancing, they also got into the punch a great deal, especially just before driving out on Route 46 for a little after-dance snack. Each song would start like this: The master of ceremonies would yell, "Ready for another dance?" into the microphone, and everyone would yell back as loudly as possible, "Yes!" Then, the host would say, "Go, Mr. Baark!" Then, shouting in a rather slurred voice, "*Ready*, one…two…three," and the music would start. Most of the music was fast music, and the teens, often sipping from the little orange paper punch cups with pumpkin faces on them, would jump about as if being electrocuted. Below the fireplace at one end of the hall that was so hot that the bricks in the fireplace glowed red, there was often heard the sound of both males and females being ill in the basement restrooms after a dance. The whole jiggly dance conducted in a hot room that warded off any late October chill from cooling the dancers seemed to have the unfortunate effect of making everyone feel ill.

The clubhouse was decorated with orange and black streamers that went from the middle of the dance floor to the wall and corners, and orange and black balloons that the Junior Leaguers had spent all afternoon filling with hydrogen. These balloons made a wonderful popping sound if they came near to any cigarette lighters. The more rambunctious of the male dancers would light off a balloon in the spirit of frightening the other dancers, occasionally blowing out some window glass in the process to the lithe sounds of *tinkle-tinkle* as the glass blew out onto the car hoods.

As the evening wore on, Mr. Baark looked at the women more intently, the music went faster and faster, and more and more bowls of punch were consumed, so that when the dance ended at midnight, everyone was pretty well three sheets to the wind, including the chaperones. The celebrants either drove out to Route 46 to Paul's Diner for some coffee to go with their Halloween snacks, or stripped to their undergarments and went for a quick wade in the cove water at the east beach, so as to feel a bit better. Some of the couple's went into the deeper dark water to express their love. And, sometimes, they met a snapping turtle with jaws and claws that worked, or a water snake in the dark water, or stepped on a left-over sparkler rod from the 4th of July, and their yells of anguish and terror put a genuine fright into Halloween night, and roused the grandpas and grandmas in their nightcaps from bed.

As Halloween drew to a close, the small children felt that it had been a success, because they had gathered lots of candy; the parents felt happy because they had given away all of the candy, and would not have to eat the leftovers; and the teens felt altogether pretty high about the holiday. It was not known how the people felt who had met a snapping turtle or snake in the dark cove water after the dance (though I'm sure you can imagine).

Christmas

Christmas is the time of year for canasta parties, and after the players have tired of that exciting game, they would go from the living room by the fireplace out onto the porch for a little holiday snack. These Christmas snacks were served on the best holiday plates sitting on little holiday doilies with holly imprinted on them. Light Eastern European pastries with white sugar on top, slices of rum cake covered in chocolate icing, white cake with red and green swirled icing, and torte cake serve as the dessert. The meat snack is often crabmeat mixed with cream cheese, shaped into some sort of animal, and covered in cocktail sauce. Another lake favorite of the holiday season is layered breads and meats. This is created by having a loaf of bread sliced long ways, installing meats and cheese on each layer of the loaf, then slicing the loaf again vertically and cubing the slices. The result is a layered snack that is quite delicious, and a favorite of the lake people at holiday parties. The layered loaf can be altered at each party by changing the contents of each layer, so that it's sort of a surprise at each holiday gathering.

The dress for holiday parties at the lake is always casual, and the guests all volunteer to help carry in wood for the fire on cold nights. Carrying wood can result in getting sawdust all over one's party clothes, so it is important not to dress up. Pots of scented water are boiled over the fire on iron rods cemented into the side of the fireplace, and what aroma does not go up the chimney pervades the party room with an enjoyable scent. Replenishing the scented water and shoveling the car out of the snow after the party are also likely to dirty clothes, so casualwear is always the rule.

Gifts given at this time of year are of a very practical nature. New boat cushions, wood-splitting mauls, flue brushes, fireplace matches, new chains for the gasoline saws, a new fancy boat anchor from Macy's in New York, wood racks for the living room, and insulated gloves for reaching into the fire are useful store-bought gifts. Homemade gifts include birdhouses, sweaters, pot holders, tile trivets, lake mussel shell wall decorations, dried flowers pressed under glass and framed with copper strips, wood carvings, knitted bread covers to keep the coal and wood dust out, and homemade small tables and chairs for the children. One of the most popular of the homemade gifts is a square stick about 10 inches long which has notches cut in it and a small wooden propeller loosely attached to the end by a small nail. If a square, short stick is rubbed back and forth over the notches in the larger stick, the propeller will whirl. The lake children, even today, love to get these little propeller toys, and the sounds of the small sticks rubbing over the notches in the larger stick can be heard all around the lake at the holiday season, like termites gnawing in one's attic.

Since the lake people like to have their pine trees standing in the summer, they do not cut them down for Christmas, but instead go get a real tree at Big Bob's Discount Tree and Decoration Hall, which is set up every year at the Lions' Building west of town. Big Bob rents the Lions' hall from which he can sell trees every year. Most people at the lake do not use artificial trees, as there is not enough room to store them over the summer. Everyone's basements and garages are full of boating and fishing and swimming equipment. The trees at the lake are decorated with many family heirlooms such as the old Victorian ornaments, and the lights often used today are the bulbs which are smaller than the big outdoors bulbs, with vertical ridges on each bulb, two wires to each socket, and which all go out if one of the bulbs goes out. As these bulbs are hard to locate today, and as the lake people do not wish to use another type, they go to the flea markets down at New Hope and Somerville to find the bulb that they need to keep the lights going. People at the lake would not think of throwing away a string of lights just because the string goes out when one bulb needs to be replaced. It just takes a little patience to check for the burnt out bulb, and the lake people have plenty of patience. After all, patience is the main ingredient in good fishing.

The lake itself participates in the decorations by providing Goose Island. On the island, a wire tree frame has been built by men wearing large boots to protect them from the piles of goose droppings. Attached to this tree frame are strings of large outdoor bulbs, and an electric cable is run each December to the western shore to provide electricity to the tree. The frame and lights remain on the island all year, where they are periodically attacked by the geese, but the electrical cable is taken up in March, when the water thaws. This tree, out on the island, looks very nice when the lake is frozen and the lights reflect off of the ice. Assorted docks are also decorated with the big bulb lights, but not everyone does this, as it's a rather cold job putting up the lights in December with the wind blowing down over the hill.

Assorted lighted wreaths are placed in the windows of homes along the lake, and sometimes the outdoor spotlights which shine on the wood piles are replaced with red and green spotlights. This makes picking up the wood difficult, but makes the woodpiles look very festive.

As everyone at the lake spends a lot of time at the woodpiles during the winter, this added touch of color is appreciated even though it makes seeing more difficult. A wreath made of pine cones, and sometimes a glass tower made of glass balls, are placed on the mantel above the fire, and then the bare spots on the mantel are filled in with pine boughs and holly, some of which is cut from the local holly trees growing by the water. A nice local touch is a birch log on the main table, with holes cut in it for red candles. Most of the lake's birch trees have died off, but many of these candle birch logs still remain in the families which have been at the lake for several generations, and their placement on the main table of the house is a tradition.

The weather at the lake at Christmas is frightful. The wind blows down the eastern side of Bald Hill, the night temperature remains at zero, and when the clouds are not snowing, they deposit frozen rain on the roads and trees.

On a winter's night at the lake, there is heard the frequent sound of branches breaking, a loud "pop" as the limb finds the electric wires, and the lights go out in another house for a week or so until Jersey Central Power and Light comes out to repair the line. Sometimes the loud "crack" of a limb breaking is also followed by a loud "smash" or "clang" as the wayward limb hurtles down through the roof of a dock or the roof of a parked car. But, as everyone has fireplaces going until the concrete lining glows red, the loss of electricity is not a very serious matter. The houses will still be warm and cheery, with the candles in the birch log and the oil lamps lit. Even the canasta game can continue by the light of the oil lamps, and at night everyone wears long red or white underwear to bed to stay warm, and the fire plays patterns on the stairwell walls, and is reflected on the faces of the sleepers upstairs in the loft bedrooms.

On Christmas morning, the children are up at 4 a.m., whispering to their parents, "Is it time yet?" And, yes, it is time, when the children run downstairs to the tree and the family opens gifts. After the gifts are opened, the lake family enjoys a large lake breakfast, consisting of last summer's frozen bass, pan fried potatoes, eggs, center-cut or smoked bacon, tea, celery strips filled with Wisconsin cheese, and eggnog. After breakfast, some people go to church, while others sit in front of the fire watching the children play with their toys. Christmas at the lake is a family day, and the children do not run off after opening their gifts. Rather, they remain with their parents, enjoying their gifts and any little food treats that the neighbors may have dropped off for the celebration. During the afternoon, many of the families shovel out the car from the side of the road, and go to the multiscreen movie theater off of I-80 west of town, which always provides at least one G-rated movie for the holiday. Perhaps, this movie is a family film, or a new comedy, but the lake families can always be identified since they always sit together as a family at the movie.

After the movie, it's time to drive around the countryside looking at the house decorations, and part of the drive for every family is around the lake to see the tree lit up on Goose Island, and then for high adventure, up to the top of Bald Hill on the slippery road to look down at all of the colored lights on the docks around the lake. This adventure is always exciting and terrifying at the same time for the children, for the one-car road to the top of the hill is always bad during the winter, and there is always the worry of sliding off of the road. But once at the top, the shining lights around the frozen lake make the children in the warm car shout, "Look, look," as they pick out their neighbors' lighted docks from the hilltop. With binoculars, the lights can be seen to reflect off the lake ice and even the small lighted pine trees in the yards by the water can be seen. Afterwards, it's home to the fireplace and perhaps a children's card game such as Old Maid or Fish, and then later, bed, with the firelight shining up the stairs and on the ornaments hanging on the tree. When the children are asleep, their parents are likely to say, while holding hands by the fire, that it was the best Christmas ever.

Memorial Day

The Memorial Day holiday at the lake is still a patriotic holiday, when the people go to the cemeteries to remember the dead who defended America, and go to town to watch the parade. At the cemetery, little American flags are placed at the grave of the veterans by the children in the Cub Scouts or Boy Scouts, or perhaps by a family member if the deceased has any relatives remaining in the area. The flags, which are on little metal rods, are placed at the foot of the graves, and after all of the veterans' gravesites have been decorated, a student band from the local school will stop by the graveyard and play taps while the Scouts stand in line.

The town parade is one of the old type parades, which is designed to honor the vets rather than just to provide entertainment. The parade always comes through the main street of town, and is led by the color guard from the Reserve Army unit from up on Route 46. Following the color guard are blocks of veterans from the VFW, Am Vets, and the American Legion. Other Reserve units follow, and then comes the town's patriotic display, consisting of floats towed by Jeeps. These floats are designed by the town's civic groups, including the American Association of University Women, the Senior Citizens, the Lions Club, the Kiwanis, the Friends of the Library, and the Churches United Association. Respectively, their floats last year were titled: "Women in History" (Revolutionary War women standing around a paper-mache cannon), "Our War Leaders" (famous generals from all eras, in proper attire), "A Great Nation" (a large paper Declaration of Independence with the population pointing at it), "Respect the Army's Flags" (Revolutionary War flags being held by teenagers), "Learn to Read About War" (a family gathered around a table reading), and "Pray for Peace" (a sample of the population praying in a veterans' graveyard, with the gravestones made from cardboard and sprayed with white paint). These local floats are always the hit of the parade. The lake people had two floats in the parade. The first, submitted by the Women's Club, was entitled "Watching for the Enemy" (a group of lady scouts standing watch on a hill). The second, submitted by the Fishing Club, was entitled "Feeding the Army" (a group of cooks handing out plastic fish and platters to WWI soldiers).

After the floats pass, any of the civic groups who wish to march follow along, carrying the American flag at the front of the group. At the end of the parade come the town's fire trucks and an ambulance, all with their sirens and lights on to put on a big memorial show in honor of the vets.

The afternoon of Memorial Day is spent eating hunks of beef from the grill, family swimming if the water isn't too cold, drinking the first iced tea of the season, and throwing a few horseshoes or playing badminton. The old men sit on the retaining walls and flick black ants into the water using wooden ice cream sticks, and watch the fish eat the ants, while the old ladies sit in metal webbed yellow rockers on the docks and rock the afternoon away.

Labor Day

Labor Day brings the end of the summer season, and also the crowing of the lake King and Queen. The King and Queen are elected at the last summer teen dance held at the clubhouse (close to the cove), built in 1931 at the behest of the women of the lake. The teen dances are sponsored by the Junior League, who handle the funding and ticket sales. At the last dance, held the Saturday before Labor Day weekend, each teen votes for a King and Queen upon entering the dance. The names on the ballot have been previously chosen by the officers of the Junior League. Only Year-Around teens are ever nominated, and only the most handsome and beautiful teens at the lake are ever nominated. No other attribute is required and there is no other method of election other than voting. Teens at the dance simply write the names of the King and Queen on two separate pieces of white paper and stick them through a little slit in two boxes wrapped in white paper, marked on top "King" and "Queen." The duties of the winners consist of two things: to sit in the King and Queen's chairs at the Labor Day dance in the clubhouse, and to stand in a stately manner in the lead rowboat during the Labor Day Regatta.

The regatta is an extremely important ritual at the lake, one that the summer-only residents never participate in as they regard it all as a waste of time, and one that the year-round residents regard with the highest sense of duty. The origin of the lake regatta, which consists of decorating rowboats with all sorts of structures and top heavy decorations, has been lost in the dimness of time. It is suspected that the 1930s property owners may have created the first regatta as a tribute to the newly finished clubhouse, when everyone on the lake got into their boats and paddled and rowed to the clubhouse landing for the first social night. This simple proud parade of boats somehow developed during the years into boats with extensive ribbons and decorations, and the ritual ended up occurring on Labor Day each year. The lake people took to abbreviating the regatta to "The L.D. Regatta," which the summer-only folks soon transformed into "The Ludicrous Display Regatta." This blasphemy did not endear the summer-only residents to the year-rounders of the lake. In fact, the summer residents in recent years have taken to recording the regatta so they can show it to their friends at parties as entertainment. The usual capsizing of some of the boats due to top heavy conditions likely make for some good laughs at a January party at the summer residents' winter homes in Florida.

The regatta had a yearly theme which was selected by the Women's Club and was usually patriotic, such as "The Revolution," "The Armistice Day," or "The Civil War." Months before the regatta, the families who were going to participate – and they were always the same – would start decorating their boats. Rowboats with double-banked oars worked best. After the boat was selected, it would have a raised platform built upon it from plywood. The rowers would sit underneath the plywood platform, while the entertainers would be up on the platform. Sometimes another structure would be built up on the platform from which the entertainers would wave to the crowds on the shore. For example, during the "Civil War" year, one boat had a replica of Fort Sumter with Union soldiers waving to the crowd. Of course, the more decorations which were piled on top of the rowboat, the more likely was the rowboat to sink or turn turtle. The simplest decorations were ribbons and bunting strung from poles, and the rowers were part of the theme. This was easy to do when the year's theme was "Exploring the West." Even the canoes could participate that year.

All around the lake on the day before the regatta, families could be seen preparing their boats, until Labor Day itself arrived. The Labor Day Teen Dance, at which the King and Queen reigned, was held at the clubhouse the Saturday of Labor Day weekend, but Labor Day itself brought a sense of excitement rivaled only by the Fourth of July. Early in the morning, the families put the final touches of decoration on the rowboats, with some families even hanging signs on the boats identifying the decoration. Some years, the Women's Club printed programs and placed them in everyone's mailbox listing the lineup of the boats and each boat's scene. The regatta was the equivalent of the Rose Parade in California.

The regatta always started at 1 p.m. on Labor Day, and always went counterclockwise around the lake, starting and ending at the Johnson dock at the north end. Everyone hoped that it would not be a windy day, as the decorations on the boats made them hard to handle in a wind. Usually, there were 20 to 30 boats in the regatta at the height of its popularity in the 1950s, although this number has dropped off today to about six boats. The boats proceeded in line slowly around the lake, with the people on shore and the people in the boats waving to each other as the boats passed 10 yards from the end of each dock. The people on the shore stoked up their grills, cooked huge hunks of steak, and combined the steaks with beer while watching the regatta. There was no wine or dainty food – just good beer and red meat. Sometimes, during the regatta, a wind would come up from the south while the boats were still headed south, providing some good entertainment for the people on shore as the rowers tried to control the boats. Should one of them sink, the people on the shore would grab a few beers to sustain themselves, and launch a few rescue rowboats to pick up the swimmers and tow the foundered boat into shore. The old people of course, looked forward very much to seeing the regatta, and often invited other elderly friends from the local area out to the lake to view the water parade. These elderly people also liked to get into the spirit of the day by eating much red, fatty, charcoaled meat along with beer, and to join in the celebration in every way possible. Older people were never left out of activities at the lake.

The people on the regatta boat were dressed in costumes, while the people on the shore were dressed in bathing suits and sandals, or shorts and knee-high socks with brown shoes for the men and shorts and short white socks and tennis shoes for the women. Each generation was dressed appropriately for its demeanor and function, but always in a practical manner. After the boats had passed by, the celebration continued by people playing badminton, lawn golf, horseshoes, and croquet. Of these games, the two with a distinctly lake flavor were horseshoes and croquet.

Horseshoes was a favorite game at the lake on holidays, especially on Labor Day, for everyone knew that the remaining nice days were few, and soon the autumn rains would begin, keeping the people by their fireplaces. The game was often played on the lawn near the water. There were no sandpits, just two iron rods driven into the dirt about 10 yards apart. The distance between the rods was never measured, just estimated to be far enough apart for whoever was playing. Thus, the distance was a function of the players' strength. The horseshoes were often rusty or had been painted over with rustproof paint. Often, this paint was whatever had been left over from painting some piece of decorative iron here or there around the yard, and so the horseshoes were often a very unusual color such as white and yellow or yellow and green. No one ever kept score when playing at the lake. People just played until they were played out, and then they would go down to the water and flick large black ants off the retaining wall and into the water with an ice cream stick, so that the fish could eat the ants. After this, to cool down, they'd sit in the rockers on the docks and watch the water for a while, while they discussed the game just finished.

Croquet was a favorite game at the lake year-round, but it was tough to set up the course. Each time one would try to put a wicket into the ground, it was probable that a root or rock would be encountered, and the wicket would have to be relocated. This resulted in a very haphazard course. The problem was even more serious regarding the two hoops and the stake in line. If they were not lined up, end play was impossible. So players adjusted the best they could, and hoped when hitting an opponent's ball out of play that the ball would not fall into a mole hole or into the water. As the balls frequently encountered trees and rocks, they lost much of their paint after a while and were painted with whatever paint was available, resulting in painted balls which astounded most of the guest players who were not familiar with ways of the lake.

Birthdays

Birthdays at the lake are like holidays, for the birthday person always takes off from work on his or her birthday and goes fishing. Catching an edible fish on one's birthday is considered very good luck for the coming year. The more fish one catches at the lake on one's birthday, the more luck one will have. It's also a lake tradition that the birthday person never has to clean the fish that he or she catches on one's birthday; this task is done by the family members or else the family members pay for the fish market in town to clean the fish caught by the birthday person. The birthday person, if the weather is not unreasonable, starts their celebration by going fishing, often at 6 a.m. while everyone else is asleep. This way, they'll have the rest of the day free for other activities.

If the birthday person catches no good-size fish, they will return to their dock and catch a couple of small pan fish for good luck by using bread balls and a single hook, and throw them back after catching them as they were too small to eat. After the traditional catching, the birthday person is ready for the traditional once-a-year lake birthday breakfast. This feast is a test for the eater's endurance, and a way to prove that the celebrant still has a youthful stomach. Breakfast starts with fried sausage patties, cheese slices, and a few beers. This coats the stomach for what follows. The next course is an egg and cheese omelet, with mushrooms in white sauce and one pound of ham on the side of the plate. This is followed by sausage gravy (from the first course) and biscuits in a bowl, with whole milk in a glass for nutritious vitamin D. The family will usually play videos of family activities at the lake. Everyone else in the family eats a light breakfast, for they take more pleasure at watching the person celebrating than they do in participating in the actual eating of the birthday breakfast. The family members thus will usually share in only one of the courses which have been prepared. Next to be sampled are assorted cold shell fish with cocktail sauce supplemented by some assorted cold cheeses, and a little blush wine to aid in digestion. After that, the breakfast is completed. The person who has lived to see the completion of another year without a heart attack now has a brief morning nap on the porch to compensate for getting up early to go fishing for good luck.

The birthday afternoon is spent in active games and activities, such as horseshoes, dart throwing, croquet, canasta on the porch table, or ant flicking off of the lake's retaining wall. The more adventurous people will try a little diving off of the end of the dock. Of course, if the birthday falls in the winter, only the canasta playing or dart throwing is feasible. The younger people may have fun by playing a little archery, though this tends to endanger the neighbors' dogs. The usual target is a bale of straw set up on a table. Should the celebrant's friends drop by to wish one the best returns of the day, they will be given a bow and a brown paper grocery bag of arrows, and everyone will shoot at the bale of straw for an hour, and then have some lime drink for refreshment. This drink always perks up the people who are now starting to gather in earnest and usually unannounced. Word of a birthday gets around the lake quickly, as word is passed from the trades people in town (who see when family members are buying the birthday breakfast) to the lake residents in town doing grocery shopping. Birthday celebrations are always open affairs, with everyone who lives at the lake invited to everyone's celebration. It is thus possible to eat almost every lunch free by buying little gifts and dropping over to someone's house to help celebrate.

The centerpiece of the day is the luncheon served to everyone present, including the pets. This luncheon may be served indoors if the weather is not too nice, but from May to October it is usually served outdoors. The indoor luncheon is usually a buffet affair, with the dishes being the best china the family has. The food is laid out on the sideboard and is always heavy on meats and seafood, and light on salads. The meats include large hams, a whole turkey, and chopped steak and gravy. Included also are potato salad, macaroni salad, noodle salad, bean salad, corn on the cob from the farmer outside of town, and pancakes kept in a little silver warmer with a candle under it, and served with Aunt Emma's homemade syrup that she made for Christmas last year. The butter for the Viking rolls is real, and used to come from the Alderney Dairy on Route 10, but now comes from the A&P store near where Mildred lives (you'll read about her later). Dessert at the indoor buffet is chocolate ice cream, birthday cake, assorted Eastern European pastries with white sugar on the top, and assorted rum and liqueur cakes which the relatives have made. The meal is topped off with imported coffee, often ground in the kitchen by a little electric grinding machine.

The outside feast is better than the inside buffet, for the charcoal grill can be used to great advantage. First, hunks of beef can be placed on the grill and allowed to burn on the outside, then covered with barbecue sauce to allow the inside to stay pretty raw. The meat is then covered with onion slices and packed around with potatoes in aluminum foil. It is later served to guests in large portions and eaten totally. It is considered bad manners at the lake to trim the fat from the meat, and in fact, the eating of fat is regarded as a way to build tolerance to the cold weather of winter. The process of building up the body for winter is a slow one and, therefore, must start early in the summer. People at the lake like to season their beef with salt, pepper, sea salt, and thyme, and then cover it in ketchup or steak sauce. On another grill, clams are boiled in pots of water, and corn is boiled on the gas stove in the house and later carried outdoors on platters. Sometimes, if the birthday person has been lucky that morning and caught a large fish, the fish can be cooked on the grill in aluminum foil and each person will eat a scalding and sometimes bony bite from his or her plastic fork for good luck.

Along with all of this are the usual potato, macaroni, and spaghetti salads which are put out early so people can start eating, and remain out all day in the July air for nibbling upon as new guests drop by. The outside desserts are much like those at the inside buffet, with a store-bought cake from town with the words "Happy Birthday Biffy" written on it in dark icing, and lots of little flowers on the cake. People at the lake like to eat the little icing flowers off of the birthday cakes, and to get a flower on one's piece of cake is considered to be very good luck, as well as good eating.

Sometimes, cookies with white filling are served with the cake, and the guests very much like to separate the two sides of the cookie and eat out the icing, then dip the cookie sides into melted ice cream and use the cookie sides to shovel the ice cream into their mouths. Also, served for dessert are fruit tarts with cherry and strawberry filling in the middle, petit fours, baskets of chocolate candy from Ohio, and small rolled breads stuffed with chocolate which look like cigars. These cigars are made near Cape Lookout by Hungarian immigrants, and are considered a must at any lake birthday party, as they are expensive and good-tasting. Dessert is followed by drinks such as coffee, pop, malts made in the kitchen by all of the children at the same time, brandy served in wine glasses, and milk for the very old and young whose digestion isn't too good.

Around 4 p.m. the presents are opened. Birthday presents tend to be store bought, rather than handmade as are the Christmas presents. That's because everyone believes that enough effort went into making the Christmas presents, and it's much easier just to run into the five and dime store and buy something than to spend weeks making something. Also, since many people attend a great many birthday parties, there just isn't time to take a great deal of care in the selection of the birthday present.

What might one receive at the lake for one's birthday? A favorite gift is matching boat cushions with cloth handles for hanging them up in the garage over the winter. Another favorite is the luminescent handle fishing pole that can be easily located in the dark on the bottom of the boat, and thus not stepped upon and snapped. Other wonderful gifts which will be treasured are the spiked horseshoe playing shoes, which can be bought at the shoe store in town and come in brown or black for both men and women, as well as a green plastic eye shade cap that one can wear while sitting out in the boat in the sun. These caps rather look like dealers' caps from the casinos of Atlantic City, as the top is open to the nice warmth of the sun, but have little jumping trout fish appliques on them to show that they belong to a fisherman and not to a card dealer. One of the most sought-after birthday presents is a boat organizer for the family. This vaguely resembles those clothes closet organizers in that it is made from plastic tubing, but it sets down, instead of standing upright, to organize all of the fishing equipment. It only comes in white, but comes in three forms: rowboat, canoe, and the sailboat organizer, which keeps picnic supplies from being lost overboard. This organizer is manufactured at Trenton, the state capitol, and is very popular with state workers and fishermen on the Delaware River. Sometimes, the lucky birthday person will receive a water slide. This slide is bolted to the end of the dock. A little electric water pump sends water down the slide to ease the way, and the proud owner can climb the aluminum ladder to the top of the slide, and slide down into the water, landing in the water with a splash and a thump on the bottom of the lake if there wasn't much rain that year.

One of the most cherished gifts is the four-leaf clover which grows in some abundance around the south area of the lake. These are found along the edge of the lagoon, and after being picked, are placed between two pieces of glass which are then surrounded with copper foil to hold the glass together. A sticky eyelet is pasted to the back of the glass, and the ornament can be hung on the wall attached to a nail driven into the wall. These clover leaves are a unique color, no doubt due to the lagoon water, and are composed of green leaves with unusual red stripes in them.

The opening of the gifts is accomplished while the guests continue to eat on the hunks of meat and the assorted salads made with mayonnaise, such as the macaroni and potato and pasta salads which have been nicely warmed by the sun and so are very flavorful. As such, the sounds of discount store gift wrap being removed from the presents is accompanied by the sounds of eating, and an occasional loud hiccup. The birthday person is expected to immediately try out the gift which has been received, and so after a while the recipient is decorated with fishing hats, poles, bright shirts and ties, sitting in a chair on top of several boat cushions. Larger gifts are set up in the yard, and if the gift is for use on the water, the water is imagined. The men tend to congregate around the grills while the gifts are being opened, and comment about the state of the fires and discuss the burning rates of different brands of charcoal. The women gather around the birthday person to see what each other has bought for that honored person, and to make sure no one spent too much on the birthday person.

As the afternoon wears on, someone will yell, "Let's flick ants!" and everyone will reach into his or her back pocket and get out their wooden ice cream sticks. These sticks came from the center of the ice cream bars that are brought from the man who drives around the lake every summer afternoon in a little white truck with an open front seat. The rear of the little truck is a cold box with the ice cream inside, with little doors on the side to provide access to the ice cream. When the doors are opened, a cold frost cloud spills out into the pavement and makes one's feet feel cold. Often, people at the lake mark their name on their ice cream stick, as people at the lake feel a strong emotional attachment to their sticks. People who do not keep their sticks loose in their back pocket keep them in little plastic boxes which they carry in their left back pockets, or sometimes taped to their straw hats. The sticks are used to flick big black ants off the concrete lake retaining walls and into the water, where the pan fish strike up through the water in a big splash to swallow them.

The lake people turn this flicking of ants off the wall into a game with prizes. Everyone lines up along the wall by the water, which is, of course, lower than the wall. As soon as a big ant runs along the wall, the ice cream stick is used sideways to flick the ant off the wall and into the water. Usually, the whole side of the stick is used, with the fingers holding the very end of the stick, which starts parallel to the water, and is then rotated towards the water, flicking the big ant off the wall and into the water, where it will start to swim, and the fish will soon attack it. Some of the more proficient flickers use only the very rounded end of the stick to flick the ants off the wall, and those people are greatly respected. The contest part of this activity is timing how long the ant survives. Good players are able to flick their ant near to a fish which is drifting by, or on a nest underwater near to the wall. Poor players just flick their ant into the water, hope for the best, and lose, for this is a game of timing and skill. The best players are able to flick their ants near to the fish's nose, which will produce the fastest consumption.

The game is played by everyone lining up along the wall, and behind each player is someone with a stopwatch which the timers carry around the lake all day on their belt loops to show that they are flicker timers. Each player flicks in turn, with people who have flicked in the current round allowing the ant to run past them without being flicked. Ants run along all of the lake retaining walls every few seconds, so there is no shortage of playing pieces. The stopwatch is started when the stick is heard scraping along the wall flicking the ant, and the watch is stopped when the ant is eaten. After a round, all timekeepers report times to a main scorekeeper, and after 10 rounds, a winner is declared. After the game, everyone will head back to the house in a very good mood, everyone talking at once about their flicking techniques, and how many games they have won over the past month. Then, it is time for a little more meat, some corn on the cob, and a little bite of the warm macaroni salad, followed by a rest in the chairs after the flicking game.

Meanwhile, the birthday person has thanked everyone for the gifts, and joined the guests who did not go off to play at the flicking wall in the consumption of desserts. The store-bought cake with words such as "Happy Birthday Biffy" written on it is eaten first after singing "Happy Birthday." Everyone hopes to get the little icing flowers on the birthday cake to eat (although each person says, "Oh, you take the flower") and the birthday person always gets to eat "Biffy." When the vanilla-filled cookies are separated so that the icing can be eaten, all of the youngsters and men stick the cookie sides into their mouths and make faces, then remove the cookie sides and dip the sides into melted ice cream and use the cookie sides to shovel the ice cream into their mouths. The fruit tarts with cherry and strawberry filling are eaten whole. The petit fours, baskets of chocolate candy from Ohio, and the small rolled breads stuffed with chocolate which look like cigars are gobbled up and are soon gone.

As the afternoon passes, the guests may play a little croquet, throw a few horseshoes, or doze in the lounge chairs. The children all go into the house to watch television and lie on the furniture in strange and unnatural positions. The men speak talk the algae in the lake and the odd color of the water in the lagoon, and the women occupy their time talking about the time that Cindy fell off the regatta float and nearly drowned, and "Haven't the wildflowers been nice this year to pick?" and "It's getting hard to find any around this week."

Prizes are always awarded for the best players of the afternoon ant flicking, croquet, and horseshoes. These little prizes awarded by the host or hostess are always of a very useful nature. The winners may receive barbecue mitts, flashlights, a fishing cap, or a whistle to call for help when one's boat is sinking.

During the evening of the winter birthday party, everyone is inside sipping hot chocolate or coffee, and by 9 p.m., it's time to shovel out the car if it has been snowing, or maybe just scrape the frost off the car windows. By 9:30, the well-fed guests wave goodbye and head home to bed and their own warm fireplace. But at the summer birthday party, the party can last well into the night hours. The adults sit out on the patio under yellow bug lights, or maybe sit in the dark on the dock, watching the water and listening to the geese over on Goose Island. This is boring to the children, who go inside to play games.

One of their favorite games to play is couch fishing. One or two of the children get on the couch and pile pillows lengthwise to form the side of the boat. They use yardsticks as poles, and string to the yardsticks as line. Then, they take something from the living room end tables to be a lure, such as Mother's ceramic ashtray. The other children lie on the floor and act as the fish. The fishers close their eyes and wave the yardsticks around, landing the "lures" on the carpet near to the couch. The "lures" are slowly dragged back to the couch. If none of the children on the floor "take" the lure, then the child on the couch tries again. Eventually, the suspense will be too much, and one of the "fish" will grab the lure. The fish may be reeled in and captured, or escape, or pull on the lure so hard that the fisher is pulled off of the couch, and into the lake. The whole game is accompanied by much screaming, gestures, and chaos.

Another favorite lake game at the birthday party is playing a game called Big Bug. Dice are rolled and a large plastic bug is assembled from assorted plastic parts. The first child to finish building the bug is the winner. Another favorite at a party is Awesome Head, when all of the children go into the kitchen and get the largest Idaho potatoes they can find. Plastic parts such as eyes and noses are added to the potato based upon rolls of the dice. The first potato head completed makes that child the winner, and the happy child gets to keep the potato, take it home, and place it in their dresser drawer as a memento of the occasion.

New Year's Eve and New Year's Day

Perhaps no other holiday at the lake is celebrated so diversely as the celebration of New Year's. The older people at the lake tend to have a little snack to celebrate the ending of the tax year in their homes in front of a blistering fire. These snacks are almost always composed of shrimp and crab, cocktail sauce, and crackers, usually wheat. Accompanying this fine food is a little sherry, rum, or decaf coffee. This group of celebrants often call their friends on the phone at 9 p.m. to wish them a happy new year and a good night's sleep. By 10 p.m., they wish each other a final toast, glasses are raised, the last of the seafood eaten, and then it's time to throw some more logs into the fire before heading to bed.

A second group celebrates differently. These are the young adults, and to them the last day of the tax year is a time to party as a group. They are not happy unless they are surrounded by people just like them. The evening starts at some of the bars on Route 46, maybe at Jimmy's Place or over at the Lakeside Bar and Grill, or the Firestone Bar. This partying starts around 8 p.m. and goes until everyone is pretty wobbly, say about 11 p.m. Then, it's off to some house for more partying. Chips, beer, whiskey, dip, little cantaloupe balls, finger food, candy, corned beef with ketchup, and ice cream are all some of the little treats served. Everyone wears a little New Year's hat and has some sort of noisemaker. At midnight, everyone yells "Happy New Year," makes noise with the noisemakers (a few fire their shotguns into the air outside the house), and head for the water. One of the traditions at the lake among the young adults is the traditional First Swim of the year. Many of the people have worn their bathing suits under their clothes, and at the water they remove their party attire and line up at the water. The host and hostess have thoughtfully provided towels for afterwards, and with a final sip of beer, the whole line runs and jumps into the water. If the water has ice on it, the host has spent the last few hours at home, instead of going out to Route 46, breaking out the ice enough so that everyone can at least get a little wet. If the lake is not frozen, then some of the happier groups form a conga line, and snake into the water, with the tallest people leading the way, so as to provide a little challenge for the shorter people. After the First Swim is over, everyone has a little drink or two, towels off, gets dressed at the house, and the party will continue until dawn. Then, it's off to Big Roy's Diner for some fast food breakfast, and a little nap afterwards.

The teens have New Year's parties, much as the young adults do, only without the first swim of the year. The teens meet in each other's basements and play music on the record player and watch TV and talk, talk, talk. It's not much different than a normal Saturday night get-together. They wear jeans and gold jewelry and athletic shoes, and they all look and sound alike as they sit in the basement together, waiting for the day when they can party on the main floor of the house, and when that day comes, they will know that they are all grown up. Sometimes, the teens all take the Lakeland bus into the Port Authority at 42nd Street, and walk over to Times Square to see the lighted ball drop, and then catch the 12:30 a.m. express back to New Jersey, and their parents pick them up in town. The teens' tales of adventures in the City will provide enough materials for several days' discussion when they entertain their friends in the basement.

The younger children look forward to staying up until midnight. Sometimes, if they get drowsy in the evening, parents will put them to bed for a nap before the midnight hour, and then get them back up at 11:45 to watch midnight arrive and see the party at Times Square. The children are given some sort of noisemaker, and they can make noise at midnight. If no noisemaker is available, the mouthpiece of an instrument, such as a clarinet, can be blown, and the parents yell in the children's ears "Happy New Year!" as the child makes noise. Usually, the children are so excited that they need a little snack of potato chips, cheese, and warm milk to coax them back to sleep.

By dawn on New Year's Day, everyone at the lake is asleep, and by 10 a.m., everyone is up again to watch the parades on television with a big breakfast of omelets, toast with cinnamon sugar, sausage, bacon, and fried potatoes. The lake family, who probably have not all seen each other since early on New Year's Eve due to their individual comings and goings, will spend quality time together as they eat their breakfast and watch television. The conversation is sprinkled with comments such as "Pass the toast" and "Wow, look at that float" and "Gee, what a big band." And so, the people of the lake spend New Year's Day in an air of friendliness and consumption that bodes well for the functioning of the family in the New Year. The family that watches television and eats fried potatoes together is often quite content.

In this chapter, you'll learn about spin-casting fishing and the types of fishing trips on Cedar Lake.

Technical Matters

In American literature and movies, the romance of fishing is almost always portrayed as being related to fly fishing. Yet, those people who have tried spin-cast lake fishing often find that it has the same romance and glory as does all other fishing. The big brother of lake fishing is surf casting, but the principle is exactly the same. It is important to understand how spin casting works in order to understand just what lake fishers do out on the lake all day.

While fly fishing depends upon a back and forth rhythm and momentum to propel the fly out onto the water, spin casting is accomplished using heavier lures than flies, and so one swing of the arm or a flick of the wrist is all that is needed to send the lure outward. The line on the spin cast reel is controlled by a wire arm called a bail. If the bail is moved to the open position, the line comes off the reel. If the bail is closed, the line does not go out. To cast out the lure, the bail is opened, the line held with the index finger to prevent the lure from just falling down into the water, and the pole swung backwards. Then, when the pole is brought forward, the line is released by the finger at the appropriate time, and the lure arcs out towards the intended destination.

When the lure lands in the water, the crank on the reel is turned by hand, causing the bail to close. The crank is then turned at the desired rate to bring the lure back to the boat. Bails come in both half and full bail types. The half bail extends two-thirds of the way across the face of the reel and is anchored at one end by a screw, while the full bail makes a complete arc across the face of the reel, and is fastened at both ends by screws. Reels come in both right and left hand models. The poles are about six feet long and have several wire loops on them through which the line goes down to the lure. The lure is fastened to the line by tying a snap hook and swivel permanently to the line. Various lures are then attached to the snap hook. The use of the snap hook allows rapid changing of lures. When fishing for pickerel, a steel leader can be easily attached to the permanent swivel and hook. This steel line has a second hook and swivel at the lure end for the attachment of the lure. This steel leader is usually only used when fishing with an underwater lure, because its weight will cause a surface lure to sink instead of remaining on the surface. The swivel between the hook and line is used to keep the line from twisting. Each lure is equipped with an eye for the hook to snap onto. The usual type of line used is 12-pound test monofilament, though some sporting types of fishermen who don't mind losing a lot of valuable lures might use as low as five-pound test. The lighter the line, the easier it is for fish to break it. Yet, if it is too heavy (e.g., 20-pound test), it will be too heavy to cast well. Of course, catching a fish on very light test gives the catcher more right to brag than does catching a fish on heavier test, as catching a fish on light test weight supposedly requires great skill on the part of the fisherman. On the other hand, losing a lot of fish and lures from lightweight line is not very good economics.

In the spring, the line is removed from the reel and new line installed. Failure to do this means that the old line may break easily after lying about on the reel all winter. The new line must be wound tightly on the reel to prevent kinks. This can be done by having one person hold the packaged roll of new line so as to keep a strong tension on it while another person cranks the pole's reel handle to wind the line on the reel. Another method that works well is to run the new line onto the reel while pinching the line between two fingers to put tension on it. Winding line onto a reel without winding it tightly will result in having a big wreck the first cast or so, because the line will develop loops from the reel which eventually will get grabbed by the line going out rapidly on a cast, resulting in three strands of line, instead of one, going out through the loops on the pole. The resulting mess of line may take an hour to unravel and rewind on the reel. Fly fishing has the advantage in this case, for in fly fishing the line is pulled off the reel by hand in what can only be a single strand at each back and forth motion of the fly rod. Nevertheless, the problem can be avoided by keeping the line tightly wrapped on the reel. Many fishermen constantly use two fingers of the non-cranking hand to keep tension on the line as it is being reeled in.

There are two other ways that line goes out other than casting the lure. The first is that the bail can be opened while the lure is out somewhere, thus allowing more line to go out and the lure to go deeper. The second is that on the face of the reel, a plate can be twisted to provide tension when a fish takes a lure and runs. The amount of tension will regulate how much pull is needed to allow line to feed out even though the bail is shut. This is important, for having the drag screwed down tight will allow no line to go out if a fish takes a lure. Thus, a hard hit will cause the line to break. A big fish will usually run for a while, requiring line, then surface, flip and turn back in towards the boat. Proper control of the line is necessary, as a lot of slack in the line will allow the fish to go where it pleases and flip the lure easily.

There are really four types of lake fishing techniques, each with pros and cons. The first – trolling – involves getting the boat up to speed, dropping the oars to cast an underwater lure out, closing the bail, and rowing along slowly, towing the lure underwater. One must be careful to keep the pole secured in the boat, lest a big hit by a fish, combined with the forward momentum of the boat, pull the pole into the water. This technique has the advantage of allowing the fisherman to cover a lot of territory, but has the disadvantage of often ending up with the lure in the weeds, so that the lure is being towed along covered with a bunch of weeds, doing nothing. This is nonproductive. Trolling is mostly used when there is some chop to the water, and it is too windy for surface fishing. It is useful for pickerel fishing.

The second method – surface casting and retrieving – involves sending out a surface lure towards brush, weed banks, trees, lily pads, or islands. This type of fishing is very productive in calm water, and is useful in the evening or early morning when going after bass. The disadvantage is that it requires good casting control to avoid throwing the lure into the tree or island, where recovery may be difficult.

The third method – underwater casting and retrieving – is tried mostly away from shore, in any depth of water. This involves casting the lure out, waiting some time for it to sink, and then retrieving it. The deeper the water, the more the line is allowed to sink when it hits the water. This method can catch any type of fish, and a fish will often wait until the lure has been retrieved almost back to the boat before taking it.

The fourth and final method is live bait fishing. Minnows will tend to catch pickerel. The minnow is hooked vertically through the jaw lips or the back fin, cast very gently out, and allowed to swim until eaten by the pickerel. Night crawlers can be attached to one hook or multiple hooks, and a red and white bobber attached to the line several feet from the worm to suspend the worm below the surface so that it will not sink. Crawfish can be hooked through the tail and allowed to sink in the hope that a bass will find them. Frogs can be hooked through the lips or the skin at the back and gently cast towards an island. The advantage of this type of fishing is that one is likely to catch a very large fish, and the disadvantage is that one is likely to catch a snapping turtle or, if using night crawlers, lots of small fish.

Live bait fishing tends to result in the destruction of whatever is caught, for the fish usually swallows the bait whole before the hook is set, and hook removal will be difficult. This results in the death of numerous small fish that could have been released if caught on a lure, because lures usually catch the fish in the jaw where removal of the hooks is easy.

The Early Morning Trip

Going fishing in the early morning – at 5 a.m., for example – is a great adventure, equaled only by the midnight trip. This type of fishing is done in July and August, for the mornings in the North Jersey hills at this time of year are cool enough to require flannel shirts, a sweater, and heavy jacket. People in the City can be sweltering on a July night, while the people in the Jersey hills are sleeping under blankets with the windows shut. Morning fishing trips planned in September and October, no matter how well intentioned, tend to not materialize when the alarm rings at 4 AM and the dark, cool air outside of the electric blanket does not seem as attractive as sleeping in. Only the young fish at 5 a.m. after Labor Day, when the mornings are very cool.

The day starts with the proper attire. Boat sneakers, jeans, red flannel shirt, old sweater, and a corduroy coat are best, along with a warm hat which covers the ears. A knife is worn on a sheath attached to the belt in case of an unpleasant encounter with a snapper or snake. The tools needed are the boat, oars, flotation cushion in case of a big wreck, pole, flashlight to see the way to the dock or landing, net, a coffee can to bail out the water which leaks into wooden rowboats, anchor, stringer to hook the caught fish onto if any will be kept, and the tackle box. Wearing a life preserver is also a good idea.

The tackle box holds the following: lures, spare lure hooks and swivels, tape measure to see if the fish is a keeper (12 inches is the normal minimum for bass and 15 inches for pickerel). Other tackle box items include fake worms and bugs, scaling and skinning knife, bobbers, steel leaders, bare hooks for live bait, and a scale for weighing fish. The lures consist of various surface plugs for bass, spinners and spoons for pickerel, and assorted fake minnows that dive as they move, fake rubber bugs and worms and frogs, and every imaginable design of lure that might catch a fish. In spite of a box full of lures, most fishermen really only have three or four favorites that they use over and over. Tackle boxes are about 12 to 14 inches long, open up at the top, and come in plastic or metal, with two or three drawers. None are designed to float, so a big wreck in the boat means the loss of the tackle box if the boat is upset. Big wrecks on the lake are caused by hitting an unexpected rock, or looking over the side while getting ready to net a hooked fish and unbalancing the boat. A disaster on the lake at 5 a.m. usually means a long time in the water, as most people who would come to the rescue are asleep.

Before the tackle box is used on the first fishing trip of the year, week, or day, most fishermen like to spend a few hours arranging their lures and checking over the box to see that it has everything needed for the trip. This is a great ritual, and only the people who will actually fish ever check over their tackle boxes. Guests and rowers don't check tackle boxes. Usually, the box is set on the porch dining table and opened slowly and reverently, as if the lures may have changed into gold since the last fishing trip. Children too young to fish are scolded to not be playing with the hooks, and to stay away from the table until they are older, and can be taught the meaning and use of each lure. All clutter is cleared from the table, the tackle box unloaded, and the contents sorted. Hooks in one pile, shot and bobbers in another, homemade lures into another, store-bought lures sorted according to the type of fish they are supposed to catch, and the equipment such as the stringer, the scaler, a knife, pliers, and forceps are removed and inspected. If any of the tools are rusty, they are scrubbed with a steel wool pad and oiled. The knife is sharpened on a curved whetstone, and the stringer untangled and checked for weak spots. Some of the old stringers were actually made from string, but the new ones are made from yellow nylon rope. The lures are inspected for broken hooks and eyes, the number of remaining bobbers and sinkers and hooks counted, and notes made on a pocket notepad. Every fisherman knows how many of each item he wishes to have in the box, and if the number of a certain item falls below the number required, then it's off to Bob's Bait Shop on Route 46 for a shopping trip. Many fishermen carry replacement lures of their favorite type in case the line breaks and their favorite lure is lost due to a mishap.

The shopping trips to Bob's Shop always last several hours, even if the trip is only for a replacement bobber. The shop is filled on the left side with new aluminum boats and wooden oars and floatable boat cushions with carrying straps, and nets. But if one goes to the right upon entering, then one is in the world of lures. There are yellow spinners and black or green plugs, and red worms (five to a pack for $2.00). Along the back wall, there are plastic frogs and plastic centipedes, all in plastic bags stapled to cardboard backing. The plastic frogs are one for $1.50, while the plastic centipedes are five for $1.80. In little cardboard trays, there are red and white spoons, gold spoons, silver spoons, and black spoons, all in different lengths according to how big a fish one wishes to catch. Silver fake minnows that wiggle when reeled in come in five sizes. Tubs of worms and minnows are in the center of the store, and the customers help themselves, putting the bait into little cardboard waterproof wax-lined boxes, and pay by the container. A tub of really good night crawlers sells for 75 cents, a non-industrial large paper bucket of 12 minnows, in water, sells for 90 cents. Up in the front of the store, still on the right-hand side, are the new lures – the ones that are motorized, have a radical motion, or light up in the dark under water. Most of the fishermen look at these lures and look at the sales brochures, but never buy the lure. Only the new fishermen from the City try these radical lures, and no one who has fished for a while believes that a lure that lights up underwater and darts up and down with a running little motor and propeller will ever catch a bass. In fact, the old timers believe that having motorized lures is a good way to have the lure wear out a lot faster than a plain lure that wiggles because it's designed well. All in all, it takes several hours to examine the new lures and bore the young high school clerks with the tale of Hoffman's big perch that he caught at the lake last week, or Gibbon's fall from the boat, or James' poor perception of things in the dark that caused him to cast a perfectly good lure into a tree growing on the south island.

Once the replacement lure or bobber has been procured and the fisherman returns home, the lures, which are hopefully still on the table, undisturbed, are returned to the tackle box. Each item of the box is placed in its compartment or drawer, and all is made ready for the next trip. Since the excitement and confusion of the very next catch will bring disorder again to the box, and indeed may result in the entire contents landing in a muddle in the bottom of the boat if the pliers are needed in a hurry, the whole box will have to be re-inspected and repacked before the next trip. People at the lake who fish several times a week are thus doomed to forever be inspecting and repacking the tackle box in preparation for the next trip. The task is never done, but is always enjoyed, for what can give such pleasure as having one's lures spread out on the dining table, picking up each one and lovingly looking at it while it drops old scales onto the table, and cherishing the ownership of tools used for the capture of another species? It gives one chills up the spine to see the afternoon sun shining off the knives and spinners and metal tape measures, and to know that in a few hours a fish's jaws will bite down on one of the lures now lying quietly on the dining table. If that lure were left on the table and not taken along on the trip, would the fish bite another lure cast into the same place, or would the fish remain free? This is a subject of much debate on the lake, for there are those fishermen who believe that a fish will take any lure cast close enough to it, and others believe that a fish will only take the lure that is right for the time of day and the water conditions. The debate has not yet been settled, but is a constant topic of discussion at the monthly Fishing Club meetings at the lake clubhouse.

Breakfast for the early lake fishers is usually a cup of coffee and a few donuts from the grocery in town. Fishermen resist having too much coffee early. The trip down to the landing or dock is done by applying the flashlight beam and making lots of noise, for 5 a.m. is the time that the skunks are out and about, and it wouldn't do to startle one of them and thus start the fishing trip smelling of skunk. There is also the possibility of a snake lying about somewhere, or a rabid raccoon. In the 5 a.m. dark, these possibilities are taken seriously, and early fishers try to make a brave racket as they head for the boats, and look about them warily.

Arrival at the boat means getting everything aboard and stowed away. If the boat is aluminum, it may have to be launched. If wooden, it will need to be bailed out, for all wooden boats leak. The oars are put into the oarlocks, the floatation cushion placed on the seat as protection against the morning damp, the tackle box placed at one's feet, the anchor in the bow, the net at the side behind the fisher so that it won't get tangled with the pole, and the pole set on the bottom with the tip out over the water at the rear of the boat. The stringer is placed on the bottom on the other side from the net, while the flashlight is set on the rear seat in front of the rower, who rows facing the rear, and the bailing can is left on the bottom by the fisherman's feet. Orderliness in the dark will result in preventing messes and unfortunate happenings and untoward events should a fish be hooked.

The departure from the dock is made under starlight, with the nearby houses still dark. The frogs will still be croaking, and a bat can be seen against the stars. The oars will make the dark water swirl in small sparkles from the stars, even though the moon has set by now. Out toward the north the boat moves, with an ever-widening view of the dark shore. The individual trees cannot be seen yet, and the individual houses are now hidden away in the shadows of the trees. The lake looks now as it did in the 1930s, before all of the houses were built. Bald Hill cuts off the stars to the west, and the truck traffic on I-80 is the only reminder that it is not 1935. By 5:30 a.m., a mist will begin to rise from the lake, hiding the shore, and making collision with another boat a possibility. These rowboats carry no running lights, and rowers stop occasionally to listen for other rowers in the dark. Up towards the north, towards the weed banks and the floating island, the shore of the southwest corner of the island can eventually be seen as a low dark mass, like the medieval German forests in which the wolves lurked, waiting for the lone traveler.

This precious time before the dawn is the time to try a surface plug or surface silver minnow that will dive just beneath the surface when retrieved. Now is the time when the big bass are up near the surface, when the lake has not yet felt the sun's heat. The water will be a flat calm, the only ripples caused by the rhythmic dip of the oars. If the oarlocks have been properly oiled, the oars will make no sounds as they move, and the fish will not be scared.

Twenty yards from the floating island, with the bow of the boat facing east, is the location which places the boat over the weed banks. Here, the water is only two to three feet above the weeds, a good place for the bass to be waiting for something to move on the surface. There is one sure truth about fishing for bass on the surface: if there is a bass near, it will take the lure usually in the first thirty seconds of the lure hitting the water. The fisherman who has carefully planned will already have the first lure of the day snapped onto the line, and now is the time, at 5:30 a.m. – when there is just a touch of light to the east, and the night sounds quiet down, and the rising water mist delays any start of the day sounds – that the fisherman makes the most use of surface fishing. All surface lures are designed to do one thing: hit the water with a noticeable sound, and float. Many bass will take a surface lure within seconds of it hitting the water. Some lures are designed to stay on the surface while being retrieved and make some popping noises, and others may dive a little, then refloat if retrieval is stopped.

As long as the dark holds, casting surface lures in all directions from the boat will often produce results. There will be a large splash of water just after the lure hits the water, the rod tip will snap down, and perhaps a little line will be pulled out. Big bass do two things when hooked: either dive into the weeds or snap right up on their tails on the surface to throw the lure. It is best to try to keep the bass under the surface. Sometimes, rowing towards the fish gently, while keeping some tension on the line, allows the fisherman to get right over the fish in the weeds, then pull it up into the net while somehow holding the flashlight in one's mouth. If a little daylight is available, the need for the flashlight is reduced. It's difficult for the lone fisherman to hold the pole, net, and flashlight and row at the same time, and this unwieldy combination often results in the pole, flashlight, bass, or net being lost, or the fisherman falling into the water in the confusion.

Out on the lake around 5:30 a.m., the geese down on Goose Island begin to awaken, and start a group honking session to discuss plans for the day. The water mist thickens as day approaches, and along the shore a few lights in the houses of people who will catch the 6:30 train to Hoboken are turned on now. The smell of wood smoke from the cabin cook stoves, and the fireplaces of the old people who have taken a night chill drifts out from the land trees. The damp water mist, which rises almost every morning regardless of how hot the day will be later on, coats the tackle box, the oars, the line and pole, and one's outer coat. The mist coats the boat seats and cushions, and the droplets run into one's pants, getting them damp. The line on the reel becomes wet, and water drips from the pole's wire loops. The constant leaking of the wooden rowboats may require a little quiet bailing now, and the water in the bottom of the boat gets into one's boat shoes and make one's feet cold. The coffee can is set on the bottom of the boat in parallel to the side of the boat, the fisherman leans over toward the can to tilt the water in the bottom of the boat towards the can, the can is lifted and the water quietly poured into the lake. The can must not be scraped along the bottom of the boat, for this sound will scare the fish.

This is the time of day when all creatures begin in earnest to anticipate the light by waking and moving. It is feeding time, when some creatures in the water and on land will not live to see the sunlight. For the pickerel and the bass, this hour before the sunlight strikes the surface of the water is the time of open jaws and swift moves. It is the time when the sunnys and bluegills stay in the shallows by the shore without knowing why. Those little fish who stray into deeper water, perhaps following the water bugs, will not return to eat the bread thrown into the water by the small children. The smart chipmunks stay in their burrows, but the small swans, who are not yet smart, are taken away by the snapping turtles. This is the killing hour, when the smart and the strong take their meals at the table provided by the slow and foolish. It is the time when the smart fisherman who knows the layout of the bottom can sense where the fish are by the temperature feel of the water, the direction of last night's wind, and the amount of rainfall runoff in the last 48 hours. Sometimes, other fishermen can be seen in the mist, wrapped in dark coats and hats hunched over their poles and oars, their boats all looking black now. They do not wave or talk or say hello, for they are too busy stalking and watching that they are not being stalked by a snake or a snapper, and they keep careful watch as they cast and retrieve in the killing hour.

Around 6:30 a.m., the daylight comes, and out of the mist, which is beginning to rise, the geese community takes off for the day. This is the wake-up bugle call for the lake, as some 60 geese take a run for the sky, necks out and wings wide, the white patches on the side of their faces marking the formation as they form into a "V" and turn east, into the sun, which is still below the trees, in search of food. Some will go over to the river in town to meet the morning commuters who will throw bread to them, and others disperse to other lakes, to feed well. As daylight arrives, the fisherman can stop using the flashlight and begin to vary their fishing techniques. Now may be the time to move a little further away from the island, out further eastward and try some underwater fishing for both pickerel and bass. The choices become critical. Is it best to try over the stumps, or up around the lily pads, or around another island? If the week has been hot, is it best to try deeper water early in the day? Might there be a big pickerel by the underwater rock piles? Everyone has his or her own opinion, and of course, the more each person fishes the same spot hour after hour, the more fish are likely to be caught in that spot, reinforcing the opinion that this fishing place is the best on the lake.

At 6:30 a.m., the shore houses are lit with the lights of the commuters. They are gobbling their waffles and eggs, taking their showers, listening to network news and the traffic reports from the City. They put on their suits and locate their briefcases and tie their ties. Others put on their expensive blouses and professional suits and black high heels and a necklace. These people may look out at the lake and say, "Nice day," or "A little fog today," and go on to watch the traffic reports while they plan what route to take to the office. The chimney smoke dies away as the fires lit to remove the chill burn lower, and the sounds of cars starting can be heard. Out on I-80, the sound of the truck traffic is louder, echoing off of Bald Hill. Neighbors' dogs bark louder, wanting breakfast. Out on the water, the first glint of the sun shines through the eastern trees, and there is the lightest of airs from the southwest. The boat drifts a little to the northeast. Some people say that fish bite best when the surface at the water has a little ripple on it, and some mornings this ripple of a breeze happens now. If the fisherman wants to stay in calm water, the best place is on the north side of an island, so the island will provide a windbreak, or perhaps it is calm in a small cove over along the protected western side of the lake. The wind on the lake almost always comes from the west, and so the western shore is often calm when the rest of the lake is covered in ripples and waves.

Now is the time to hunt for the pickerel in the weed beds, when they can see – not just sense – a shiny spoon-type lure twisting along over the weed bed in imitation of a frightened minnow. The early sun will slant down through the water at 7 a.m., illuminating the small particles of floating weed, and along the weed or mud bottom, one may see a turtle swimming along, or sitting on the remains of an underwater stump. The mist burns away in a ripple of wind, and the bass head for deeper water and a nap. The lake is not so threatening now. The dark shapes of 6 a.m. compose common sights now, and one may be able to remove the outer coat, and pack it and the flashlight and belt knife away. The other fishing boats, which were invisible battleships and PT boats and cruisers off of Guadalcanal earlier, ready to open fire on an enemy, are now just other rowboats with old men in them, tired now from the early cold and the rowing and casting, who want to go in for coffee soon. The ducks have left Goose Island now, sailing along the shore looking for handouts. Sometimes, with the coming of the sun through the trees, the wind will pick up a lot, ending the fishing as the boat is blown about, or sometimes the rising sun will eat the wind, forecasting a hot and unbearable day out on the water. Sometimes, but not often, the sun will fade away, and the fish go to the deep, and thunder will be heard behind the hill, and then all of the boats will head for home, for soon the rain will set in for the day, and the fishing is over for 24 hours.

If rain is coming, by the time one reaches one's dock, the rain will start to patter through the trees like an elf walking through October's leaves. It will drip off the eves of the docks, making circles in the dark green water, and will drip off the cabin eves, dripping out of overflowing gutters, and pooling on the stone patios. Boats are tied away from the dock and retaining walls to prevent them from being battered as the wind raises waves on the lake. Some people tie their boats to plastic jugs floating in shallow water and anchored down to concrete blocks on the bottom. This system requires wading the last few feet to shore. Other people tie their boats at an angle from the dock to the shore, tying a bow rope to a hook screwed into the side of the dock, and tying a stern rope to a tree on the shore. Enough slack will have to be left for the boat to move as the waves pass, but not enough so that the boat will hit the dock or retaining wall.

The fish will sink to the bottom, all of the animals will stay out of the rain, and the fisherman will plod up the gravel path to his house, with the rain on the oak leaves above sounding like the whisper of the twilight elves. The oars are stacked on the deck and the pole and net tucked under the overhang by the door; the flashlight, knife, and coat thrown on the floor by the door, and the fisherman lights the kindling in the fireplace and makes some coffee, for an early rain brings the damp and wet for the day, even in July. Nothing can be done except to sit by the small and smoky fire, watch the flames, wait for tomorrow, and read a little Plutarch, perhaps about the life of Lycurgus, the lawgiver of Sparta, for all of the lake residents are avid readers who regard fishing as the enactment of the classical struggle of good and evil, with themselves as good and the vile and mean-tempered pickerel as evil. Be that as it may, a fire, a good book, a recording of the opera, and some coffee are very useful at the lake on a rainy day. There is no point in fishing in the rain.

After reading for a while, the fisherman will lie down on the enclosed porch and listen to the "snap" of the wood in the fire and the steady "drip, drip" of the rain off the trees and the downspouts, and dream of landing large scaly fish, or of mother bass spawning in the sandy shallows, or of rowing valiantly through choppy waters in search of the big white fish of the lake. This big white fish of the lake is a legend among the old fishermen who tell of a great white fish – not to be confused with a whitefish – who lives deep in the lake and has since 1941 when someone had it on the line, but it got away and was never caught again. The story is told over lunch at the Fishing Club meetings, with much speculation as to the species of fish. The fishermen always comment, "Why didn't someone write something down?" as they search for more information about the fish. They ask questions about what type it was, and exactly how large it was, and where it had been hooked. Many people don't think that it was white at all, but just sick and diseased, and don't like to think that it might still be alive down there, maybe mating with other healthy fish to make little fish that will grow up and be eaten by the fishermen now having lunch and drinks at the Fishing Club meetings.

The Midday Trip

Fishing in the middle of the day is thought to be a daft exercise by many fishermen. During this period, the sun blazes down and the wind is silent. It is the time when the beaches are crowded with mothers and screaming children waiting for the porta-potty, the sailboats which stayed out too late in the day are being towed to shore by the canoes, and the fish have gone deep. This part of the day belongs to the non-serious fishermen such as the children on the docks fishing with children's poles, using bread for bait, and catching the sunnys and bluegills.

Out on the lake, an occasional fisherman tries his luck, looking for pickerel who are still hungry after the morning feeding. If it hasn't rained for a week, there is a chance of catching something during the day, but if the rainwater has washed bugs and worms into the lake, the fish will not bite during the day.

Equipping the boat, especially an aluminum one, for the day trip is worlds apart from early morning fishing. Several towels will have to be loaded to use against sunburn, as well as suntan oil. Some type of footwear is needed, as the bottom of an aluminum boat will be very hot after a few minutes in the sun. A cool floatable cushion is also needed. The other gear needed are the net, tackle box, oars, and pole. The stringer is not needed because no one keeps a fish caught in the middle of a hot July day. Sunglasses and a cool hat are needed, too. Usually, a lunch of pop and a sandwich is taken along also, and maybe a radio for entertainment.

There aren't many boats out at this time of day, but the only good place to fish is out in the middle, in the deepest water. Getting the lure deep enough in the water takes some practice. After the lure is cast out, the fisher begins counting. After a count of five, the lure is reeled in. If the lure comes back without any weeds, then the count may have been too short. If the lure comes back covered with weeds, then the count was too long.

There are only two fish out in the deep that will bite in the middle of the day: the pickerel and the perch. Both will take spoons and spinners, but one must fish down deep, away from the sun and the warm surface water, which can reach 75 degrees in July. When one gets tired of casting, one can always troll, or stop and eat their sandwich and drink their pop. If a fish takes a lure, it can be played with, brought up to the boat slowly so that its swimming motions can be watched. The pickerel underwater in the sun are a shiny green, with pale fins and the dark chain pattern on their sides. They will allow themselves to be pulled up to the boat, then dart straight downwards toward the darker water. If given enough slack, they will surface and flip the lure and save one the trouble of unhooking them, for fishing during the middle of the day is done to kill time, and is not serious. It is not as good as taking a nap on the porch, but better than cutting brush or poison ivy.

The Evening Trip

The evening trip is the serious fishing trip of the day. It usually starts about 4 p.m., when people wake up from an afternoon nap and start checking their tackle box and getting their oars, net, and anchors together. If it's a weekday, then people will soon begin arriving home from work in the City, and the first thing they do is to change their clothes into their fishing clothes with white boat sneakers, and then to look out at the lake to see how rough the water is, and from what direction the wind is blowing. Of course, if rain is falling or it is very windy, then the departure will have to be postponed, with everyone looking out the porch windows every 15 minutes to see whether or not it is still possible to get in some fishing time. Some people like to fish in the rain, but they are teenagers. Adult fishermen don't fish in the rain.

The fishing evening involves a schedule related to the time of year, the weather, and the wind levels. In summer, when the day is longer than fall days, fishing can go until almost 9 p.m. In the fall, darkness arrives around 7 p.m. It doesn't do any good to go fishing before 4 p.m., as the fish won't bite until dinnertime. Supper before the fishing trip is eaten hurriedly, and consists of macaroni and cheese or frozen fish sticks. Everyone eats with an eye on the water, with the fishermen positioned at the table so that they can see the lake, for often in the evening the wind will die away suddenly and the lake will be calm enough to see the reflection of the trees and the mountain in the water. As soon as the wind dies, it is time to stop eating, collect the gear, and run for the docks for a long evening of fishing.

Rarely, the opposite may happen, when everyone will be out on the lake fishing, and the wind will pick up instead of dying away, the waves starting to slap against the sides of the boats. The chop will make it difficult to reel in a fish on the line, or to accurately cast towards an island, and so if the wind picks up after everyone is out on the lake, people will say, "Oh, well, hell. Let's head in," and the boats will be seen plodding into the waves while the passengers secure the lines and lures, and make everything ready for arriving at the docks.

Bringing a rowboat into a dock in the wind is a tricky thing, not to be taken lightly, although not as difficult as docking a sailboat or a canoe. Most fishermen like to dock parallel to the end or side of the dock so that the gear can be unloaded, followed by the passengers. This maneuver often requires turning the boat into the wind, reversing down towards the dock with the help of the waves, and then backing with the oars to provide a gentle arrival. Failure to back with the oars results in a crashing arrival that may knock the whole end off of the dock, especially the older ones, and even damage the boat. Of course, the rower must remove the oar on the dock side from the oarlock and bring it into the boat at the last moment before contacting the dock, or the oar will be caught between the dock and the boat and possibly break in half. This is embarrassing – a dead giveaway that a City person was rowing. After docking, the gear will be piled onto the dock in a heap to be sorted out later. Should the arrival be late, all of this action must be done by flashlight, for on the whole lake, no one ever bothered to equip their docks with permanent electrical lights. After the gear is removed, then the passengers climb out onto the dock. This is accomplished in one large step and is difficult for people who have short legs. Each time one person gets up onto the dock, all of the remaining people in the boat must lean the other way to avoid swamping the boat. As people at one end of a large boat get out, the other end sinks lower and sometimes a wave will be a little too high, and wash into the boat. This event is greeted with much shouting, pointing, and assigning of blame between the male and female fishers. Usually, when a wave washes into the boat while unloading, the rower will criticize the passengers who get defensive. The rower then expresses scorn, and passengers withdraw from the conversation. The rest of the evening is spent in silence and wet pants.

De-boating from an aluminum boat is extremely tricky, much more so than getting out of a wooden boat. Each time a person pushes with the feet as he gets up onto the dock, the aluminum boat will tend to scoot in the other direction. Experienced boaters try to step up rather than sideways when getting out of an aluminum boat. These boats are unforgiving if one stands in the well-known comic position of one foot in the boat and one foot on the dock. The aluminum boat will immediately move outward toward the lake, landing the person into the water. Assuming that the weather is not windy, the evening trip will not have to be cut short, and three or four hours of fishing can be enjoyed.

Since most fish are caught in the evening, there exists a sense of anticipation that fish are going to be caught, unlike the noon trip when no one really expects to catch anything. The first decision of the evening is where to fish. People tend to fish different places based on the amount of sunlight available. It is a general rule that the fish head for shallower water the later it is in the day, so people tend to fish in a little deeper water earlier in the evening, and then closer to the land or islands as the sun nears the mountain.

Evening fishing is a family event. When the men in the family go onto the water, the women often go along to see the lake, or visit with friends who are out sitting on their docks. As a boat goes from a dock to a fishing area, it naturally passes other docks, providing a perfect chance for everyone to visit. If the fish aren't biting at all, after the fishers grow weary of catching nothing, the family may row along the shore, visiting. These visits do not consist of getting out of the boat at all, but rather follow a certain water ritual. A family will row along the shore until a dock is approached with a family they know. The family on the shore, represented by the father, calls out, "Catching anything?" for all conversations on the water begin with a fishing comment. The family in the boat, again represented by the father, will reply, "No, not much," while rowing towards the people on the dock. Strict protocol is observed. No further conversation ensues until the boat is a few feet from the dock, because people who are rowing have no time to both row and talk. But when the boat nears the dock, the women carry on a little conversation about their children and flowers and pets, while the men smoke their pipes. It is the rower's job to keep the boat near enough to the dock to carry on a conversation, yet not too near so that the wind will blow the boat into the dock and damage the boat. When the women have finished visiting and the children on the shore have shown their latest pets to the children in the boat, then the men have a quick howdy-do, a comment about the weather and the fishing, and then the boat proceeds along the shore in search of the next shout of, "Catching anything?" In this manner, even though the fish aren't biting, the evening can be passed in a very pleasant manner.

Visiting doesn't happen only between boat and dock. It can also happen boat to boat. These visits require more diplomacy than boat to dock conversations, because it is a great faux pas to row towards another boat for a visit if the other boat occupants are actually fishing. Threshing along briskly through the water towards another boat will scare the fish away for sure, and make the other boat's occupants irate. It is the kind of social goof that identifies the visitors as summer people. The boat to boat visit starts in the same manner as the boat to dock visit, with the father of the first boat heading in towards the second stationary boat shouting, "Catching anything?" and the father in the stationary boat replying, "No, but I have a new lure. Want to see it?" It is up to the boat who answers the question of whether anything is being caught or not to issue the invitation to meet. If the second stationary boat just replies, "No, nothing," then no invitation has been issued, and the boats will not meet. The first boat must not invade within casting distance without an invitation. But if the second boat issues an invitation to meet, then the first boat will row over to the second for a visit. The second boat will drift, allowing the first boat to approach so that they are lined up parallel, about three feet from each other. This arrival takes some skill not to overshoot the stationary boat, and at the same time not to get the oars entangled. This arrangement of placing the boats parallel to each other results in a wonderful way to carry on a conversation, for the people can converse with each other directly opposite, allowing multiple conversations to be held at once. As many of the boaters carry along little snacks and beer, some exchange of treats can be made if the boats drift against each other and the oars between the boats are removed from the oarlocks and laid inside the boats. These exchanges of treats must be done with care, with the exchangers carefully handing over the items to be traded while trying to sit still in the middle of their seats, and everyone else leaning the other way to prevent a capsize. Sometimes, if the fish really aren't biting, then three or four boats will gather out on the lake, fumigate the air over them with bug spray, string rope between the boats so they won't drift apart, turn on a radio, and have a little water party. Of course, should a heavy wind come up, then the lines will have to be cast off, and the boats can soon be seen in line ahead, heading through the waves back to their respective docks.

But, if the fish are biting in the quiet summer evening, then what an evening it can be. There is no talking in the boats, for this is the time when the biggest fish of the year can be caught, and the gift certificate from Bob's Sport Shop won. Now is the time when the big pickerel and bass will take a lure with a powerful snap of the jaws, when the anticipation rises with each cast of the lure into the quiet, flat water. People on the docks use binoculars to watch the fishermen, so that a large caught fish can be reported to the grapevine. People in the boats sometimes also use binoculars to see what lures are being used by the other fishermen. The result is many binoculars being used on a quiet evening.

The best fishing spots are up on the north end of the lake, out from the old stone boathouse, along the edge of the weed bank where it drops off to deeper water, and up over the weed banks east of the floating island. The little cove on the north side of the floating island, the north shallows, and the rock pile off of the point back down at the middle of the lake are all good evening spots. A few people try their luck out in the deep middle, but the results are unpredictable.

The catching of fish not only depends upon the location, water temperature, and timing of recent rain, but upon the lure. Everyone on the lake has favorite lures, usually a mix of surface plus, diving lures that float when still, and underwater spoons and spinners. Artificial, exotic lures such as rubber frogs and centipedes do not work very well. It's best to stick with tried and true lures to catch fish.

In the evening, the sun gets behind the top of Bald Hill, the water may have just a slight ripple to it, and the trees on the shore will be reflected off the water. There may still be teenagers swimming out on the float, and people having cocktails on their docks, or eating little hot Chinese snacks out of the oven. The evening will get cool later, but now it's still the time for sunglasses and a light shirt. If the water quiets down while the sun is still above the hill, then it may be possible to look into the water and locate the stumps and weed banks, and determine the depth of the water. A quiet lake makes the fishing go well, for a lack of wind means the boat will not drift.

Fishing requires patience, and cast after cast, the fisherman must be patient and believe that the fish will bite eventually. Some people troll, and a few use live bait and a bobber, but most spin cast. In its own way, spin casting is as pretty as fly fishing, with the lure and the line arcing out over the calm water. When the fish hits the lure, the pole tip will dart downward, and the fish will either dive and run, or surface and flip off the lure. If one really wants to catch the fish, it is best to keep the pole tip low. If the fish goes into the weeds, then the boat can be rowed so that it is above the fish, and the fish pulled up into the net. Sometimes netting the fish is also thrilling, as many fish will flip or run when they are near the net, occasionally causing the fisherman to lose the net and pole into the lake where they can be seen if the sun's rays are at the right ankle. Sometimes, they can be recovered by using another pole with a large hook at the end of the line, but this is embarrassing as everyone will be watching from the shore using their binoculars. People at the lake use their binoculars a lot, and usually on each other.

After the sun goes behind the hill, the bats will come out. If the water hasn't quieted earlier, it will now, and it's time for a jacket, and a cap to keep the evening bugs away. After the sun is hidden, there will be about 90 minutes of fishing time left. This is the time to fish up in the shallows for the big bass, while on the docks people light their oil lanterns and candles to keep the flying bugs away, and the teenagers on the swim float watch the evening stars come out. There may be as many as 10 boats up in the north end looking for bass. Boats which have been successful will have a yellow rope stringer hanging over the side of the boat with the metal loops inserted through the fishes' mouths and gills. While fish will eventually drown because they cannot close their mouths all the way, leaving them on a stringer keeps them cool and fresh for cleaning. Of course, many fishermen just catch fish and let them go, and still consider that the evening was most successful.

The evening concludes around 9 p.m., when the last light is going, and the boats follow the shore to the home docks. Many times, families will be waiting on the docks in order to lend a hand with the boat ropes and to help unload the fishing gear when the fishermen row in. The younger members of the family are always ready to carry the fish up to the house for cleaning on the patio, while the adults may sit on the dock a few minutes longer to watch the stars come out over the water. One reason that many people do not keep the fish is that cleaning takes about 15 minutes per fish, and so the night may seem never-ending if several fish need cleaning. It's easier to go to the A&P and get some frozen fish filets than it is to clean the fish. But, if they have to be cleaned, then eventually they are wrapped in aluminum foil and stored in the freezer, or wrapped in wax paper for tomorrow's dinner, and at last, it's time for bed.

The Night Trip

The night fishing trip is like the night train – sort of mysterious, frightening, and impressive at the same time. There is an air of the unknown danger on a night trip, for not only is it hard to tell what has been caught until the catch is up to the boat, but the difficulties of fishing in brush and along the islands are compounded by not being able to see where the cast lands. The inability to see what has been caught until the last minute can be extremely exciting, and is the reason why most night fishermen carry a belt knife. At the last minute, if a turtle has been caught, the line can be cut and the unwanted catch released. The same is true if a snake has somehow been caught inadvertently. It is always a thrill to pull in a bass lure and find a six-foot water snake on the hook.

The night trip starts much as the early morning trip, with the gear being loaded into the boat, and plenty of flashlights and lanterns taken along for visibility. Only the men and older teens go on a night trip, for participation in this type of fishing is a recognition of adulthood. The women see no need to be damp and bug-bit in the middle of the night, and so rarely go along. Falling into the water in the dark or meeting a snapping turtle can be dangerous, so the youngest fishermen are left at home to wait on the dock or on the porch for the return of the fishing party. Over dinner or while sitting in the rocking chairs on the dock, the members of the night expedition will have discussed the destination of the night trip. Sometimes, the neighbors will go along, and so several rowboats can head into the night water together, with much waving and blinking of flashlights towards each other. The usual destination is the north shallows, or over the old stumps in front of the stone boathouse on the northeast shore. Bass are known to stay around these stumps, and this is a good place to fish with night crawlers.

Once the boats have arrived over the stumps, everyone tries to be as quiet as possible, so as not to scare the fish, and everyone keeps the flashlights shining down into the boats, instead of into the water, if possible.

Occasionally, a fisherman will grunt in pain as a hook misses the worm but finds the finger, but everyone is a good sport and considers pain from mishaps to be part of the adventure. The men drop their worms into the water after attaching a bobber to the line two feet from the worm, then hunch over in their corduroy coats against the cool night air while keeping an eye on the bobber. Of course, in the dark, the bobber can only be seen by the light of the stars and moon and an occasional shore light, so after a few minutes the flashlight must be used to see if the bobber is still on the surface indicating that a fish has not yet taken the worm. If a number of people are in the fishing party, then sooner or later everyone begins flicking flashlights on and off for just a quick check of the bobber to see if there is a bite. This flicking is easier to do than holding the pole for a long time, so that after an hour over the stumps, the pole is lying tilted against the side of the boat while the owner sips coffee and flicks the flashlight on and off every 30 seconds to see where the bobber is. If there are a number of fishermen over the stumps, this flicking on and off of the flashlights creates a firefly effect which looks very nice from the shore, but may disorient the bass under the water so that they do not know where the worms are to eat. The night fishing trips have not produced any more bass on the hook than has the morning trip, but the tales of huge bass caught at night by someone's grandfather are numerous.

When someone does hook a bass in the dark, there is much action. At the shout of, "I've got one!" everyone reels in his own line so as not to get a tangle when the bass runs, turns his flashlight beams down into the water (several flashlights have been lost overboard this way), and peers over the side looking for the bass as the lucky catcher reels it in. Only the good-sized fish are kept at night, for keeping a fish caught on the night trip means that it will have to be cleaned on the patio or in the kitchen later that night, when everyone would rather be asleep. Many a good excuse is made not to keep a fish caught at night, rather than have to clean it at midnight when everyone else in the family is asleep.

Cleaning the night fish in the kitchen is not recommended, as bass scales get all over the floor and sink and countertops, sometimes reappearing in the cereal the next morning. Yet, cleaning the fish on the patio under the light of the living room floor lamp is not recommended either, for not only are the bugs out in legions, but the smell of the gutted fish attracts the raccoons and the skunks, and a person is liable to have an unpleasant encounter just when the task seems done, and all of the fish are in the clothes washing metal tub being rinsed for the last time, prior to being wrapped in aluminum foil and placed in the freezer.

When the bass are not biting over the stumps, the night party may try the north shallows, using a surface plug along the edges of the rocks and lily pads to search for bass. This type of fishing requires a great deal of fishing sense, for one is casting a heavy plug toward brush or trees. When one does not have this sense, the plug is likely to fly into a tree, and from the shore flashlight beams can be seen shining into the trees, while the lure and line, wrapped around a branch, are located. Occasionally, the curses of the fishermen can be heard on shore where people are sitting on their docks drinking a night bottle of wine. The fishermen try to get the line out of the tree and not fall out of the boat at the same time. This mishap is one reason why fishermen at the lake do not use too strong a line, for a very strong line has been known to break the limb which it is wrapped around due to a bad cast. When the line is vigorously pulled, the limb comes down on the fisherman's head. Sometimes, it's just better if the line breaks and the lure remains in the tree.

Those fishermen who tire of catching nothing on the night trip usually row out to the middle of the lake and drift while they drink their coffee that their wives put in an old green plastic thermos for them, and eat a cheese sandwich. It is not proper for the night fishermen to return before 11 p.m. They will be regarded as unmanly and earn no points toward entering heaven. In the world of the lake fisherman, points towards entering heaven are earned by superb casting (3 points if the lure lands within six inches of the lily pad), good line handling (no kinks in the line = 5 points), excellent rowing (shipped no water during a choppy trip = 1 point), and outstanding fish catching (caught a fish over five pounds = 10 points). If the fish were the largest of the season for its type, another 5 bonus points toward entering heaven are earned. Showing a child how to fish gets 7 points and releasing a fish back into the water to grow larger gets 4 points. All men who fish the lake waters instinctively know the male point system, and as they grow old, they mentally add up their points earned while fishing to see if they will get into heaven, where the water is always calm and the fish bite quickly. Women who fish have a different point system related to getting into heaven, usually related to how many times they have to suffer through a long cold fishing trip without complaining before they are considered for sainthood.

On the water at night, the fishermen see the bats swooping by eating the bugs, the shore lights shining white on the water, and the lights from the jets going to Newark Airport looking so much more colorful and enjoyable than the plain old stars that the romantic poets wrote about. The geese down at Goose Island make night goose noises in their throats, and a "plop" indicates that the muskrats are out and about on the lake. Once in a while, a duck will quack in the dark when a goose has bit its tail feathers, and the sounds of the teens out on the float, or people on their docks, will be heard out on the water. The fisherman who listens for it can hear the sound of trucks on the interstate, or the sound of the train to Dover blowing for the crossing in town where the station used to stand before vandals burnt it down, or even the whine of the jet engines overhead. But the primary sound is the sound of water and animals and the creatures in the night, all awake and listening to the world.

The night trip ends when the fishermen decide that they have had enough. The row to shore is just anticlimax – a chore to be done before bed. By 10 p.m., the families have gone back up to the house to prepare for bed, and the exhilaration of the trip has worn off. Many a fish caught in the night and on the stringer is released back into the water if it is still alive. The men are tired and ready for bed.

As the boats leave the lake, the night creatures take over the water: the bats fly low over the water, the bass come towards the surface now that the boats have gone, the pickerel head towards the shallows looking for dinner, and the muskrats prowl through the floating island. Out on Goose Island, the geese and ducks stop making noise and finally settle for the night. On land, the skunks and raccoons and foxes come to the water for a drink, and to pick over the leftovers from the families' evening snacks. The only night owls on the lake are the ones in the trees. People do not stay up after the 11 p.m. news on WPIX. When the weather forecast is over, it's off to bed, for there is much outdoor work to be done early such as cutting brush or going fishing at 5 a.m. The downstairs lights in the houses go out – one by one, and then in whole bunches – the upstairs lights come on briefly, and then the houses around the lake are dark except for a night light in a youngster's room here and there.

And then it's time to dream lake dreams.

Bob dreams of the big one that got away last Saturday over by the south lily pads. Cindy dreams about the sailboat she wants for her birthday. Susan dreams of winning the swim meet coming up next weekend, and Cathy dreams of being the queen of the lake at the next Labor Day celebration. Sara dreams of going fishing with John in the dark, and Maureen dreams of dancing the weekend away at the lake clubhouse to the most modern sounds. Mary dreams of electric automated fishing reels, and Kath dreams of eating Mary's fish. Margaret dreams of perfect watercraft shopping trips, and Bill dreams of a Paris eatery transplanted to the lake shore. Linda dreams of opening a jazz club on the lake which turns out to be a success, and Mary dreams of training the turtles to sing opera. Sam dreams of eating ladyfingers while watching a purple dawn over the swimming float, and Gail dreams of the perfect suntan that everyone admires when she walks on the west beach in her new red bathing suit. Beverly dreams of the winter wind in her hair and her eyes freezing shut forever, and Doris dreams of driving 90 miles an hour with no traffic across the surface of the lake. Edmond dreams of the frog he stepped on 10 years ago that scared him when it jumped, and Bobby dreams of falling out of the canoe into the dark water during a morning fishing trip. Jacob sees Kevin rowing towards him but not getting any nearer, and Matt sees Mark shooting baskets on the swim float. They all see the lake in their own way, and in their own way they also fail to see the lake and what it means to each of them. In their dreams, they see the lake as a center for action, for frenetic activity, for interaction with other humans. But they never dream of the lake as it really is: a center of beauty in a tiny state.

In the night, when the boats are all ashore and their rowers asleep, the fish rise to the surface – hundreds of bass, pickerel and bluegills, and they just break the surface of the water and look up at the moon without thinking, enjoying the white glow. The raccoons, skunks, and foxes look up, too, at the big white orb in the sky without any concept of what's up there…just that it's bright and makes the night hunting easier for all. And under that bright glow, the fish swim at the surface, the bright glow reflecting off their scales and fins and black eyes, and they move through the lake water in a clockwise direction, almost as if on parade, moving through the simmering water with the lake to themselves. They enjoy the glow in the sky and wait for a small neighbor to pass within reach of their jaws. Instead of watching television, the fish in the lake watch the moon, and their fins make a little night music in the dark water. Rather than having some chips and salsa for a snack as humans do, they have each other for a little night snack while they all swim along together, under the moon.

Safety Suggestions

Even though the waves on the lake are only two feet high in a wind, that wind is enough to make one pay attention when handling a small three-seater aluminum rowboat or a canoe. Wooden boats are more stable and due to a broader beam, they handle waves and wind better than do aluminum boats, which tend to be skittish. People venturing onto the water should check the weather forecast.

The wind on the lake is most always from the southwest or south. If one wishes to fish in calm water, it will be found along the west and south shores, or on the north side of the big island up north. If one has fished along the west shore but lives on the east side and the wind is worsening, then one must select the route home. There are two water options. First, proceed around the lake rowing within 10 feet of the shore. The trees and structures will tend to block some of the wind. This is the safer but time-consuming choice.

The second choice is to go across the lake in a more direct line home. This option requires that one follow some guidelines that generally apply to any boat in wind. Do not go broadside to the waves and wind. The rolling motion will be much more pronounced than if one meets the waves at an angle or bow into the waves. It may be when traveling west to east with a wind from the south that the boat track is a long leg southeast and a short leg northeast to the dock. Aluminum rowboats tend to move at the same pace as following waves and so broaching (a wave coming over the stern of the rowboat) is not an issue unless the rowboat is heavily loaded.

If waves and wind become unmanageable, there is a rule for all boats: bow into the wind until in the lee of the shore, then follow the shoreline home. Most aluminum boats have flotation material beneath the seats to keep the boat at the surface if it should fill with water. Boaters should have flotation seat cushions, life vests, a whistle, and a flashlight at night.

If a lightning storm is coming, boaters should go into shore anywhere and seek shelter. It is not unheard of to have 70-mile-per-hour storm gusts on a small inland lake, which are strong enough to flip a boat that is beam to the wind if loaded lightly.

Having some bailing device such as a can is useful. Wooden boat seams tend to leak so some bailing during any outing is required. But having something to bail with may be useful even in an aluminum boat.

Passengers should be warned to sit in the middle of their seat and not to stand when away from the dock. A passenger falling overboard is likely to turn the boat over due to last second efforts to not fall into the lake. Sometimes one sees people fishing standing up in the rowboat. A strong pull from a fish could unbalance a person.

Passengers being rescued from a water-filled boat, such as a canoe, by a rowboat, should not attempt to climb into the rescuing boat, but hold onto the stern until towed to shore. Boats should have a long line in the bow for towing which can be done even if the boat is full of water. The boat will remain near to the surface. This author has done three of these rescues. Two cases were identical: aluminum canoes with one person in the rear, a high center of gravity, and a heavy load in the stern so that the tip of the bow was above the surface. Both canoes capsized in a breeze. Occupant and canoe were towed to shore.

The other rescue was different. Two children not wearing life jackets or having any boat cushions or parents with them were backing their rowboat into waves when the boat was swamped by waves coming over the stern. The boat and children were towed to shore. Remember: if you can't wade to shore, stay with the boat!

A person in the water should not attempt to get up into a rowboat. However, if he or she must try, the procedure generally is for the person in the boat to move toward the front to balance the increasing weight in the boat from the person getting into the stern. Boarding into the side should be avoided as the boat might roll over. The bow is usually too high or is smooth.

For certain, it is dangerous to go from the rowboat into the water for a swim. If the swimmer is diving from the boat, the boat's reaction to the loss of weight in one part of the boat is unpredictable. If sliding over the rear seat facing outward, there is the possibility of hitting one's head. Trying to go over the stern facing forward means all sorts of risky contortions.

Reference is made to an incident on this lake on the evening of August 10, 2009. Fatima Younes, 26, drowned after going out to the swim float in the middle of the lake with two companions after working all day on a very hot day. The three jumped into the lake. Fatima did not come to the surface. It is interesting to note that the boat involved in this trip was an aluminum rowboat. Such a boat is unpredictable. If empty, the slightest breeze can shift it. If one jumps out of it, the boat will kick in the opposite direction from the jumper. Public sources did not identify the cause of drowning. Sunset on that date was 8:02 p.m. The high temperature was 91 with a dew point of 69.7. Civil twilight ended at 8:32 p.m., according to the *Old Farmers Almanac*. The incident was reported to first responders at 8:22 p.m. These times mean that it was nearly dark on the water, especially considering that Bald Hill is on the west side of the lake. During February, the sunset is on the south end of the lake. But during summer, it sets behind the hill, causing earlier darkness. The body of Fatima was pulled from the water at 11:57 p.m. The combination of tired swimmers, an aluminum boat, swimming at the float in the deepest part of the lake, and darkness resulted in tragedy. A memorial service was held with people in their boats around the swim float.

There was a time in America, now long passed, when a community was proud to involve the residents in civic associations for the common good at the lake. From 1930 to 1960, these civic associations flourished. Almost all of them are gone now, but in their day they were the glue that held together the people living around the lake. To be elected to an official position in one of these organizations gave the office-holder a sense of destiny which was generally reflected in national politics. Much as America was changed by World War II, the associations at the lake faded away after the war, until by the time of the Kennedy killing they were, as Hamlet might have said, a shadow of their former selves. Once at the lake there existed the Property Owners Association, the Community Club, the Club Auxiliary, the Lake Women's Club, the Lake Recreational and Athletic Association, the Lake Fishing Club, the Water Safety Corp, the Junior League, the Literary Club, the Lake Flower Club, the West Side Improvement Association, and the East Side Cottagers Association.

The civic groups were thus divided into semi-governmental groups, such as the Property Owners Association, the Improvement Association, and the Cottagers Association. Among other good things, these groups assessed dues and managed the common boat landings. The Property Owners Board towed the swimming float out to the middle of the lake each May, and towed it in again every October. The other accomplishment that the Property Owners Board achieved was to design a complicated system of boat identification tags. But the board created a system of boat tags designed to keep outsiders out, which changed every year. First, the Board designed nice brass boat tags which could be attached permanently to the bows. Dallas' boat had one. Then it was carved wooden tags which looked nice. Then came self-sticking weatherproof tags, and finally the newer stick-on non-rainproof paper tags, which mostly fell into the lake and had to be replaced every month. By 1975, most of the boats' bows were covered with 20 or more tags that their owners stuck on year after year.

The social organizations held the important social power at the lake. There were three classes of families at the lake. The "Pioneers," who often were also the "Old Money" families that had arrived before 1940. The "Summer People," who came up to the cabins from the City and Newark-Elizabeth areas. They were looked down on by everyone who stayed at the lake all year around. The final group was the majority, the "Year-'Rounders," who had winterized their cabins, built houses for both winter and summer use, and who worked in town or commuted to other towns along the railroad. These social groups were the Community Club, the Club Auxiliary, the Lake Women's Club, the Lake Recreational and Athletic Association, the Lake Fishing Club, the Water Safety Corp, the Junior League, the Literary Club, and the Lake Flower Club. Some are worthy of a closer look.

The most important groups were the Club Auxiliary and the Women's Club. The Auxiliary was for the younger women, who assisted with the events to be held at the clubhouse. They helped cook for the Saturday dinner dances, helped with the holiday bake sales, and made sure there were enough supplies at the bar on Friday night. The Women's Club saw to it that the clubhouse, envisioned as far back as 1890, was actually built in 1931. It had a large dance room on the second floor, and a bar next door overlooking the cove. The first floor contained meeting rooms and a kitchen. In 1931, 90% of the Women's Club marched in the mile-long town parade in honor of the bicentennial of Washington's birth. They all waved American flags, the officers carried large American flags, and they all wore white dresses, wide white hats, and white stockings and shoes. They got to walk in front of the horses, not behind.

The Lake Recreational and Athletic Association and the Water Safety Corp battled each other from 1930 to 1950 for control of the water and the regulating of what went on in the water. Both were voted out of existence at the annual Property Owners Meeting in 1951.

The Fishing Club met the first Thursday of each month over lunch at the clubhouse. The club was composed mostly of retired men, although in the summer some of the younger men and women on vacation might drop by to discuss lures. The club never met during the winter when things might be iced up. The club elected a President, Vice-President, Treasurer, and Secretary for one-year terms. There was little change in office holders from year to year and the typical agenda was the same from month to month:

Reading of Last Minutes and Approval

Discussion of Recent Catches and Fish Size

Mention of New Lures

Discussion of Fishing Techniques

Proposal to Send a Letter to the State Asking for More Fish to be Stocked

Lunch

The meetings earnestly went for about an hour, with the discussion continued over a hamburger lunch and a good smoke afterwards. There was thoughtful discussion about night fishing, the use of spinners in weed banks, the effectiveness of poppers over stumps, and the best time of day to fish. The men were earnest and loud, and, as the bar was usually open during lunch, quite red-faced. For these retired men, the monthly meeting was a chance to restore some of the self-esteem they had lost when they retired, and to associate with good fellows of their own kind. After lunch, they would head home to overhaul their fishing tackle and get ready for a big evening. The night of the monthly fishing meeting was the night of the month when everyone fished in a setting of good friendship and joy.

At 7 p.m., when the sun was on the top of Bald Hill, scores of rowboats being rowed by junior fishermen, with their grandfathers sitting in the stern seats, could be seen pulling for the islands and weed banks. And, after a few minutes of earnest fishing, many of the boats grouped together to share a few beers and some more discussion. Sometimes, friends would cast towards each other's boat with the intent of tangling the lines, and thus providing an excuse for a little chat and a beer handed from boat to boat. It was, like much of the 1950's, a genteel way to pass the evening without playing canasta, out in the wild with the grandsons, in search of adventure. The grandsons often noted, though, that any fish caught were returned to the lake rather than face the cleaning chore on a hot patio under a floor lamp, borrowed from the house for the task. When the bats started to fly on the lake, it was time for the grandsons to row the boats home. The old and young fishermen would all sit on their respective docks and watch the bats fly and the stars come out, and all over the lake one could hear the creak of rocking chairs, some going fast, and others slow, and so night arrived on the lake on the first Thursday of the month.

The Junior League was composed of earnest future business people, mostly male, whose mission in lake life was to raise money for lake projects. The group was composed of high school seniors and junior college students who hoped to move to the City and make their mark. A few of them had been arrested for driving drunk, and so made their mark in an unfortunate manner by having their name listed in the weekly "Police Report" in the Morristown newspaper. They did much good at the lake, for without their efforts, funds might not have been available to beautify the community boat landings and beaches. They were the people who had sacrificed their time to build the swimming float that the Property Owners Board towed out to the center of the lake every May.

The members of the Junior League, in addition to the beautification programs, sponsored the monthly teen dances at the clubhouse with the overflowing roof gutters. The 30-year-old chaperones at the dances were often heavily into the punch bowl, and after about the fifth dance, they discreetly sat while the Junior Leaguers plied them with punch. The punch was served in the same bowl used by the Flower Club at its shows except the punch was not diluted, but rather added to until it was strong enough to drop a dancer in their tracks. The higgly-jiggly music of the 1960's often resulted in the dancers being ill in the paint-flecked restrooms in the basement. The emcees often shouted out, "Let's get all the men to higgle, and all the women to jiggle, here comes a real *fast* tune," followed by a blast of music. The swing band was sometimes directed by Mr. Baark from the local Catholic school, who thus lent the dance an air of respectability. He conducted religious music during the week, chamber music as needed, and dance music for spice. He sweated while waving his baton. The dance band often came from the local Catholic school also, hired for the evening, but they were dance makers, not music makers, and so felt free to produce music which suited the audience, unlike most of the school's musical groups. They picked the songs, and Mr. Baark waved his baton, and there was music echoing out over the water of the cove. Mr. Baark was ecstatic! He jumped and swayed, and sweated in a black suit and narrow tie, and when each song was done, he'd beam at the teenage boys and say, "My golly, *what* a song, huh?" Then, he'd pant a little from a bad heart while looking at the women, and wait for the emcee to chatter a little before starting the next song.

The dances went from 1941 to 1965, and then stopped when the Junior League at the lake disbanded. As it is in nature, there was no particular reason why either the Junior League or the dances stopped – they just did. But the Flower Club was happy, for the halting of the beautification and clean-up program meant that more of nature's weeds would grow at the boat landings to be picked for table decorations. Today, those ex-Junior Leaguers own stores in town and car dealerships and see each other at the high school reunions held at the restaurants on Route 46.

The Literary Club was the elderly ladies' club. It was loosely associated with the town's Friends of the Library, and many women at the lake were members of both groups. It was composed of 20 to 35 ladies who were often also members of the American Association of University Women. In their day, which sadly had set years ago, they had been teachers and managers of a literary nature. They prided themselves on reading and being up to date about the *New York Times* Sunday literature supplement. They planned their meetings so that they always met during the summer at the homes of members who had lakefront houses. During the winter, they met at the homes of members who did not have icy steps down which   to navigate.

Their meetings were planned around little snacks, usually ham sandwiches, cheeses, Viking pastries, ice cream, and plenty of sherry during the summer. The winter fare often consisted of beef sandwiches, oyster soup, Viking pastries, crackers with cheese spread and an olive slice on top, and sherry. The food was served on the old wedding china with gold, non-microwavable trim on little white paper doilies. The topic of discussion was usually a new romance novel. An exchange table was set up in the living room of the hostess, and the ladies would place the book they had finished last month on the table and take a replacement to read. This plan saved on costs and ensured that the ladies' reading was pretty much all the same. At every meeting, two ladies would get up and give a book review about the romance novel they had read last month. These reviews ranged in time from two to 20 minutes. The two-minute reviews were caused by the speaker forgetting what she was going to say, and sitting down to have some sherry. The 20-minute presentations allowed everyone time to sip sherry.

The use of sherry to break the ice at the Literary Club meetings worked very well to make the ladies chatty and get them through the ordeal of giving a presentation. But it often interacted with the ladies' medication to make them sleepy so that during the book presentations, there were occasional snores from the ladies gathered around the luncheon table. Nevertheless, the ladies drank their sherry and reported about the romance novels they had read, and they felt as if they were still applying their college educations in the area of adult learning and in promoting reading.

The Lake Flower Club was composed of those older women who were interested in the natural aspects of the lake; specifically, the cutting and taking indoors of the lake's flowers and weeds. These two categories – flowers and weeds – differentiated the members of the Flower Club. Some ladies cut weeds and some ladies cut flowers, but the members of this club could be easily identified by their earnest search for beauty with a pair of scissors in their hands. There were many unnamed weeds which could be cut and arranged as the centerpieces on the porch tables, from which they often released their seeds into people's dinners when the right time of the season arrived. Such weeds were pokeweed, flax and cattails. The members who went after flowers cut down the blue bells, tiger lilies, irises, and roses. As the ground was stony and wet, the best flowers to be obtained, as with most things in life, were those provided by the wild, rather than those which were planted and gardened.

The best harvest times of year were summer and fall, and every year in August the Flower Club would hold the annual Lake Flower Show at the clubhouse. The flower show had numerous categories such as "Wild Herb," "Iris," "Natural Arrangement," "Arrangement in Wood," " Patriotic Arrangement," "Rose," "Wild Flower," and "Best Money Plant." These shows were a social highlight at the lake, and were accompanied by Viking Pastries, an assortment of snacks, and diluted wine punch in a bowl containing a circulating pump that created a waterfall of punch that was closely examined by the men. The music was provided by the chamber group from the local Catholic high school. The group was composed of several clarinets, flutes, and three violins under the direction of Mr. Baark. He was baldheaded with a thin mustache, and a round and increasing middle, and he always wore a severe black suit and dark tie. His life must have been one of great frustration, for having been trained at Julliard in the City, he knew what good music was supposed to sound like, yet rarely heard any such result from the swing of his baton.

The flower arrangements themselves took second place to such social niceties as who was attending the show, what the raffle prize was (plant food), and the quality of the snacks. The show was held from 1938 to 1960, when more and more of the women went to work and fewer were roaming the hills armed with scissors. Like the hemmed-in buffalo, they were increasingly thwarted by state and federal laws which said not to pick the roadside flowers along state and federal roads, and by new property owners who posted "no trespassing" signs at the roadside. By 1960, the flowers in the show had lost their wild side and were more and more the homegrown, unhardy varieties, mostly all roses. As the extravagance of the shows faded, the chamber music was dropped and the snacks became commonplace, as did the flowers. After the club disbanded in 1968, a few last survivors could still be seen early in the morning fog gleaning nature's beauty with a pair of scissors to enhance their patio table centerpieces. The passing of time generally meant the passing of most of these clubs, but in their prime they added much to life at the lake.

Dallas and Margaret

Pictured above (center) around 1965, Margaret lived with Dallas in the big stone house on the hill by the north side of Bloody Gulch, which was a narrow little one-lane road between their house and the lake which was cut through a hill of solid rock. It was called Bloody Gulch because of the head-on vehicle collisions that occurred there. Dallas and Margaret had no children, but Margaret's father lived with them and wore a vest with a heavy gold watch chain to which was attached a very fine watch from the Illinois Watch Company. To a child, that gold watch was Margaret's father. He never said one single word, let alone a sentence – he just stood above Bloody Gulch with the sun shining on that huge watch chain hanging across his large belly.

His son-in-law, Dallas, was one of those string-bean types of lake people, while Margaret had wide hips and a long nose. Dallas and Margaret both had brown hair, and on Fridays at the clubhouse, people said, "What a shame that there are no children who would also have thin brown hair," and "Who will inherit the house eventually?"

The house was built in the 1920's of rock with a big granite fireplace and lots of mice in the basement. No one except the unfortunate furnace man ever went into the basement, and at night, one could faintly hear thousands of mice busily at work on mice business. There was no cat. It was sort of a fortress, or at least uncomfortable to get to, because it had 29 steps up from the main road, and seven steps up from the Bloody Gulch road. With a smoky fireplace and mice in the basement, winters in the house were unpleasant. Dallas and Margaret moved to the lake in the 1950's from East Orange, which was entering an economic decline. They arrived as a couple and were always thought of as a couple, though rather aseptic.

Margaret wore long dresses and flat heels and a lot of pearls. Her glasses hung from her long neck by an invincible chain, and no one ever made a pass at her or flirted with her. Her life was full of afternoon tea parties held on the patio under a metal umbrella that occasionally fell onto the guests if any wind sprung up on the lake – and tile. Not big tiles, like bathroom tiles, but millions of little tiles that she cemented onto the tables and trays by using ring-covered fingers in a studio over the garage by the main road. Every gift she ever gave was covered in tiles. She made trivets and tables, stools and ashtrays, all covered in tiles of every color and shape, though mostly square. She gave these fine gifts to everyone, and to her friends, Lois and Anne, she gave matching little tea tables. The tiles were stored in bursting cardboard boxes that couldn't stand the strain and so could never be moved easily again. This lent a certain obstacle course aura to the studio that children loved, for Margaret always let the children visit whenever the studio door was propped open with a maple tree limb.

Dallas fished. The people at the lake never knew what else he ever did in life, but when he was at the lake, he fished. He fished at 6 a.m. and 6 p.m., and at those times in the summer one could hear the crunch-slap of his old brown shoes through open windows on the gravel path to the lake, and one knew it was time either to get out of bed or watch the evening news. Dallas never fished in the middle of the day. He said it was a waste of time. He fished in an old wooden red boat that resembled a destroyer with its pointed bow. It was a beauty, with a little seat right in the bow for a child, two seats with oarlocks in the middle, and a wide seat for two ladies across the back. Sometimes, Dallas would let the next door kids borrow the boat, and they would row with two sets of oars on a windy day, playing at a battleship cutting through the waves. It was a good fishing boat. It weighed 379 pounds and wouldn't drift 10 feet an hour in a gale. When Dallas stopped rowing, the boat stopped. In the summer dawn, Dallas could be seen sitting still in the fog like something from 1820 off Cape Hatteras. He wore a bent brown hat and smoked a pipe, and as the boat and fog were both gray, the only thing of Dallas to be seen at 6:10 in the morning was the brown hat out on the lake, with a little smoke over it.

When Dallas came in from fishing, all of the neighbor children would carry the fish up to the road. When he would be seen pulling into the dock, the children in the area would run down the gravel path with their sneakers going pop-pop-pop on the little tiny white rocks. They'd run onto the far end of the dock and look to see if there were a stringer tied onto an oarlock. If so, it meant fish for dinner, because Margaret didn't eat fish at all. Dallas either ate his fish alone or gave them to someone to cook, and he and Margaret would then go to that person's house for supper, Margaret bringing some casserole leftovers for herself rather than eat fish. Dallas' great goal was to catch the big pickerel that he knew lived in the lake. He almost caught it in 1955, but it got away. Dallas had a theory that the fish lived somewhere off the weed bank that ran under the water between the stone dock and the hill to the west. Dallas spent every trip trolling between the stone dock and the west shore trying to catch that pickerel.

One day, on a June morning in 1959, he did. Caught on a yellow Abu spinner, it was huge for a little lake. About 36 inches long. There was a great deal of excitement when Dallas rowed in and held up the fish on the stringer. Word got around as fast as usual, and the kids came running and there was a lot of talking. Dallas didn't say much, just looked at his fish that was dead from being pulled along under water on the stringer. He took it to Bob's Sport Shop on Route 46 for weighing and had it mounted, and for years it hung on the front porch overlooking Bloody Gulch, out of reach of the mice.

Dallas died in 1965 of a stroke, and was buried in New Jersey. Margaret moved the fish to the studio over the garage, and then gave it to the people of the lake. The big fish whose photo had been in the Morristown newspaper once was hung at the Clubhouse in front of the bar. Today, no one knows who caught the biggest pickerel ever caught in the lake, or when it was caught, as the little brass plaque on the mounting board is not there.

Margaret gave her last tea party in 1967 and moved to Florida for the winters. She had her 3,574 pounds of tiles shipped to Florida also, where they finally went to a women's craft club. She died of heart failure, and was buried in Florida in 1972.

The neighbor's daughter bought the mousy house for $35,000, got married, and had twins. There are still 29 steps up from the road and 7 steps up from Bloody Gulch. She had a little tan pet dog who had little pups which grew up to be little dogs. They were all given names starting with "S" in honor of the twins' names, "Sally and "Susie," and given away around the lake.

The boat from which Dallas caught the championship pickerel is still there (pictured below), sitting off the ground on flower pots, and painted each year in red lead preservative in the hope it will float again. (The wooden boat outlasted Dallas by 38-plus years.) The oars are still in the top of the dock that Dallas used every day. They are still painted green and gray, with oil on the lock stems.

The brown hat and pipe have been trashed, but the twins celebrated their seventh birthdays with a party in Margaret's former studio. When the old red couch was moved back to provide more room for games, a shy, sly little blonde neighbor girl, visiting for the summer, picked up a two-inch long piece of brass with engraving on it and quickly put it in her purse. She later took it home, and forgot about it in the daily excitement of that long ago summer. In 1981, the purse went to the Salvation Army in Dover, with the brass oval still in the bottom of the purse. On the brass oval was etched:

Congratulations, Dallas

Biggest Fish Ever Caught Here

June 12, 1959

36", 14 lbs, 10 oz

Becky 1 came to the lake from California after the collapse of the aircraft industry around Los Angeles. She rented a small frame two-story house on the west side of the lake with a newly added front porch. The porch was made of aluminum and shone in the morning sun, while the rest of the house was wood, and so the porch looked as if it had been added on to the house years after the house was built, which was essentially true. Becky loved to party, a trait which she had acquired in California, and on Saturday nights her porch was always full of lake degenerates who munched on antidepressants and wine coolers spiked with assorted liqueurs. A lot of people threw up on Becky's porch, but at least she wasn't lonely on Saturdays, and the porch always had a vague after-smell on Sundays.

Becky's parents were pretty well off, and they were always going off somewhere and sending exotic postcards back to Becky. On their sailing trip to Sweden, they sailed right past Mildred who was there with the Senior Citizens group tour, but of course, they never knew it. Becky had a brother with whom she had an interesting trait: they both had good chest muscles. Becky often went out to Picnic Island to sunbathe topless during the weekdays, which made the day for Earl, sitting in his rocking chair with his binoculars and oxygen tank. Earl's use of the oxygen tank prevented him from having to breathe the New Jersey air, which was always rather putrid on Wednesday mornings when the oil tankers were unloading over near the New Jersey Turnpike, and made him look so feeble and close to death that the girls of the lake were always giving him a good look at things to try to get his heart rate up a little, without killing him by getting it *too* high.

Becky was a writer who wrote at night when everyone else was asleep around the dark water. She wrote porno under another name. Her books carried such literary titles as *The Little French Maid and Me, Drilling Deep for Love,* and *Ten Ways to Play While Hung up with the Phone Cord.* She didn't make a whole lot of money as a writer, but enough to live from Saturday to Saturday.

Becky wore bizarre clothing in a style she picked up in California. She liked lots of bright colored printed flowery stuff, skin tight, so as to shock the old ladies shopping at the Grand Union in town. Sometimes, she wore her hair in spikes, with purple eye shadow and long jingly earrings, or she might be seen in a skimpy red bathing suit as she lounged about the parking lot of the Dairy Queen. Her dresses had lots of gold on them, and her hair was always full of little décor she bought at the five and dime store near the Grand Union.

Becky loved to fly all night. Having worked for an aircraft company once in computer flight design, she actually thought that it was safe to be going 500 miles an hour at 30,000 feet above one's dock. She was not afraid at takeoff, and could put on her lipstick in the plane's restroom without error after punching her ticket again as a member of the Mile High Club. Her greatest thrill was to board an early Delta flight at Newark, get 14 drinks on the flight, and land at San Francisco in time to catch a cab and watch the sunrise find the Golden Gate Bridge while she meditated and chanted. After 14 drinks, most of them served free by the friendly male flight attendants, her chants were a bit fuzzy while she looked at the Golden Gate Bridge, but she felt pretty mellow and assumed the chanting worked well in promoting a mellow and placid life.

Then it would be off to some sort of chic neon place for a breakfast of ice cream and eggs and a little vodka, and a night flight back to Newark. She would deplane at 4 a.m. in Newark, while everyone at the lake was asleep except the man sitting on the gray dock at the cove, completely soused from too much tranquilizers and whiskey on the flight, and take a limo home in time for a short nap before the next party on Saturday.

The Saturday parties were in the Roman tradition, with everyone sitting on cushions on the dark porch. In the reflection of the moon, teeth could be seen moving in unison through the food that Becky had bought at the Grand Union three days before the party and stored in the crème-colored General Electric fridge until it was time to get the food out for consumption. The food was always the same imitation crabmeat, salads that were premixed, fat-loaded dressings, meatballs in red sauce, sausages and sausage buns – all accompanied by plenty to drink. The guests never went into the water, it being regarded as a sort of horrible fishy dark place to die, and their motto was "Never get off the porch…*never* get off of the porch." And so on Saturday nights, they stayed on the porch, well away from harm.

She was the modern extension of Billie and Wally (you'll read about them later). Instead of traveling around her dock in an inner tube, she traveled around the country, and instead of having a few beers on a Saturday night, she had a few other power punchers to make life bearable. She found that prescriptions were a good substitute for a good paying job, and that if she couldn't quite be young anymore, she could at least *act* young. She liked her men smart and innovative, and with muscles developed from rowing. She was the leader of the fast crowd who had slid off of the Santa Fe rails somewhere in the 1980's, and ended up crashed on the lake hill. Of these folks, the more "on the track" people lived down by the water, while the people who had really been derailed by life and the economy lived up higher, away from the good waters full of fish droppings and teeth.

She had eaten on the Queen Mary at Long Beach, danced at all of the best L.A. nightclubs, strolled the streets with the grunge people, and carried a year Disney admission pass with her photo on it from when she was 18. She hated the California traffic but missed it, and was happy again when she discovered that I-80 near the lake was impossible westbound at 5 p.m. She bought a used gray Porsche that was pretty much a piece of crap, seduced the mechanic at the Shell station by the railroad station into really tuning it up, and she'd run up I-80 to the Water Gap doing 90 miles per hour with her blonde hair streaked with red, her shirt unbuttoned and no bra underneath, cruising for cop flesh. She often found it, and her gray Porsche allowed just enough room for some interesting aerobics.

She died in May 1995, completely whizzed out on whiskey and pain killers, two hours before John died on I-90 (more about him later), when, at 95 mph, she hit a smiling, happy buck with great looking pointy antlers near Exit 2 on I-80 westbound, two miles from the Gap. Her brother buried her near Long Beach in a California cemetery full of bizarre-colored headstones. Her brother had a little saying first written by Sallie Ezard of Illinois on July 13, 1888, inscribed on the headstone in the California tradition:

May all your days be spent in bliss

May all your plans succeed

Be but as happy as you wish

And you'll be blessed indeed!

Marilyn

Marilyn came to the lake late in life also, in 1992, when she was 43 years old. She bought a brick house on the northwest side of the lake with a wooden open porch with wooden columns across the whole front of the house. The house had a small brick chimney and a small fireplace inside, and everything was neat and orderly in the little house. Marilyn had deep lost blue eyes and blinding headaches that reduced her days to inactivity and darkness in the living room. She had taken a medical retirement from the State due to these attacks, and had hoped that a change of scenery might be best for her ailment. The change in scenery made no difference at all. Sometimes, in the dark of the night, when the pain in her head wasn't so bad, she'd sit in a chair on the rickety dock and look at the planes headed for Newark, and wish that she were on one, and that all of life was still ahead.

As a schoolgirl, she had wanted to be good at everything, but especially at playing the flute, and sometimes at 1 a.m., she'd sit out on the dock playing "Little Church in the Dell" over and over, with an occasional version of "Amazing Grace" just for variety. Some nights it was Bach and some nights it was Beethoven, and some nights it was just a haunting, flowing melody over and over and over. With a State medical retirement income, she didn't have to do much. She stayed indoors in the dark little house all day, coming out at night to shop if her head didn't hurt. Like the other people of the night, she was in tune with the night sounds and could identify all the creatures of the night by their individual sounds. To her, the owls in the timber north of the floating island were as individual as the ladies of the Garden Club, each with its own rhythm and tone. She could identify the geese out on Goose Island by their individual honks, and could tell the early morning birds apart.

As if to make up for the chaos in her head, she dressed well, with each outfit coordinated and in color for the season. It didn't matter to her that no one would see the outfit at night, for it was important to have order in the places where she could. Each night, she dressed for a late dinner, cooked fresh food that she had bought from the Grand Union in the middle of the night while she was wearing sunglasses, and then went out to eat it on the dock. People who saw her at the Grand Union at 2 a.m. thought her strange, and she didn't want to talk about her disability that would probably turn into a tumor later in life. Painkillers helped a bit, and like many of the lake people who were in pain, she carried on with the best fortitude she could muster.

Eddie

Eddie lived in a 1934 Cape Cod with a brick chimney on the east side across from Goose Island. He'd been in France during the Great War (he never called it World War I) at about the same time as his friend Ralph had been in France as a civil engineer. Eddie had been a combat soldier who lived to tell about the experience over and over. Eddie and Ralph often met at the Thursday afternoon Fishing Club meeting held at the Clubhouse and told stories about France when they weren't talking about lures. Eddie had a couple of stale-smelling boxes of war letters from his deceased wife, pictures, newspaper clippings, and French coins. Sometimes, he'd invite Ralph over to examine the souvenirs, and sometimes Eddie would talk to the veterans groups or school classes about the war. He always marched alone in the town's Armistice Day Parade in front of the two town fire engines and behind the color guard. Ralph went fishing instead.

Eddie's prize from the war was a British bayonet, with the little royal crown stamped on the side of the blade near the hilt. It came with a metal scabbard and hung by two small hooks over the fireplace. Every month, Eddie took out the bayonet and oiled it with auto oil to prevent rust.

Mornings during the summer, Eddie went out along his large wobbly dock with the round wooden support posts buried into the mud to the flagpole at the end of the dock, and raised the American flag, and every night when the sun fell behind the top of Bald Hill, he lowered it down again. He would never accept a late dinner invitation or any other social event that would prevent him from lowering the flag at sunset. In the summer, from June 1 to September 31, Eddie would stand at attention, bareheaded, on the end of the dock at the flagpole and sound taps on his bugle before he lowered the flag. He knew all about taps, such as the fact it was written by General Butterfield during the Civil War as a regimental identification method, and he knew all the variations of it that could ever be played on a bugle.

Everyone on his or her dock or out fishing would stop talking and listen when Eddie played. He never played in the rain or cold, as he was 65 years old in 1950, but on every quiet summer evening for 18 years, just at the time when the bass would hit a surface lure the quickest, the long, sad notes of taps would echo out over the lake to remind everyone that Eddie had seen a war. He died in his sleep at 5 a.m. on a fall morning in 1963. The house was sold to a couple from Montclair. The bugle and flag went to his grandson in Manteo, North Carolina.

Billie and Wally

Billie and Wally lived in a one-story white frame house built in 1928 as a fishing cabin. They were professionals. The house was near to the water and had a red-trimmed roof. They were in their 30s in 1959, and moved to the lake after a four-engine airliner hit their apartment building in Elizabeth. They threw their big black lab dog out the third story window to save him, and since the firemen caught the dog, the lab lived to swim in the lake under a full moon and chase foxes through the neighbors' flowers.

They both worked "in the City," and every day they would drive to town and get on the Lackawanna electric train to Hoboken, where they took the ferry to the city. Their absence all day gave the insects a chance to play, and by 1962 the whole roof was full of termites and flying ants. There was a wide, screened porch across the front of the house facing the lake, and at breakfast on that porch insects would fall out of the ceiling where they had eaten through the wood and fall into the scrambled eggs and bacon. Billie was a fine cook and everyone liked to be invited over for dinner. When invited to dinner at Billie and Wally's, however, one soon learned to watch one's food while eating. This constant watchfulness on everyone's part (without, of course, them ever mentioning it), resulted in giving a monastic air to the meal, with everyone's head bowed towards his or her food while each person kept an eye out for termites and flying ants.

Billie and Wally danced at the clubhouse on Fridays until midnight to tunes such as "The Witch Doctor," "The Lion Sleeps Tonight," and Hush-a-Bye," took moonlight dips from their dock, barbecued huge fatty hunks of beef, served drinks with little pink umbrellas in them, tried the hula hoop, and were generally bouncy people. Billie planted hundreds of non-frost resistant flowers using a bent trowel with her hands encased in green plastic gloves, and blushed at off-color jokes. Wally suntanned, flipping back and forth every minute or so on the gray wooden lopsided dock where he found an occasional splinter in his ass. Much like the ghosts in *Topper*, they were like two-dimensional busy flies who were always hyped up and cool. They drove big red Oldsmobile convertibles with big engines and loud AM radios.

Their bounciness, which reminded everyone of a pair of Tiggers from the Pooh stories, came to an end in 1962 on Route 30 between Gap and Kinzer, Pennsylvania, when a trailer broke loose from the truck pulling it and rolled downhill over their car. The big black lab survived again to bark about the adventure, and went to live with Billie's sister at the third house north of the New England-style white church with a spire on Route 306 at Kirtland, Ohio, near I-90, and had lots of pups. The lab died of old age in 1986, but the descendants live near I-90. The house was sold by the sister to Ray and Julia from Westfield. Written on their joint tombstone was "In

Memory's Casket, Reserve One Gem for Me" originally penned in Sept. 1988 by Nellie Cummingham of Virden, Illinois.

Mildred

Mildred didn't actually live on the lake, but all her friends were there, and she was thought of as a lake person even though she lived alone in town by the railroad in a two-story, four-bedroom, two-bath wooden house without a fireplace. This last deficiency was overlooked by the lake people due to the fact that she owned something which no one else in town did: a 1965 bright green VW Bug with only 56,000 miles on it in 1994.

She was 5'2" of go-do-it person. She polished and washed the car herself, revved it up when she shifted gears, and drove just as fast in the snow as she did on dry pavement: the speed limit, and no more. All her little dogs had names starting with "S," such as "Spot and "Skip," and came from the lake area. Her life was social. She went to the Women's Club Meetings, the Literary Club meetings, the Senior Citizens Center, birthday parties for her friends, and dinner at the Marriott or Red Lobster. When she wasn't eating or celebrating, she cruised the ocean.

The house had an open front porch on which massive wooden square pillars supported the second story. There was a handy-dandy city fire hydrant right out front which the dog wet on, useful in case the house ever caught on fire. She collected Hummel figures and plants. She placed the Hummels on the built-in white-painted bookshelves in the living room, and placed the plants in the kitchen. There were so many plants that there was no room for anything else in the kitchen. The plants were on the tables and countertops and in the tub in the downstairs bathroom. She hung her clothes on the door to the downstairs bathroom so that it could never be closed, but since only she and the current small dog lived there, it really didn't matter.

Her favorite activity was making brownies to give to her friends. She used her mother's recipes and wrapped the brownies in used plastic sandwich bags, then aluminum foil, then in a box, and then wrapped several rubber bands around the whole package. The brownies were always delicious. Friends came to tea, were jumped upon by the current little tan dog, and ate brownies. The rubber bands came from Lois, who saved every rubber band she ever saw and gave large sacks of them to Mildred, who sent most of them back wrapped around boxes of brownies.

At holidays, she drove the little green bug to visit her family in Boston doing a steady 55 mph in the middle lane, while surrounded by trucks doing 75 mph. The little dog went along, digging at fleas while sitting on the passenger bucket seat. Mildred was a short sprite of activity, a female Puck, darting about in her air-cooled car.

87

Emabel drove one of those four-door big tan cars made by GM that older people drive. It was 10 years old with 21,000 miles on it when it arrived at the lake. Emabel was a slow and careful driver, and never went out on Route 10 or I-80. She was a lady who knew her limitations. She liked getting mail from Idaho and Illinois, kept the family genealogy charts, and shopped from catalogs. She was short and thin, with white hair piled up on top of her head, and she always dressed for every meal. Earl was short and thin and had no hair on top at all. They were married 64 years.

Emabel hated every Hispanic person she ever saw, and blamed the Hispanic people for the loss of the cantaloupe industry at Rocky Ford. She thought that, at best, the Hispanic people were okay to mow the grass and rake the yard, and in fact, her gardener, as well as her maid in Colorado, had been Hispanic. But that was the limit. She would never go to a Hispanic doctor or talk to an Hispanic neighbor. She liked to cook, but her real passion in life was bridge. Upon arriving in New Jersey, she immediately joined the Women's Club Bridge Group, as well as the Senior Citizens Bridge Group, and happily played three times a week.

Earl had a good friend, Ralph Swink, who was the son of one of the founders of the town of Rocky Ford, who had played pool with Earl in Colorado, and made the flight to New Jersey twice after Earl moved just to play pool with Earl there. Ralph was a jolly, balding large man who liked good food and easy pool. Although they growled at each other fearfully during a game, their games had an air of finality about them that was sad to watch. In his later years, Ralph could hardly hobble around the heavy pool table, while Earl panted with each stroke of the cue stick. A pool game was often followed by strong coffee and a nap, the coffee having no stimulating effect at all. Earl was able to find friends at the lake who were just as pleasant company as Ralph Swink. Earl was content with all he had done in life – a man with no regrets, a nice arrowhead collection which eventually went back to the Rocky Ford museum, and many years of fine pool playing. He has spent his younger years fishing from a cabin at Florence, Colorado, so moving to the lake gave him a chance to relive many pleasant memories. He died at the age of 93 in his sleep, no doubt dreaming of playing the perfect bank shot. He was cremated.

Emabel, as of 1994, is still in the white lake house, still playing bridge, and giving away packets of wild rice at Christmas to her friends, which her daughter grows on her wild rice farm in Idaho. The neighbors think she'll live to see 105.

Nick was seven years old in 1986, and could never sit down, it seemed. If the theme of the lake was that there was always something to do, then Nick represented the lake fully. He *always* found something to do. He and his mother rented a one-story ranch brick house with no porch, but with a nice brick fireplace on the west side for several years, starting in 1984. Nick always asked questions, and because they were intelligent questions, adults answered them, and so Nick became smart.

He had big round eyes and collected rocks, pine cones, and gold coins, of which he didn't have too many. He bounced when he walked through high grass along the shore of the lake, and played with small fish and talked to the birds. He didn't remember much about his father, who had vanished away voluntarily when Nick was four years old, but Nick inherited one of his Dad's favorite activities: eating at fast food places. The day was perfect for Nick if he could go get fast food fries and burgers twice in one day, and Nick's mother, being kind, allowed him to do it from time to time on special occasions, such as Christmas.

Above all, Nick wanted someone big to hold his hand when the bats were out over the water of the lake. He wasn't afraid of the turtles or the fish that might bite, but he didn't like the bats. He liked to walk between two people who would swing him off the ground by his arms, and he liked piggyback rides up on someone's neck rather than on a back. He played with wooden interlocking logs and trains, and knew what was what. He rode elevators, and chased dragonflies and darning needles that flew over the water.

In the warm April of 1995, while looking through his night binoculars at 5 a.m. on a Saturday from his room, he saw a man sitting alone on the end of a gray dock at the cove. Nick watched this man be there from time to time, always sitting on the end of the dock, looking up at the sky. Nick wondered who the man was, and why he was out on the dock doing mostly nothing, and he pestered his mother over and over to row him over to the gray dock in the cove to meet the man, until one Sunday morning, she took out the canoe, put Nick into his lifejacket, and they paddled over across the lake to the gray dock to see the man looking at the sky. As they drifted past the dock, pretending to be out on a leisurely paddle about the lake, Nick shouted out, "Want to come along?" For the first time in many years, the man went for a ride on the water with someone. He slid into the canoe from the end of the dock so smoothly that it was obvious he was used to lake boats. He was silent, sitting properly still on the floor of the canoe, allowing Nick in the front seat to chatter along about the ducks and the geese, while Nick's mother paddled in the rear seat, and as dawn approached, said only: "Take me back to the cove landing now, and next time, come earlier." At the cove landing, the man stepped out of the middle of the canoe, into the shallow dark water, went to his red car, and drove away.

The next time that Nick was awake, looking out his window, and saw the man sitting on the dock at 4 a.m., they all three went for a ride, when all the houses were dark and the fog drifted over the water. The routine never varied, and the man found that the mother and Nick started coming over earlier, about 2 a.m., as if they had been keeping watch for his return. On the rides, the man and the mother never talked; rather, they allowed Nick to keep up a steadily running conversation about the wildlife and the lake. One night, when they picked up the man, he set a wooden box with a hinged lid into the canoe, and after the ride, Nick was allowed to open the box to find it full of 1950s toys: a Monopoly set with metal pieces such as a battleship and a hat, drawing boards made of slate with wooden borders, a wooden ball on a string that could be flipped into a wooden cup, a notched stick with a little propeller tacked into the end with a little stick to rub over the notches to make the propeller spin, and metal cowboys and Indians. Nick played with the toys.

In late April, 1995, Nick found a letter in the canoe that said, "Pick me up at 6 p.m. tomorrow at the cove landing. Bring your mom." So, Nick and his mom took the red wooden canoe and met the man at the cove landing by the clubhouse with the stopped-up kitchen sink. He had brown eyes, and carried a bag of coins for Nick, and a single rose for Nick's mom. He wore a cap with a cloth fish through the top, and he sat silently in the bottom of the boat, watching the old familiar docks slide by, watching the people on the shore as the sun set over Bald Hill. People were cooking out and having their wine on the docks, and though many of them waved to the red canoe, and Nick always shouted and jumped around in greeting, the man never said anything, only commenting once that, "A big black lab lived over there once, by that long dock. Survived an airplane crash. She was the nicest thing alive on this lake. I hope she did okay in life." And that was all he said. They brought him back to the cove landing after dark, and he handed Nick's mom the red rose, and handed Nick the bag of coins that turned out to be U.S. gold coins. He then drove away, and that was the last time they went boating together.

In May 1995, little Nick received a letter from Pepper and Pepper, Attorneys at Law in the Village in New York City, informing him that he had inherited the house with the gray dock at the cove, all of the stored contents, and over $20,000 in additional gold coins. Nick was never told what happened to the man who sat on the gray dock in the middle of the night and said almost nothing to the people of the lake. Among the items Nick inherited in the stored stuff were a woman's old furs and some black and white photos of a couple on their honeymoon in Europe, with the date "1939" written in pencil on the back. The woman in the photos had eyes very much like the eyes of the man who sat on the dock at night.

Grace

Grace retired from a good job as a bank manager in Manhattan and came to the lake in 1980. She had loved a soldier during WWII who was killed in Italy, and so she never married. She was friends with the realtor, Judy, who had selected the house for Earl and Emabel. Grace was one of those professional people who came to the lake but never really learned the lake ways. She bought a house up on the northeast end, facing west, with a beautiful granite fireplace which she never lit, an aluminum rowboat which she never rowed, and a dock onto which she never went. Unlike her business sense, which had been acute, her sense of buying a house in the lake country had not functioned to its fullest. The house was perched on the side of a hill, next to last on a dead-end downhill switchback. It was 17 steps down to the dock and 39 steps up to the door which was on the north side of the house and opened into the living room. No sun ever shone on the little one-car wide road or the 39 steps, and the township plow did not come down over the hill for fear of getting stuck. The result was that Grace rarely got out after the snow started to fall, even when she revved up the studded snow tires on her '78 Zephyr and sprayed pieces of asphalt back towards the doctor's house next door.

On snowy days when she really had something important to do (such as get to the bank), she'd line up the Mercury towards the one-car wide road up the hill and take a daring run for the top. She was able to achieve this acrobatic attempt several times before sliding sideways into a huge boulder right next to the little road, thereby denting in the door area on the right side.

The garage was a two-car version under the house at a right angle to the road. It was a tight fit with each car space having an individual set of swing-open doors. On one snowy day, she misjudged the center line of the left door, and took all of the trim and chrome off the driver's side, which was a nice balance to the destruction already done to the passenger side of the car.

The steps were the crowning aspect of winter at Grace's. No matter what the weather, the ice on the steps, which formed as the snow melted off the roof and dripped onto the steps, never melted. Carrying groceries, which Grace entrusted to the local delivery boy, always ran the risk of being fatal. Her friends never set foot near her house from October to April. But in the summers, Grace's house was nice for parties. She's pictured below (middle) in the 1970s.

The front porch had a fine view down on the lake, and in front of the side door was a circular picnic area carved into the side of the hill and supported by concreted rock. It was not for the faint-hearted, as possible failure of the rock supports did not bear thinking about, but the picnic tables and hand-built rock grill were the setting for many picnics when her family from Long Island or friends came to visit.

Grace was Swedish, and her love in life was parties and food. She loved to get take-out lunch from the Viking Deli, and early in the morning she could be found, along with most of the lake folks, buying a huge supply of pastries at the Viking Bakery and picking up a copy of the *Star Ledger* and *New York Times* at the newsstand and soda fountain shop next door. The result was that Grace became somewhat overweight later in life, though she was quite jolly about it. She was active in the Senior Citizens group and a member of AAUW, and liked to visit friends for a little something such as honey and biscuits during the afternoon. She was not too mobile even at the best of times, and there occurred several unfortunate incidents in which Grace pulled the handrails out of the wall or concrete as she attempted to hoist herself up someone's steps to the bathroom or road.

She had no pets and didn't talk about fish. She mostly ate and visited, and sat a lot. She had a fall in 1987 and another in 1988, which damaged her knee. Although she had the kneecap replaced, she declined to do the exercises or reduce her caloric intake. The attraction of the Viking donuts was simply too much for her to overcome, with all of her remaining family out on Long Island. Her increasing lack of mobility and the 39 steps proved to be more than she could cope with, and in 1989, without really needing to, she gave up and went to a nursing home on Long Island, where she died three years later of inactivity and boredom. Her nephew bought the house from the estate, and now comes out from Long Island on weekends to enjoy some drugs and a little time in the country with his friends he brings along.

The black Zephyr with both sides dented in was sold to Lois' son by the executor of the estate, with only 20,200 miles on it. In October 1993, the car was sold to two teenagers from Beavercreek, Ohio, with 94,687 miles on it. The car was still running well and in the glove compartment were all of the registration folders with Grace's registrations in them, along with Grace's New Jersey maps. Glued to the dash was the Shell station's plastic reminder that the next oil change was due at 21,000 miles. The Shell station, located by the railroad station in town, still places these reminders in its customers' cars. In May, 1994, Lois' son saw Grace's Zephyr, still with the dents in both sides, at the corner of Woodman Avenue and Colonel Glenn Highway in Dayton. The car was still running and no doubt Grace's registration was still in the glove compartment. Tied to the mirror was the little plastic red flower Grace had gotten by donating to the AMVETS in 1973 by the Grand Union.

Fred and Ethyl

Their names reminded everyone of the famous pair in the "Lucy Show," but they were not common nor particularly friendly people. They were an "Old Family," which meant their family had moved to the lake when settlement first began and the few families who wintered over could afford a very large house. Theirs was huge and old, and the fireplaces not only worked, but were lit every day during the winter. (Pictured below is Ethyl's ancestor, Maude, around 1880.)

They did no work themselves, but hired companies to care for the yard and deliver firewood and decorate for Christmas. There were only a few "Old Families" on the lake who could trace their family's settlement in the wilderness back to the 1920s. No one knew what Fred and Ethyl did for work, or if they did work, or had worked. They were polite and surveyed their land daily to see that no limbs had fallen in the night wind. They didn't throw parties or go to parties, did not lower themselves to swim or fish, and rarely commented to the neighbors, who were in their same social condition, about anything. Their house was the only three-story house on the lake with a magnificent view not only across the lake, but down the whole length, as it was built on a point of rocky land. The locals always told visitors that the big house was the only one on the lake which had three septic tanks, which was true.

In due course of time, they produced two daughters to pass the estate on to. The elder, June, never married, became introduced to Viking donuts thanks to Grace, and stayed at home to manage things and eat Viking take-out. The younger, Mary, got married and had twins who liked little tan dogs and parties.

Ethyl in due time developed colon cancer, perhaps from eating the lake fish in the 1950's, went to the hospital for an operation, and never came home again. The funeral was a quiet, dignified affair at which no one cried. Fred and his daughter, June, continued to manage things in the largest house on the lake until Fred died in 1968. No doubt the twins will inherit the mansion someday, and come to like parties and social chitchat less and less.

Anne and Milt

Anne and Milt had two granddaughters who lived in Scranton. They came to the lake in 1950 from Westfield. Milt had been in shoe production and Anne kept house. Milt was bald, and several neighbors made the unfortunate error of mistaking him for the vegetable man who came to all of the side and back doors every other day. He was not the vegetable man, though for a couple of days until people got things sorted out, there was a scandal to the effect that the vegetable man was hanging around Anne.

They were a shy couple, the opposite of Billie and Wally. They had a couple of cats given to them by Myrtle, who was always happy to give away cats to a better home whenever the opportunity arose. Their house was the dollhouse type, with a brick chimney and screened porch in the pines. They lived more by the road than by the water. Milt liked to swim at night under the moon, but as he got older, his swimming was reduced to sitting in an inner tube and drinking a beer. Sometimes, he would float downwind over to Billie and Wally's dock at night for a free beer. Wally would later put on his flippers and push Milt back upwind to his own dock. One night after a few too many beers, Wally put on his flippers and, since there was no moon, lit a red road flare and gave it to Milt to hold to show the way back to his dock. This improved the visibility but sunk the inner tube when a hot spark from the flare hit the rubber. As it was really not deep, Milt and Wally waded in to shore through the lake mud, and each went his own way home, both weaving a little. The path home was pretty clear for Wally, but Milt had a rough time of it in the sticker bushes without the moon or the red road flare.

Annie kept house and went to the Senior Citizens meetings and the Annual Lake Shareholders meetings. She was one of the few on the lake who did the latter, most people being more interested in living than in the business of living. She encouraged Milt to go to the Fishing Club meetings and stay active. She was a good swimmer, taught the granddaughters to swim and fish, and coached the lake swimming team. Her great goal in life was to be active and involved in everything. She was athletic at heart and dreamed of the wild lifestyle. Milt kept her from ever really achieving this, but she was content to wait. When Milt dropped over from a heart attack, Anne began to live. She went to the movies in town, the Senior Citizens Center, the Volunteer Firemen's dinners, took over as the head swimming instructor, and bought a sleek red car which made Billie buy a bigger red one. She was short – just as short as Emabel, whom she lost to at bridge once. She died in 1974 of colon cancer, two years after Margaret, her favorite bridge partner.

Edna

Edna came to the lake in 1948 after her husband died in an accident. She was tall, wore pearls, and wrote a daily diary. Her son, George, was a professor at the local community college, and they shared a brown one-story house with a brick fireplace on the west side. Their house was on a point of land with a good view of Picnic Island. She was one of many who loved the lake in the summer and loved Florida in the winter. At the first sign of the leaves turning, Edna would shout at George, who was not too young either, "Let's go!" and within a few hours, Edna's bag would be in the trunk of the black four-door GM car, and they would be off for Florida. As George was not a fast driver, and the trip was often started without proper rest, the trip down often took five days. Edna would be deposited at her condo, and George would return slowly to the coming winter.

Edna was good friends with Mildred, Margaret, and Lettie. Like Lettie, Edna could not see or hear too well, but still had spirit. She liked pearls. Edna used to rent a summer cabin up on top of Bald Hill, and came to like the lake so much that she went in with George to buy a house. From the shore, one had a clear view up the lake to Fred and Ethyl's house, and across to Teddy and Helen's house. One of the lake beaches was to the south from Edna's house, and the screams of the children playing on the sand, which had been dumped by Young's Coal Yard during the summer of 1948, would have deafened anyone except Edna, who was already pretty deaf, but who found her deafness useful sometimes when salesmen came to the door.

While many of her friends valued activities, Edna valued her friends. The best days were spent merely sitting in the wood-paneled living room visiting over a weak cup of tea with every lady who happened to drop by unannounced. Edna found this habit most of her friends had of dropping by unannounced troublesome, because it meant that taking an afternoon nap was risky, for as soon as she went to sleep on the couch, someone carrying some treat or other was sure to pound on the door for a visit. The result was that Edna frequently nodded off sitting in one of the kitchen chairs closest to the back door by the road. Most people at the lake had their front door built on the lakeside, which meant that visitors were always entering through all sorts of kitchen clutter at the back door which faced the road, where everyone parked. No one at the lake parked in his or her garage, as the garages were full of boats, shovels, firewood, and wood cutting tools. She still, at the age of 64, happily commutes between her condo in Florida and the lake.

Ralph

In his younger days, Ralph had been on the team which had improved the vacuum tube for RCA. He had little education but lots of experience in radio, having worked for Wired Radio in Washington, D.C. He was born in 1894 at Woodson, Illinois. He and Myrtle bought a summer cabin at the lake in 1955, so for several years during the summer, Ralph got up at 5 a.m., before Dallas went fishing, and drove to town in the Buick to the railroad station where he took the Lackawanna electric train to Hoboken to work, returning in the evening. As he usually carried gum for the children, he was often met by a few of the neighbor kids, who would sit by the road waiting for him to come home, and give them each a piece of gum.

He wore a brown hat with brim and an open collar shirt, and never forgot the Depression. He was thankful to have a job and a wife, and cherished both. He was 5'7" tall with brown hair that never thinned or turned gray. He was the proverbial good employee, never late for work, and several years after buying the lake cabin, he retired honorably from RCA when they still made the best televisions in America. He liked to fix things, and his Bible in this regard was a 1952

Popular Mechanics encyclopedia of home repairs and improvements. The set of red books told him how to do everything, from using the car battery to making a burglar alarm, to making a radio receiver and pouring concrete, to making a dog carrier to sit over the trunk of the family coupe. Ralph loved to build the projects shown in the red encyclopedia. He especially loved taking movie pictures with a wind-up eight-millimeter camera of the family using whatever he had built.

He was President of the Fishing Club for four years, and Secretary for four more. He liked writing letters to the State asking that more fish be added to the lake for the benefit of the sportsmen. He fished seriously, wearing loose khaki pants, white boat sneakers, and carrying his lures in a gray metal tackle box. He bought all his lures and bait at Bob's Sport Shop on Route 46, and each spring he put new 12-pound test line on his reel and oiled the reel well. He liked the adventure of night fishing for bass, and actually caught some big ones. When out in the boat, he would yell gleefully to any other fishermen within shouting distance, "How ya doin'? Catchin' anything?" and they would shout back, "No, not a thing," even though they were. He answered the same way so that no one would discover his favorite fishing spots.

He had a custom-made sign which read "Ralph and Myrtle Live Here" hung on the garage over the white swing-open doors, with the big black metal hinges that were getting rusty from Billie's dog peeing on them every morning. He liked to have his friends over for beef grilling in the new cooker he bought at the hardware store next to the bakery in town. He never drank after he was married, and supposedly never smoked either, although he had a box of Pall Mall cigarettes hidden in the trunk of the Buick. His life was full of reliable brand names such as Buick, RCA, Sears, and Pratt-Whitney.

The only thing he really disliked about life on the lake was the fact that every winter the water pipes under his cabin would split under the northwest corner of the house even though they had been carefully drained and disconnected every October. This then required the horrible experience of crawling under the corner of the house and into the deep old well, and then soldering the splits in copper pipes. Each spring, it was the same story: the pipes would be reconnected, the water turned on at the road, and then a loud hiss as the water sprayed down into the old unused well. Before the soldering could be done, the water had to be shut off again, the pipe drained again, cleaned with sandpaper, covered in flux paste from a white tin marked "Nokorode Soldering Paste, Providence, R.I." and heated with a propane torch. He had the torch's predecessor out in the garage, an oil-filled burner with a hose attached that the user blew into to make the flame into a point.

Ralph's greatest day came late in his life after he developed a bad heart. His fishing had been generally restricted so as to prevent exertion, but he still went out to the floating island several times a week for an hour to fish for largemouth bass. His spin casting, which in his prime

97

had been able to land a popper within inches of a fallen branch or lily pad, had been reduced to a distance of 10 feet from the boat.

One June evening, he was fishing by the floating island over a weed bank using a red fake worm. This was one of Ralph's favorite lures and he was the first person to use one at the lake with successful results. But by now, the fish were too smart to typically fall for a fake worm, and whereas once huge and scary bass had struck time after time, now a bass rarely took a fake worm. Natural selection, probably. All of the foolish fish had been caught. In any case, Ralph cast a fake red worm about five feet from the boat, in much the way that Elsa cast, and hooked a five-pound bass that must have been incredibly stupid not to see the boat overhead. It made Ralph's day – and week, and year. He exclaimed to everyone in the Fishing Club that red worms with two single hooks still worked, and he had been proven right. He took the fish home and cleaned it on the patio with a floor light from the living room shining on his sweaty, round, proud face. Myrtle baked it wrapped in bacon and stuffed with oysters, and Ralph walked a little taller again. That fish probably added two years to his life.

He died of heart failure in 1973 in a nursing home at Cranford, but right to the last week when he went to the nursing home, he cleaned his reel and organized his lures. Each week, he would take them out of the gray metal tackle box, and examine each one for damage from pickerel or bass teeth. He was cremated, and is buried in the Smith family plot near Dalton City, Illinois.

On his marker stone are carved these words, penned by one of Ralph's favorite writers, Katie Henry, on 29 April 1888:

Remember me when the years have fled,

And I am numbered with the dead.

Remember me though still I lie,

Dear Myrtle, meet me on high.

Jan

Jan came to the lake in 1972 as a retired teacher from Darien, Connecticut. When she retired, she sold her house in Connecticut which she had shared with her mother, who died in 1960. She already had one vacation house on Cape Cod which she rented out, and because her mother's husband and Myrtle's husband had been in the Great War together, she had heard stories about how pretty the lake was, so she decided that having no family, she would move to the lake. She settled in on the west side in a small Cape Cod style white house with a brick chimney and a cat (given to her by Myrtle), and settled down to retirement.

As she was an active oval-faced women with no hobbies at all, she spent her time at the lake planning her travels, and was always going up to the Cape or on a cruise. Much like Grace, Jan had, like millions of women, loved a soldier in World War II, and never married after her intended was killed. She was always running out to the road to the rusty mailbox to see if the mailman had come and left any mail for her. She often heard from her other teaching friends who had retired to travel. (She's pictured below in Miami Beach, Florida.)

Her one passion in life besides travel was investing in small hand-blown glass figures. They could hardly be called a hobby – more like an obsession. She had 10 wall-mounted wooden, lighted display cabinets into which she placed all of her glass figures. She even had a small padded case in which she could carry five figures to coffee and Viking donut parties to show her friends. Unfortunately, carrying this display case was a job in itself, and she almost always did not have room to carry any food to the parties. While the other women brought coffee and donuts (and cider in the fall), Jan brought glass figures to pass around.

She was a tough teacher who had taught the worst pupils in Darien and survived. She wore thick reading glasses that she stuck in her left pocket when she was not reading, brown longish dresses, and flat heels. She drove a four-door Pontiac, just as her father always had. In the 1940's, her father and mother, along with Jan's sister and two brothers, had all gotten together with Ralph and Myrtle's family for Thanksgiving dinner in Roselle. The third generations of the families continued the tradition for no particular reason other than it had always been done.

She shopped using coupons, put on the snow tires every November herself, and checked the oil regularly. She kept her days organized after she retired just as well as she had while she taught. She used a pocket planner, positioned the snow shovel by the back door on nights when snow was expected, and always stocked spare light bulbs in case one should burn out. She died in 1992 of liver cancer, and was cremated. The glass figures went to her niece in Minneapolis, and are in a display cabinet bought at Kmart.

John and Marie

John and Marie were early arrivals at the lake, with John's parents arriving in the 1940s when the lake was still pretty wild. They seemed middle-aged when just about everybody else was young. John remodeled houses and so by 1970, most of the houses had his mark on them. The summer cabins were renovated into winter houses with the addition of insulation, wood stoves, and buried pipes. Along with these changes, John would add bookshelves and paneling, and change what had been uninteresting fishing cabins into the young professional version of the fishing cabin, with plenty of fish art, room for books, built-in stereo systems, wooden wall-mounted fish painted pink and blue, and chandeliers. People who began coming to the lake from the City truly thought of a fishing cabin in New Jersey as a great adventure, although most of the City people gave parties rather than fished. John smoked a lot while he worked, and while he never burnt down a house that he was working on, he pretty well burnt down his lungs, to the point that John wheezed almost as badly as did Earl on the other side of the lake.

Marie stayed home and cooked and waited for John. She wasn't interested in the church or town, but she liked to rake leaves and visit with the neighbors. At the lake, there were no fences between neighbors who proved Robert Frost wrong by being good neighbors without them. Marie was a trellis for the lake grapevine, and she helped spread the oral news in the medieval tradition of town crier. She'd pass along the latest news to the widows on either side of her each morning by shouting from her porch to theirs when they let out their cats, and the news would spread along the lake in likewise manner. Each time a cat was let out or in, neighbors would take a minute to open their doors and shout news at the person letting the cat out or in. This manner of spreading the news was the main reason why even today, most people who live by the lake do not bother with having a telephone. What would one need with a phone?

Life for John and Marie was pleasant. Because of John's housework, they were invited to most lake social events and came to know everyone at the lake. Their son went to work for the township as a snow plow operator, and so came to meet everyone else at the lake his parents did not yet know. John and Marie's grandson went to school at Rutgers, and came back to the lake to live on the northeast side, managing a clothing store in town.

John died in 1991 of lung cancer, and Marie died in 1993 of breathing John's smoke all those years. Their son still drives the township snow plow and their grandson still works in town, and both still live by the lake in their own houses.

Lois' mother had graduated from Milliken University back at a time when women rarely graduated from a university, let alone went into teaching science and math. Lois was born in East Saint Louis in 1918, and survived scarlet fever.

She received a Master's degree in microbiology in 1950 from George Washington University after having a son. For years, she managed the city laboratory of Elizabeth, and then moved on up to a job with the State of Trenton, where she became a roving laboratory inspector, inspecting hospital laboratories. In that job, she met one of her lifelong friends, Doris, who was also a microbiologist. Doris later developed muscle trouble in her microscope hand and became a building manager, but Lois continued in her professional field until retirement. She was a single mother, her husband having gone off to Europe to work for the U.S. Department of State to find a better job as an economist than could be found in the States.

In 1954, Lois took the Blue Comet B&O train from Washington to Elizabeth and came to live with her parents. They all got along well. Lois worked and paid rent, and when her parents bought a cabin at the lake, she naturally went along to enjoy the wilderness.

Lois' personality was both dependent and social. She thought that her mission in life was to recognize everyone's birthday by sending a card, and bought little gifts for people to celebrate the holidays. She lived for social events. Her 5'3" was often encased in real furs and dressy suits. She was a social aspirant who, because of her job, never climbed the social ladder at all. As a member of the New Jersey Bicentennial Committee, she had the chance to make new friends in the upper class. Her Saturday trips to the Metropolitan Opera in the City and light lunches at the Grand Tier Restaurant offered the same opportunity, but it never quite worked out.

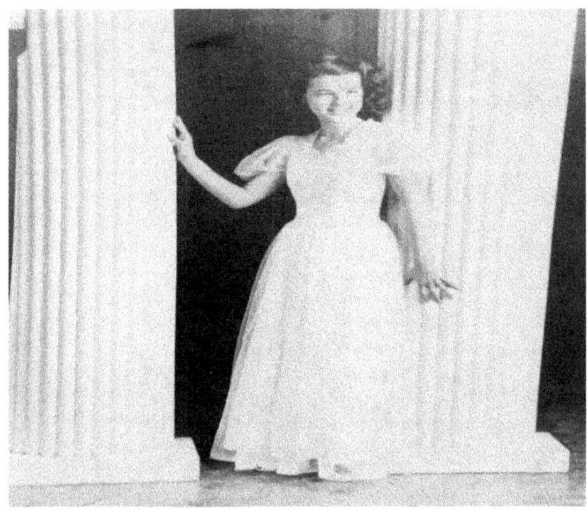

At the lake, Lois rowed the fishing rowboats, and joined the Flower Club. She was a hostess for the Literary Club, where she served sherry and little sandwiches, and reported about the romance novels she read daily. On Saturdays at the lake, she would go to town early in the morning to buy the *New York Times* and some Viking pastries to start the day. Like the other working women, she lay on the dock and sunned during the afternoons, and planted bulbs for the spring (which the squirrels dug up a week later and ate when the neighbors' cats weren't looking). Her life was filled with weekends of social events such as bridge parties and club meetings, and she worked herself to death all week in Trenton. The drive from the lake to Trenton was about an hour and a half, and many other people who worked in Trenton lived up in the lake country. At 5 a.m. every Monday, the traffic on Route 206 to Trenton from the north was nose to tail all the way from I-287. Like Lois, most of these people found that it was not feasible to drive the trip daily, so they rented apartments on West State Street near the Holiday Inn, and every Friday at 5 p.m., Route 206 would be nose to tail northbound to the lake country.

No one in New Jersey who could afford to leave stayed in Trenton over a weekend. They either went to the lake country or to the shore.

As life went on, Lois found that she could not keep up with all of the holidays, birthdays, work reports, and social events. Something had to be delayed, and what Lois chose to delay was reading the mail. Each day at the lake, she'd go to the mailbox by the road and get the mail. She'd read the handwritten letters from her friends and son, and the rest would go into brown paper sacks. At Trenton, the same was true. She'd read the handwritten mail and place the rest in a sack for later reading. This later reading never occurred. The sacks piled up at both the lake and Trenton, until they got to be about four feet deep.

When Lois' parents became older and more ill, she was forced to commute from Elizabeth to Trenton almost every day, or from Trenton to the lake. This commuting, along with the driving required to visit hospitals, wore her down but raised up her blood pressure. Along with her pension, she acquired heart trouble, diabetes, and like all of her friends at the lake, colon cancer. After her parents both died of heart failure, she retired, sold the house at north Elizabeth at 845 Kilsyth Road, had John winterize her cabin at the lake, and moved to the lake permanently. It was too late to save her health. The house at the lake was packed full of the furniture from Trenton and Elizabeth, papers from 1940, and hundreds of sacks of mail which included such goodies as dividend checks, stocks, and thousands of "Bill Due" notices that she never had the pleasure of reading.

In fear of another Depression, she bought supplies well ahead of time. The bedroom contained years' worth of new Christmas cards and wrap, the living room was piled with 22 sacks of canned food and crackers for the winter that her son had hauled to New Jersey from Ohio, as food was cheaper in Ohio. Her clothes were piled on chairs, and the mail she did read was piled on the glass table on the porch. The kitchen was piled with glassware from Elizabeth and Trenton since there was not enough cabinet space for it all. She had a cat called Amber and a Bichon purebred dog named Missy. Amber delighted in knocking down piles of stuff onto the floor where Lois sometimes tripped over the stuff on the way to the bathroom in the night, and Missy loved to play tag with the cat.

Each day, as she grew older, she planned what she wanted to accomplish during the day, and got almost nothing done. The preparation of breakfast, dressing and feeding the animals took all morning, then an hour to prepare a healthy lunch, followed by a social event or a nap. Then, it was time to fix dinner and feed the animals, followed by a romance novel and bed. The cat and dog slept on the bed with her, and for all of her natural warmth and need for love, she lived alone with the animals at the lake for 15 years after her parents died.

After retirement, she suffered little stroke after little stroke, sometimes lying on the floor for a day or two with Missy lying next to her for companionship, until she felt well enough to get up. In 1989, what she told herself were hemorrhoids turned out to be colorectal cancer. She was operated upon at Morristown in October of 1989 to have most of her insides removed, the same week that her friend Ethyl was operated upon for the same illness. Lois survived the operation, while Ethyl, who went to the local hospital, did not. In December 1989, she came home with a private nurse from Newark in time for Christmas. The first night home, a raccoon pried the screen off the upstairs bedroom window to get at the crackers in the food sacks downstairs, and scared the nurse who was sleeping upstairs nearly to death. Lois, who was in a hospital-type bed downstairs in the living room, woke up, heard the nurse's screams, and threw several bottles of hospital cleaning solution at the stairs to drive off the raccoon. The raccoon went back out the window, and the house was well fumigated by the cleaning solution splattered on the walls and stairwell. The nurse quit the next day and went home, and a new nurse from Cranford came to work at the lake.

For nine months, Lois was able to get back to her routine of placing the mail in sacks and sending out birthday and holiday cards late. Her son commuted from Ohio each weekend to help out. Then, in July 1990, she took a turn for the worse. The constant chemo drip to fight the cancer caused her to have no appetite and her weight dropped alarmingly. Her son took her to a nursing home in Ohio for the coming winter, along with much of her stuff and many sacks of unopened mail, and rented the cabin to Greg, the son of one of the town's women bankers, Anna Marie. Missy and Amber, the dog and cat, found a new home with one of the lab techs from the hospital who lived in Morristown, and had three children who loved animals. When Lois' son visited the animals in 1991, they were both doing fine.

Lois made friends in the nursing home in Ohio. Her greatest day was in October 1990, when her team won the West Ohio Nursing Home Trivia Contest. Five nursing homes entered teams of three people in the trivia contest, and Lois' team won. There were pictures in the local community newspaper showing all three of them in wheelchairs. Lois wrote weekly to her friends Mildred and Doris at the lake, worried about the house, and went to all of the nursing home activities such as Thanksgiving dinner and the Christmas show. She took third place in the Halloween costume contest with her costume of a railroad engineer, and took 16 different medications daily, including insulin.

Her kindnesses in life were generally rewarded, as she received letters from the ladies in the Literary Club, the Women's Club, and the Flower Club. Her friends were always sending her dried weeds and flowers, which fell apart when removed from the shipping box. Doris shipped Lois 40 romance novels a month, and Mildred sent photos of her and her new dog, a little short-hair which dug up the carpet.

Lois died on February 12, 1991, at Greene Memorial Hospital of a blood clot caused by chemotherapy, without ever returning to the lake. She was cremated. Lois' lake house, where she hosted the monthly Literary Club and put flower arrangements into little glass vases, was rented to Frank, a weapons designer from Picatinny Army Depot. Much of Lois' furniture is stored in the spare upstairs bedroom, her china is still in the breakfront, and in the bathroom corner a dried arrangement still hangs years after her death. Doris and Mildred and Lois' son ate dinner together at the Red Lobster on Route 46 several times a year, and remembered her fondly.

In the spare bedroom of her house at the lake, in a broken-down dusty cardboard box next to the closet where her furs still hang, are some black and white photos of Lois' honeymoon trip to Europe in 1939, gold invitations to American Embassy parties in the great countries of Europe, and pictures of her with prewar dignitaries. In these photos, she can be seen in elegant, flowing gowns wearing gloves, and looking adoringly at her new husband, enjoying the rich, dignified social life that she assumed would always be hers. Fifty-seven years later, eight people went to her funeral, and there were two flower arrangements on the floor by her casket, one from her son and one from her friend, Doris.

Alice and Frank

Alice and her husband, Frank, weren't from the lake at all, but spent a lot of time there. They were from Margaret's old neighborhood, East Orange, and they came to the lake on Saturdays to serve at Margaret's parties which were held on the patio with the metal umbrella which often blew over onto the guests when the wind blew up the lake from the south. As the patio was 20 yards from the house, servers were certainly needed when the guests exceeded 10 people. Margaret believed in serving by courses, starting with drinks, followed by soup served in shallow sloppy bowls with gold edging, several meats and vegetables, dessert, liquor, and coffee and mints. The serving was done on trays decorated with tiles by Margaret, which sometimes made the plates slip and slide. Should a thunderstorm blow up suddenly, as was probable during the summer, the guests could all be seen also slipping and sliding across the wet grass, carrying their plates on the way back to the house, where dinner would continue on the porch.

No one ever knew what Alice and Frank thought about the lake people. Alice and Frank were both about 40 years old in 1963, and were jovial. They took the train up from East Orange and were met first by Dallas, and after his death, by Margaret herself. After Dallas' death, the number of parties increased and Alice and Frank became a frequent sight at the lake. Their dignity and competence, especially as compared with Margaret's increasingly bizarre behavior (perhaps due to poor circulation), made them well-respected lake favorites. They would arrive at 9 a.m. on a Saturday after a 30-minute ride, and Alice would head for the kitchen. The groceries would have been delivered from the Grand Union in town the day before, carried up the seven steps from Bloody Gulch by a hardworking high school student. Margaret never shopped for groceries – she preferred working in tiles. Frank would take Margaret's car back to town to purchase the wine and liqueurs.

The basic division of labor was that Alice cooked and Frank carried. Alice was properly dressed in a round black dress with white apron, and Frank wore a black suit without gloves. They laughed when spoken to, seemed happy together, and never spoke unless addressed. They were good to the children, who would always count on getting a few cookies from the kitchen, and maybe a small sip of apple wine.

Because of them, the parties held under the big metal umbrella went exceedingly well. When storms came, Frank would fight a losing battle with the big umbrella, while Alice hurried to set a table either on the porch overlooking Bloody Gulch, or in the sun room on the west side of the house off the kitchen, facing the patio. This was actually the more convenient room in which to have a luncheon, as it was next to the kitchen, while the front porch required that food be carried through the living room, thus risking the droppings of food on the imported carpet. The children always wondered why Frank was never electrocuted while he struggled to keep the big umbrella upright in the storms, but the umbrella was never hit. Perhaps there were better targets out on the water for the lightning. After Frank lost his valiant battles, he would come back to the house dripping wet, and help Alice manage the kitchen and pour drinks for the guests.

Alice and Frank were never really thought of by the lake people as hired help, but more like the inheritors of Margaret's old neighborhood who had come to the lake for a little visit, and stayed to help with the party. Frank was tall and muscular, and Alice was round and short, and no doubt they made more money at the lake than they would have on a weekend in East Orange. They represented a stability in the early 1960's that was later proven to be an illusion by the 1968 riots in Newark, but they fit into lake society remarkably well. Whatever hell they returned to in East Orange was perhaps offset by the time in Margaret's heaven.

The parties stopped when Margaret started spending much time in Florida. After a busy winter of social engagements, she looked forward to the quiet of the lake during the summers and entertained herself by working on her tiles and watercolors. Without Margaret to make them appear, Alice and Frank faded away into the turbulence of the late 1960's, no doubt condemned to stay in East Orange to make a living. They were a remarkable and well-loved couple, who not once showed in any manner what they thought about the lake or its people. Maybe they really didn't think anything about the lake people. Maybe they saw their trips to the lake as just a job, and they were content to go home with Margaret's money in Alice's purse, which might not have happened if Margaret had been able to shop, cook, or plan with any sense at all. As it was, Margaret's parties were well planned and executed, and everyone had a jolly time.

The lake people do not know whatever happened to Alice and Frank. It would be nice to know.

Linda came to the lake when she was six years old, in 1959. She had two brothers and two sisters, a mother who was a nurse, and a father who was an FAA inspector. Like many of the lake families, they moved from one of the local cities that was going downhill. They bought a very big house with a brick fireplace along the lagoon by the one car bridge.

Linda was a stockbroker who loved animals and junk. She could be seen in the evening driving around the lake road in her red pickup truck, collecting anything useful that could go to charity. Likewise, she collected injured animals. Birds, raccoons, squirrels, and fish all found salvation at the hands of Linda. She had a broken down wonderful cat named Ashley who watched animal shows on television, and who was always trying to get out the house and run over. Thankfully, it never succeeded in doing so.

Linda loved pickup trucks, but often drove small, dull cars because they were less expensive. She was elected Lake Queen one summer and wore the crown at the regatta and dance. She swam in the swim meets, rowed, fished, and lived to cut brush with a 16-inch Stihl chainsaw. She knew the ways of turtles, theater, tonsils, teenagers, and tuna. She read and wished for stability. She was a packrat. The top of the garage was filled with old rockers and trunks she found discarded along the road, and after her brothers and sisters moved out and married, she took over the whole top floor of the big house for her antiques and junk. Ashley loved to run through the collections and knock everything over, much as Lois' cat Amber did, and then howl with glee.

Linda should have been rich, or successful in business, or famous in business. She never was. But she did well in other ways. She gained riches in heaven for her good works. She visited the elderly and cared for her nieces and her parents. She was successful at showing other people their successes and failures, much like a mirror to others' souls. She was famous for knowing everything there was to know about the lake and the people who lived there, as well as everyone in town. While most lake people stayed at the lake, Linda roamed between the lake and town, knowing everyone. Animals who would have died lived because of her kindness and trips to the vet with critters who tried to cross the lake road. All in all, she was one of the kindest and most well-liked people on the lake. She still hopes to win the lottery and still lives on the lake.

Doris

Doris spent much time at the lake, because like many of the people in town, many of her friends lived at the lake. Doris was Lois' friend, and they had known each other for many years. Doris lived in a split-level house with no fireplace off of Route 46, on a corner lot, and shared the house with her daughter. Doris' husband died of a stroke at the Newark Airport years before, and the other children were grown and out of the house. Doris lived for two things: to work and to help people.

Of the first characteristic, Doris was a feminist without using the label. She enjoyed work, and at age 58 did not want to retire – ever. She got up every work day at 4:30 a.m., left for work at 5 a.m. to avoid the New Jersey rush hour, and drove her white GM car to Nutley, arriving home at 5 p.m. The refrigerator was always stocked with food in case friends dropped by for dinner, but eating out was the norm. She came to know every little neighborhood restaurant in the area, and enjoyed dinner out during the week, and breakfast out on weekends.

Of the second characteristic, Doris lived to help those elderly friends who needed help. If her friends were housebound, Doris would show up at the door bringing breakfast or dinner. If her friends were in the hospital, Doris would show up at 7 a.m. with a hot breakfast. Being in the medical field, she was never put off by the visiting hours sign, but instead went anywhere in the hospital, whenever she pleased. She spent her weekends shopping for people who couldn't go themselves, ate at the Red Lobster with other friends whom she drove about collecting for the evening, and was kind and considerate to everyone. She donated bags of romance novels to ladies who liked to read them but couldn't afford them. When her friend Mildred was in the hospital for a hip replacement, Doris appeared out of the rain at 7 a.m. at the rehabilitation center on Route 202, bringing novels and breakfast. When her friend Lois was operated on for cancer, Doris sat at the hospital for the whole evening, waiting to see if her friend did okay, and then was back at 6 a.m. to sit by her bedside.

There were two cats at Doris' house, both of the indoor type, and both black and white. The older one slept on Doris' bed at night, while the younger one, a new arrival, spent the night clawing the furniture and running up and down the hall. As this cat had long back legs and short front legs, the cat was always running turned sideways while proceeding forward, and very likely to trip up anyone in the night who was headed for the bathroom off the hallway.

The yard was sterile, with short grass and a couple of small trees. Once upon a time, her husband had grown vegetables in the garden which took up most of the back yard, but after his death the yard was allowed to return to suburban New Jersey style, which meant that it was generally without country excitement.

Doris was tall, with wide shoulders that were good for shoveling snow and moving cats along who clawed the furniture. She wore efficient clothes, dark and businesslike, and expounded upon the futility of solving the New Jersey traffic problems. The wonderful new highway, I-80, had been designed to carry traffic smoothly from eastern Pennsylvania to the City, but by 1990 was so congested that even at three lanes on each side, the last 35 miles into the City was covered at a mere crawl between 7 and 8:30 a.m., and the same 35 miles out of the City was covered at the same crawl between 4:30 and 6:30 p.m. In 1992, a fourth lane was added to each side of I-80 for these 35 miles, but this addition had no effect on the rate of movement. That was why Doris went to work at 5 a.m., in addition, of course, to being bored at home and enjoying her work.

While her profession was microbiologist, she had been forced by muscle trouble in her hand, and a botched operation, to switch jobs in her company to one of building manager. Instead of a microscope, she was now concerned with air ducts, heating plants, and blueprints. She did such a good job at creating order out of disorder in the running of the buildings which she managed, that she was placed in charge of managing the two newest buildings the company had just built. This new responsibility meant more and more hours of work, which suited Doris just fine. When asked if she wanted to retire, she'd always reply, "And what would I do?" as if there were nothing to do in life except work. Really, nothing interested her other than working or helping people, and since helping people depended upon her having a good salary, working was a part of the overall play of enjoying life. Unlike Mildred, she had no interest in cruising, and unlike Emabel, she had no interest in bridge. So she worked, and fed her cats, and did the most caring, splendid things for people who were old and ill. She shopped for others, drove them to the hospital, visited them when they were ill, and in all ways led what the people of the lake called "a good Christian life." Most of them never knew that Doris was Jewish. She even put up a Christmas tree so that her friends would feel comfortable when they dropped in for a visit during the holidays. If ever there were a saint in northern Jersey, it surely was Doris because of her many kindnesses to others.

Dave was a three-star retired general who was short. He had married a woman who hated the military life and made him leave the active service and go into the Reserves. As a political climber, he still made rank and thus provided a good life for the family, which consisted of two sons and a daughter. Dave owned a big one-story modern house on the west side with a fireplace and a town-tended green yard right by the water. Being right by the water, Dave had a good problem for several years. Whenever the town lawn care company would spread grass seed in the spring, the geese, newly returned from the south, would eat it up. This eating was not just accomplished by one or two geese, but rather by 10 or 20 geese, their black necks with the white side patches bent lovingly into Dave's yard by the water. As the house was only 20 yards from the water, early in the morning the geese would be evenly spread out across all 20 yards, eating the grass seed. The town lawn tenders happily reseeded over and over, along with the usual cutting and raking of the grass on the other side of the modern house, until Dave's lawn bill exceeded the national debt.

Dave grew alarmed, and went out one day and strung three strands of wire parallel to the water at heights of six inches, one foot, and one-and-one-half foot levels, then tied white strips of sheets onto the wire. This did not work. The geese enjoyed chewing up the strips of sheet, then merely flew over the wire to land on the 20 yards of new seed. Adding more wire would have restricted access to the water for swimming, so Dave's solution was to get a large collie, and tie it on the 20 yards of new grass to protect the young grass. This worked well as far as solving the goose problem, as the dog chased off the geese who tried to land and eat the grass seed. But, by the time the costs of the dog's food, vet bills for goose bites on the nose, and broken leashes were added together, it might have been cheaper to feed the geese imported seed. But Dave at last had a nice green lakeside yard, although there were dog droppings all over it which detracted somewhat from the beauty.

Things were frequently like that in Dave's life. He had money and power, and controlled the Property Owners Board for 20 years, but the little things always went astray, causing vexation. This constant vexation at never getting things in life completely under his control made him generally unhappy. There was never a military trip to Europe that Dave did not go on, but the glitter of three stars on his shoulder made anything that he wanted so easy to obtain that he endured a general boredom with life. He knew how to fish and row and swim, but never bothered, as he saw no useful purpose to doing these mundane lake activities. He was more interested in writing rules and regulations for the lake in government style, going to board meetings, and chastising neighbors who failed to display their boat or swim tags, and in general trying to manage the lake people as if they were sergeants. As he influenced everyone on the Board, and his wife wielded power in the Women's Club, he pretty well had his way in everything.

The only trouble was that his successes in life did not bring him much happiness. He commuted between the lake and Washington, attended the society parties, drove an imported automobile with a car phone (the only car phone at the lake back then), and had a condo for winter in Florida. But no one loved him nor ever would. His children liked sharing in his money, for he owned a cleaning business in addition to being a general, but they did not love him, and his wife, who loved running the Women's Club without having to bother holding office, thought he was uninteresting. Much like the "Short Happy Life of Francis Macomber," he was the all-powerful male who was also all alone.

He could be found on the phone in the living room with the sliding glass doors that looked out to the water while he was wearing tan slacks and black shoes, or on his car phone, or on the phone in an airliner, or flying in his private plane. He was irked by common people who talked about fish, and was even more irked when Linda's dad failed to certify his plane as airworthy at an annual FAA inspection, although Linda's dad was rather pleased to raise his blood pressure a few points. The failure of the flaps to move smoothly cost Dave a few thousand dollars in payoffs to a mechanic to sign off on the work that was not done, and to another FAA inspector who had more debts than honor.

Dave kept the plane over at the Bernardsville Airport, about an hour from the lake, and he liked to buzz the lake during summer afternoons. He enjoyed nosing the plane over at 4,000 feet and making strafing runs towards the swim float anchored in the middle of the lake, violating the 1,000 foot minimum height requirement, then pulling up sharply with a full throttle. Linda, who knew everyone at the lake, heard about the practice from Ethyl's daughter, and told her father, who arranged for an FAA plane to follow Dave one afternoon, and he paid a $3,000 fine in court in Newark two months later. Much like the Viking kings, Dave drifted through life, insulated by money and power, but he never understood the beauty to be found in a goose happily eating grass seed.

Billy was a lake boy. He fished for dinner and caught frogs for their legs, crawdads for stew, and regarded the lake as a grocery store. He had the slickest way of catching frogs. While most of the boys used nets, Billy would drift up to the lily pads and hold a long rod with a trout fly just over the lily pads. He would wave this fly back and forth, and sooner or later, even though he might not see the frog in the early morning mist, the frog saw the trout fly, and thinking that it was a real fly, would eat it. Billy would set the hook, and the frog would become dinner. In this manner, he would catch far more frogs than the other boys using nets, for once the frog sensed the close approach of the other boys, the frogs would jump into the water and be gone, or eaten by a bass.

The catching of crawdads for gumbo or stew was so easy that all the boys on the lake would catch them and bring them home in pails for their mothers to boil, and then remove the tails for eating in the stew. One boy would row, while the other would lay in the bow of the boat holding a small tin can. A large can would be too big to lay on the bottom of the lake, in the shallows between rocks. The rower would move the boat, hopefully an aluminum one without a keel, into the rocky shallows. The boy in the bow would position the can on the rocky bottom next to a rock with a dug out pile of sand in front and a little hole between the pile of sand and the rock. This was the indication that a crawdad was living under the rock. As bass ate any crawdads dumb enough to be out on the mud bottom or weed banks, all of the living crawdads lived under rocks, and would pop out to eat a minnow whenever possible. Flat rocks were best because the flat rock worked well to nudge the crayfish into the can. The boy, having laid the can facing the rock, would gently lift the side of the rock by the can. The crawdad, which could not back up because of the rock behind him, would hide in the can. The boy would then raise the can and dump the crawdad into a pail in the boat. This technique was best done in only a few inches of water. If the bottom were firm and sandy, the same technique could be done by wading around, but if the crawdad escaped the can, then the catcher was liable to get a nasty nip on the toe.

If the crawdad were under a retaining wall along the shore, a small worm could be dropped in front of the crawdad's home, far enough away to entice it completely out. A piece of wood could then be dropped behind the crawdad while it ate the worm, preventing it from getting home, and a stick used to drive the crawdad tail first into a waiting can. Billy was an expert at these techniques.

There was only one thing that ever showed this lanky boy that the lake held a few leftovers from the early days. In 1962, Billy was out fishing along the south shore of the floating island at 6:30 a.m. in July. The sun was just shining over the trees on the east shore, and Billy was fishing with a floating minnow, the kind that dive as the lure is reeled in, but float when not moving. These are a particular favorite of bass at daybreak. Billy's rowboat was drifting over a weed bed that was only about two feet beneath the surface, when for no particular reason, Billy looked over the side after reeling in the lure. It took a few seconds to realize the dark green figure moving slowly north was the largest snapping turtle he had ever seen – half the size of the rowboat. The turtle would have filled the whole rear half of the boat, with its dripping feet sticking out over the side. And it was almost under the boat. If it came up, it might have upset the boat, throwing Billy into the water with it. Now, a small snapping turtle can easily take off a finger, and many of the small swans at the lake are eaten in the spring by the snapping turtles. Any reasonable fisherman avoids even the one-foot diameter turtles, and wears a belt knife in case a lure retrieval brings in an unexpected snapper. But this turtle was huge, its head the size of Billy's hand. He could see the turtle's head and four legs and tail and armor plate as it swam along the top of the weeds, searching for breakfast just as Billy was. Billy grabbed the oars and rowed for home, and for weeks he never again went near the floating island. He never told anyone, for people wouldn't have believed that a turtle so large could have remained undetected for so many years of fishing and civilization.

Billy climbed trees, was elected Lake King in 1968, and won boat races. His specialty was the boy's single canoe race. His father owned a short aluminum canoe that was no good for fishing, but was especially good for racing. Billy was a powerful stroker who won most races, and who had a whole display of plastic trophies with gold cups and black bases. On the bases were glued paper labels identifying the year and type of race that Billy had won. Sadly, the only races remaining today of the Men's Single or Double Rowboat, Men's Single or Double Canoe, Boy's Single or Double Rowboat, Boy's Single or Double Canoe, Women's Single Rowboat, or Women's Double Canoe are the Sailboat races sailed by middle-aged men. The boys rarely bother now to catch crawdads or frogs. They are too busy going to the mall or the movies.

Sandra 1

Sandra 1 was married to Dave. Her nieces used to play by the stone boathouse over at the cove. Her goal in life was to be always well-off, and being married to a three-star general was a way to guarantee this security. The result of being well-off was that she had time to do whatever she wanted, only to find that there was nothing she really wanted to do at all. She spent her time working around the yard, getting in the way of the lawn care people from town, raking leaves and planting frost-resistant flowers and bulbs. By the 1970's, her two sons and a daughter were grown and gone, along with her beauty, so life became a sort of sampler, composed of jogging one day, yard work the next day, shopping the next, a family barbecue the next, and so on. It was very easy to predict what she would do from day to day. As with most ex-military wives, she always thought she was the one who had earned the rank, and so she did not demean herself to attend any of the lake functions except the Women's Club. This club she greatly influenced, although she did not bother to run for office nor do any of the administrative tasks.

She had been jealous of her husband's career, forcing him to go into the Reserves instead of remaining on active duty, and having won that critical fight, found that her husband simply ignored her in all remaining matters in life. Sandra achieved the stability she craved, and puttered around the house by the water, and spent her winters at the Florida condo. She did nothing of any importance with her husband, but cared greatly for her three grandchildren and carried on with a stiff upper lip, managing the important political decisions at the lake, moving in the best society.

She swam well but did not fish, and no matter how down she dressed in her old sneakers and shorts, she was not part of the mainstream of lake life. If she did attempt to join in, people suspected her motives were power-based, and if she did not join in, she was regarded as haughty. So the equality of her life was reduced gradually to babysitting the grandchildren and raking the yard if the lawn care people missed a few leaves. She had no particular interests in life except the grandchildren and the organizations, and as life went along she found that neither of these really needed her any more than her husband did. She could be seen at 7 a.m. picking up twigs or jogging alone along the lake road, dressed to upscale jogging wear. If there was any passion remaining in her life, it did not display itself.

Marv and Kath

Marv and Kath were happy. They had three children who all graduated from college, and after the children moved away, Marv and Kath retired to the lake in 1987. They bought a small brick house by the water, directly west of Goose Island. This made them almost neighbors to Earl and Emabel. Marv had been a high school electronics teacher, and Kath had been a nurse. Their life, in marked contrast to Dave and Sandra, had been one of mutual love and respect. They met in Cleveland when Marv worked for a radio station, and Kath worked at a local hospital. In retirement, Marv wore a white goatee and was hefty, and Kath was slim and tall. They often held hands when they walked down the street.

Their three children all ended up living in the Midwest. Mark became an accountant, passed the CPA exam and had two sons and a daughter. Maureen became an accountant also, and worked for NCR. Margaret became a lawyer and worked for Legal Aid. This was quite an accomplishment. Marv's mother and sister both lived in Denver, where they did Colorado stuff such as watching the Aspen turn yellow and shiver in the fall, and watching the snow on the Rockies.

Marv and Kath were concerned with the happiness of people rather than the efficiency of things. They didn't care much whether the cars worked or not, or whether the furnace worked well, or whether the dishwashing machine got the dishes dry. They did care about the grandchildren and the family get-togethers. Kath liked to read in the evenings, and Marv watched the Weather Channel for hours during the winter, read travel, shortwave, and flying books, and worked on old radios.

All of the family came to Marv's and Kath's house for the holidays. On Christmas Eve, the family would gather from all over the U.S. to eat a cold buffet, open presents, and go to Midnight Mass. Marv would videotape all of the jocularity. In fact, the earliest remembrances of the three children involved spotlights for the eight-millimeter movie camera.

Among the family traditions were the retelling of the children's exciting events of growing up. These stories were retold over and over each year, so that the grandchildren would come to remember them. For example, the story was told of how Margaret was afraid of Santa, would cry when set on his lap, and would scream if she were taken into a store with a Christmas Santa display. Her fright necessitated careful screening of which stores were entered at the holiday season.

The story was often told of Maureen and Mark at Easter, when Maureen, who was the youngest, would spot a hidden egg during the backyard egg hunt. Mark, who was the oldest, would hear Maureen shrieking in excitement at discovering an egg, run over, and pick up the egg and place it in his own basket while Maureen was still excited. This left Maureen with almost no eggs after the hunt, and Mark with all of them, while Mark let Maureen do almost all of the hunting.

The best story involved the day a neighbor gave Marv and Kath, who were still living in Cleveland, a live crab for dinner. The crab got away, went out the back door, and was happily playing with the three children when Kath looked out and saw the children and the crab playing together. Her shrieks of despair brought the postman running to help, and the crab was removed forcefully from the game.

Vacation for Marv and Kath was centered at the beach. Many of the lake people, wanting to see larger waves, spent their vacation by a larger area of water, usually the ocean. So it was with Marv and Kath. As a former teacher of electronics, the departure for these vacations could not be accomplished in a slap-dash manner, but had to be carefully planned. Planning started months ahead with the booking of the reservations. This was done by examining the listings in AAA travel books and catalogs of rental shore houses sent each December by realty companies. Weeks ahead of the departure date, Marv would make lists of things to take on the trip, as well as a list of how to close the house for a week. While Marv worked on the lists, Kath read. The Weather Channel would be blaring in the living room while Marv laboriously wrote down such important entries as, "Shut water off to toilet" and "Board dog." The actual closing of the house for departure took from 3 a.m. to 7 a.m. on the day of departure. The family car had to be equipped with a CB radio for emergencies, with the antenna carefully tuned by Marv for the best broadcasting. Sometimes, the neighbors would join up with Marv and Kath, and everyone would have his or her car outfitted with CB radios so that the drive to the shore could be safely accomplished with a background of constant chatter. This constant chatter drove Kath nuts.

They were happy in their routines of birthdays and weekend antique hunting trips, and stood on the Atlantic shore at sunrise, holding hands for no reason they knew of, watching the sun and the porpoises, content in all ways. They wished upon shooting stars and cooked each other breakfast, and comforted each other when one was ill. They always thought that the way to bring up a family right was to eat dinner together.

John

John came to the lake with his mother when he was five years old. His grandparents wanted a place in the country for relaxing on weekends away from Elizabeth, so they bought a fishing cabin. This turned out to be an unfortunate decision with regard to John's development, for no group of people were treated worse at the lake than were the children of the "Summer People." Adults could restart their friendships every summer with the neighbors, but the cliques of year-round teens and children allowed no summer people to associate. The summer children grew up in isolation, cut off from their friends in the cities, while making no friends at all at the lake. They could be easily identified in town, following their parents from store to store every May while the parents stocked up on groceries for the summer, or sitting on their docks alone, or playing in the shallow water by themselves with rocks and crawdads. Because there was no social framework in which to meet other people like them at the lake, cliques of summer-only children never formed. These children never met anyone to play with.

This enforced loneliness resulted in the development of practical skills, none of them social, which made these children very good at some things. This excellence at things such as fishing and racing rowboats and canoes infuriated the year-round children, and made the social division permanent. The summer-only children were very likely to win the Boys' Rowboat Race in front of the whole lake population year after year, simply because the boys had nothing else to do all summer other than to row around the lake, developing muscles and timing. In later life, of course, this made them excellent lovers, and in great demand by lake women. The summer children, having no social engagements, were also likely to be very good at spin casting into brush where the big bass hid, and in many years the awards for the largest bass and pickerel went to summer-only children, rather than the children whose families had lived at the lake for generations.

The silent summer-only children ended up learning many of the lake skills that people at the lake took for granted during the 1930s. These children, rather like the strange children in a Stephen King novel, learned the calls of ducks and geese when all of the other teens were at the clubhouse dances, learned the names of the stars while sitting alone on their docks while other

116

teens were at the movies, and learned to take a sailboat out on the lake in heavy wind and rain while other children went bowling. Because they had the time to practice, they won the Hub Lakes Swim Meets, as well as the local lake swim races. They learned to hit a target with an arrow at 50 yards, how to repair a fishing net, and how to pour a concrete anchor. They learned where the fish schooled, where the cranes nested, and where the painted turtles hid. The children of the summer missed their friends in the cities, and never forgot what it was like to be considered second rate. Unlike the teens who grew up in the Junior League to become store owners, the summer children became M.D.'s, Ph.D.'s, and J.D.'s. Anger turned out to be a wonderful career motivator.

When young, John had chores to do at the lake typical of those that children were tasked with. In the late fall, his job was to carry in the cannel coal, shipped to Young's Coal Yard from Pennsylvania, and put the coal in the fireplace grate. Twice a day, he shoveled out the ash from the fireplace and carried it outside to dump out back in a 50 gallon drum by the large black glacial rock.

In the spring, he helped carry the furniture from the living room, where it had been stored for the winter, out onto the screened summer porch. He also helped to rake the winter's leaves and burn them in the large 50 gal drum, with holes punched into the bottom, like everyone at the lake used. He loved to see the white leaf smoke roll up towards the house, making his grandmother cough as she fixed a motivating lunch of cold tongue and fried turnips.

In the summer, he scraped paint from the frame house and painted the worn spots, spread white gravel on the path to the lake, cut brush, got poison ivy rashes, picked wild blackberries, painted the gray dock, and cut more brush. With all of the rain at the lake, brush grew at an incredible rate, and boys at the lake were always being sent out to trim.

In 1961, he and a little friend filled a six-foot balloon with water from the bathroom tap. While they attempted to carry the balloon down the three steps to the living room, and then outdoors, the balloon broke, sending a huge stream of water down the three steps and into the living room. John's mother started screaming and his grandfather, who had been reading the paper in the corner of the living room, said, "What's all this?" two or three times, before swatting both boys around the ears. The water stains are still visible near the bottom of the living room walls. John thus learned not to do annoying things around people who might object.

John didn't want to go to high school, so his mother sent him to a college prep school. In 1961, he won the Boys' Rowboat Race, the Boys' Canoe Race, and the Boys' Double Canoe Race, and received his plastic trophies in the rain at the east beach. In 1968, he won the award for the largest pickerel caught that summer on a yellow spinner near the float, occupied by the Junior Leaguers, at 6 p.m. on a July evening.

He didn't want to go to college, preferring to work in a warehouse, but he got his BA degree. He didn't want to be a teacher, but he got his MA degree and taught. Then, much as it had been to be a summer child at the lake, he found that he would be second rate without a Ph.D., so he got one. After that, he wasn't second rate any more. He ignored people such as Dave, inherited the cabin at the lake, and retained his talent of timing and muscles learned while rowing about the lake, and made the ladies happy.

He never forgot those early years, or the importance of not being second rate. He had his three boat race trophies on the bookcase in his college office next to his Ph.D. diploma. Of the two, he regarded winning the plastic boat race trophies as the greater achievement in life. Since he found that he really didn't need to visit with anyone at the lake at all, he would drive over to the lake from Ohio, where he taught college students, to visit his house and dock in the middle of the night when the tenant was asleep. He'd park his car over by the clubhouse with mold on the north walls, and wade around the cove to his dock.

John would sit alone on his dock at 2 a.m., drink cheap apple wine under the half moon, and listen to the geese out on Goose Island. He'd remember all of those times in his life when life seemed to be full of contentment and happiness, only to know with certainty that he would end up with the thing he wanted most to avoid: dying all alone. Sometimes, he'd walk up through the yard from the dock and stand looking at the dark house he owned, but never entered, and remember his mother full of cancer on her sick bed in the living room, or his grandparents at the dinner table, or those rare visits from his father when no one had anything to say at all. He remembered the time he threw up on the dinner table when his mother asked him if he ever missed having a father live with him, and he didn't care to ever think about his father again.

He never even knew why he came to see the lake house, except for him it was not possible to walk away from any memory. Everything everyone had ever said to him, every erotic touch, every holiday moment, every Christmas present, every wonderful vacation trip, was stored inside John's memory, and could not be escaped or forgotten. That was the price of learning to be smart. When the memories in Ohio were unbearable, he'd go to the lake and watch the stars. When the memories at the lake were unbearable, he'd go to Colorado and watch the sunrise, sometimes flying from Newark on the early Piedmont nonstop flight to watch the sunrise over

Stapleton Airport. He'd go to the Broadmoor Hotel at Colorado Springs, look at the swans on the pond and remember the dinners and the dancing, and the next day he'd stand in his classroom in Ohio and talk about 17th century literature and writing research papers, when he knew he should be talking about life and living.

Holidays were spent on the run from the memories of a hundred women who had said they would never leave him, but always had. He remembered every Christmas tree under which he had found a present to him signed, "Love, always, Cynthia," or "Love, always, Jewel," or "Love, always, Mandy," and he remembered every ribbon, what each family had eaten for dinner, and what everyone had gotten for Christmas. He learned to record holiday activities, and he'd sit in his office at the college with his Ph.D. diploma nearby, watching videos of different families' Christmases that he had filmed, seeing himself in the mirrors of the living rooms with someone beautiful next to him, and everyone waving and happy. And he knew not one of those families ever thought about him now or missed him at Christmas. He kept in his office a little Christmas gift of pencils with his name on them from his mother that he unwrapped each year and then wrapped back up so that he would always have a present to open each year.

On Christmas Eve, he would take four calming pills, drink two rum and pop, and board a Delta airliner to anywhere, and drink and fly until the day after Christmas. It was the only way to try to forget that no one in the whole world ever meant anything she had said about loving him, and that the brilliant person who was so successful in the classroom was a fraud at the more important job of living.

Sometimes, at 5:30 a.m. at the lake, he'd leave the dock and go over to town for breakfast at the diner on Broadway, and then drive back to Ohio without sleeping. In the last years of his life, no one, including the tenant who rented the house, ever knew that John came home to look at the stars over the lake. He always carried his old ice cream stick in his pocket, and flicked an ant or two into the water as they ran along the top of the white concrete retaining wall by the water at 3 a.m., just for old time's sake, as people at the lake had always done at birthday parties.

He died instantly on April 10, 1995, after 42 hours without sleep, on I-90 at Kirtland, Ohio, when, on the way back to college from New Jersey, he swerved a rental car to avoid running over a big black Labrador that had loosed its collar and was wandering along the interstate in the middle of the night. The lab lived through the scare to bark at many things, later died of old age, was buried in its backyard at Kirtland near a church with a white steeple, and kept its parents and grandparents company in the ground. At Kirtland, the story was often told of how the original black lab had lived through a National Airlines DC-6 airliner crash at Elizabeth, New Jersey, on February 11, 1952, by jumping out of a 3rd story window in an apartment building.

John was buried in a Catholic cemetery at Springfield, Illinois. The priest from the college was the estate executor. The little boy at the lake, who never sat down, quietly inherited the lake house, the stuff in storage, and a whole bunch of gold coins. On John's headstone, the boy asked that the following be inscribed, as originally written by Lucy Henry of Illinois on January 13, 1892:

When the evening dews are falling

O'er the dark and lonely sea

When the whip-poor-wills are calling

Will you ever think of me?

Sandra 2

Sandra 2 cleaned house for Lois, had three children, lived in a mobile home on the Pennsylvania side of I-80 near the Delaware River, and was married to a husband who wouldn't work. The porch on the mobile home consisted of a wooden overhang above the door. There was no fireplace. She was poor, but had a heart of gold, second only to Doris. Every Wednesday and Monday, she'd drive her old Pontiac down the 38 miles of I-80 to the lake to Lois' house with the porch that been screened, but was now winterized, to help Lois clean the house.

These cleaning sessions often turned into other sessions, such as going through the sacks of mail that Lois had stored up for the future, and had forgotten to ever go through. Sandra would get the task of reading some outdated letter to Lois because Lois' eyes couldn't focus well. She also opened old bills and generally tried to put some order into Lois' house. As Sandra was only at Lois' place twice a week, the task of putting order in the house always failed over the weekend when Sandra wasn't there. In addition to opening the mail and doing the floors, Sandra fixed lunch, went through boxes of old family junk that Lois had forgotten but never wanted to throw away, and generally visited with Lois, who lived alone. Lois thought it well worth the money to have someone in the house who would do as she was told to do, and yet was not too concerned about working hard all the time. This situation was fine with Sandra, who worked a legion of jobs, most of them involving really hard and demeaning work, and who was pleased to be treated as if she were a person with dignity.

Lois told all of her friends in the Garden Club and Literary Club about Sandra, and the friends began to hire her for housework too. One of the ladies, Betty Funderstein, sent Sandra to a training school to learn house and table service, and began to use Sandra to serve at dinners. Sandra's thin body and bobbed hair looked well in a white and blue serving uniform, and as she received more and more training, her salary began to improve. She left her husband, took a live-in serving job in Mary Placegate's mansion over at Mount Tabor where she was allowed to have her kids live with her, received a car to run errands in, and eventually became the housekeeper at the Placegate Mansion. Sandra left her other jobs when she moved to the mansion, but she always went back to the lake to visit Lois, driving her employer's Chrysler, for Lois had made social connections for Sandra that she couldn't have made herself. Lois and Sandra would get sandwiches from Peer's Store, sit on the porch overlooking the lake, and talk about Lois' friends. Lois' house never did get ordered or cleaned much after Sandra received her promotion, but until Lois became ill with cancer, the two friends sat on the porch and talked about people without ever running out of gossip.

Dale and Libby

Dale and Libby came to the lake in 1969 after Dale retired. They bought a two-story red frame house down on the southeast corner of the lake with a red brick chimney and a white screened-in porch. Libby liked to collect English teacups, so Mildred always brought Libby back a cup from the trips to England. Mildred and Libby had met through Lois, who knew them both from the Senior Citizens Center in town. Libby had gray curly hair, walked with a stoop in practical brown shoes, and liked to eat out on Route 46. She was always angry when hordes of relatives appeared in the short driveway for a week's visit to the lake. Libby spent a great deal of time preparing for and cleaning up after relatives who liked to swim and fish, and who had nowhere to accomplish these enjoyable activities except by coming to visit Libby. The relatives who thus appeared were always Libby's and not Dale's, as Dale's relatives lived in Colorado and seldom made the trip east. Libby had been raised over in Philadelphia when it was a nice city full of non-angry people, and the relatives who had now moved to the burbs liked to spend a good deal of the summer with Libby, which really made her quite angry.

The appearance of relatives never bothered Dale, who spent most of the day in his workshop anyhow. He didn't like to fish or swim, but he did so anyway because most of the lake people did, and he became friends with Earl and Emabel, as they originally came from the same part of the country. Dale had a wonderful little machine shop in which he could build all sorts of boilers to supply steam to operate little model steam engines for the relatives' children. If he did go out, he wore baggy brown slacks and a brown straw hat with a band around it. He had a big smile and little hair, and was vigorous and slim, and happy with retirement. He wrote illegible letters to his friends in Colorado in the hope that they would also come to the lake, and they could all work in their workshops making little metal models that operated. In this endeavor, he had some success, for he had been noticing that men who built metal models also outlived their wives by a number of years, instead of the other way around. This proved to be true; when Libby's asthma got steadily worse, she passed away one evening while watching the ABC network evening news in October 1975. Dale kept on building models, got his friends to move to New Jersey, and plans to live to see 100.

The relatives stopped coming to the lake after Libby died. She was buried out on Route 10 on half of a joint plot. Dale is in no rush to join her, and happily works in his shop with the big bay window which gives him a fine view of the whole length of the lake. Due to his attempts to get his widowed friends to move east, he has plenty of company to talk to.

George 1 had been married to a fine little stocky woman who died in 1985 of severe arthritis. He lived on West Platte Street in Colorado Springs for years, after moving there from Massachusetts for his wife's health, along with a smelly little white dog who never got a bath. After George's wife passed away, he and the little dog stayed on in their one-story white frame house with a black wood-burning stove in the middle of the living room. George was talented. He painted nature scenes, played the piano, and was a leader in the Odd Fellows Lodge, where he was a major of the military honor group. George had a metal working shop in his garage out by the alley that ran parallel between Pikes Peak Avenue and Platte Avenue, and in this shop he built working models of steam locomotives. He was part of a little group who were interested in the same hobby, and of which Dale had once been a part before moving east to the lake to retire. Each year, George received a Christmas card from Dale which included pictures of the lake. Soon, George also began receiving a card from Earl each Christmas, who knew the Springs well, and who had met Dale through Lois.

As George had lived in the east for many years, and had no reason to remain in Colorado after his wife was gone, he sold the little white frame house in the Springs, hired Allied Van Lines to move all the furniture (including the piano and shop equipment), and bought the house just to the west of Dale's place. At the age of 68, he moved east to the lake to build model steam engines with Dale. They started their own steam model company called it the Pikes Peak Model Steam Engine Works, and produced a few very nice working steam engine models every year for sale. This kept them nicely busy without doing more than they would have anyhow. Earl, often abandoned while Emabel played cards, started to walk over to visit George several times a week, and found that he had some new friends who were more alive than was Ralph Swing, who didn't move to New Jersey.

George always wore a bowtie, never wore blue jeans, and was every inch the gentleman. Like Marilyn, he dressed for dinner, never cursed when something fell on him, and had his shoes shined at the cigar store in town. Like Dale, he didn't care to fish or swim. His white frame one-story house was equipped with a wood burner that George used to heat the house during the winter, just as he had in Colorado. George sent letters and pictures back to his friends in

Colorado, suggesting that the Homestead Act in New Jersey made the taxes less than in Colorado, and that everyone should come to the lake and live it up. Some of them did, forming a little community of ex-Coloradoans, all of whom outlived their wives. The smelly white dog is doing well in New Jersey also.

Joe

Old Joe wasn't older than anyone else at the lake, but he was a mess. He had hair that came down to his shoulders, had outlived his wife by many years, and at the age of 75, sold his 14 acres above Garden of the Gods in Colorado Springs, and came at the invitation of George to live at the lake. Joe made $1.3 million from the sale of the family land that would be carved into wonderful, very expensive apartment views of Pikes Peak. It bothered Joe not a bit to sell the family historical land to developers, instead of retaining it for his family, as no one in his family liked him, and he didn't like any of them. Joe's greatest claim to fame was that he had played a hobo for 20 seconds in a PBS documentary about Colorado in 1981, over at Joe's old home near Pueblo, Colorado, which he kept because no one would buy three acres on the hot Colorado prairie. The three acres was full of old prospecting junk left to Joe by his father who didn't like Joe either, part of which eventually was donated by Joe to the Mining Museum of Colorado up north of the Springs off I-25, on the basis that the donation would not require Joe to pay to haul the junk on a lowboy up to the museum. Joe figured once he settled at the lake, he was settled there for life – and he was right. He bought the house by the little one-lane bridge that had been owned by Linda's father until he died, and Linda's mom went to a retirement complex over by the river in town. Pretty soon the whole house was a mess. Joe lived on potato chips and pop, and as he was very much alive at 75 when he moved to the lake, this diet clearly did okay for him. The floor was full of dust and potato chip crumbs which Joe never cleaned up, although George's dog did a pretty good job of clearing the chips.

Joe didn't own a vacuum cleaner or a dust rag, and so every place that someone wasn't immediately occupying got extremely dusty. The bathroom was gross, and people avoided using it if at all possible, preferring the bushes on the point of land by the lagoon to Joe's bathroom. The kitchen was full of dusty old dishes that were never used at all. Joe, like many of the older

124

people at the lake, used paper plates and fine Chinette plastic ware, but he often never bothered to throw away the used paper plates. Other than potato chips and pop, Joe liked to eat hot dogs and beans, which sometimes gave his living room a gaseous smell. Joe boarded up the fireplace because he didn't want to mess with it, shut off all the bedrooms and slept in the living room into which he moved his old brass bed, and never cut the grass. He believed that grass would only grow so high and then stop, like prairie grass, and he was right. The New Jersey poison ivy did *not* stop, however, but instead spread everywhere, until it finally overran the grass so that the whole yard was composed of lush green poison ivy.

Joe, of course, came to know Dale and Libby, and Emabel and Earl. Emabel did not approve of the manner in which Joe lived, and thought that he lived pretty badly. Libby thought that Joe needed a new wife, and Dale thought Joe lived pretty free and well, and sort of envied him. While Joe's house tended to repel visitors, Joe had thought of a surefire way to get guests over to the house: he fed them. He had learned years ago that men without wives did not eat well, if at all, and so he arranged for monthly catering by Big Ben's Fried Chicken at lunchtime, and invited all of the men whom he met at the lake. Word soon got around among the retired men that free chicken could be had at Joe's, and one did not have to be too particular about table manners and language. The Fishing Club even scheduled some meetings at Joe's house due to the informal atmosphere and the chicken. Joe made it known there would be more free food if people wanted to do a little work around the yard, and pretty soon the grass was cut, the yard raked, and the house painted – all in trade for free fried chicken. The inside of the house was always awful, but the men were happy to putter about in the yard in return for chicken, which was a lot more fun to eat than their wives' healthy cooking. Joe also had a stock of porno books in the living room that he bought in town at the cigar store and which were actually written by Becky 1, although Joe did not now that, and so on rainy days when one could not fish, one could go to Joe's and read dirty books and chip in to get more chicken, chips and pop to enjoy.

Joe owned a big yellow backhoe that occasionally ran when he wanted it to, and so on cool mornings (Joe was not too active on hot days), he would attempt to start the backhoe, which would eject lots of blue smoke, and dig muck and leaves out of the lagoon that ran up against his retaining wall. When operating the backhoe, Joe wore a cap of green with red spots on it and dark glasses that made him look something like a music star with his long greasy hair flying over his face every time he cursed the backhoe. As the hydraulic lines were old, there were frequent incidents of blasts of hydraulic fluid flaying both Joe and anyone near him at the time. Joe's acquaintances had learned from long experience that Backhoe Day was going to be fun to watch, and so at 8 a.m., all the men would gather to watch Joe start and operate the backhoe. The backhoe rarely operated for more than 10 minutes without some disaster striking the operation, and then there would be several hours of cursing and yelling by Joe while he tried to get the yellow, rusty thing going again. At lunchtime, everyone would chip in to get some chicken, and on mornings that had not gone well at all, maybe some pastries from the Viking pastry shop for dessert. Over lunch eaten outside, of course, Joe would retell the morning's events as if they had happened to someone else a long time ago, instead of just a few hours ago, and make the whole morning's fiasco seem like a story of wonder and magic. In the afternoon, it would be too hot to work much, and so the men sat along the retaining wall, using their ice cream sticks to flick spiders into the mud and watching them run away to the far shore. The later in the year it was, the less water there was in the lagoon, so that by August, there was little water and a lot of mud up against Joe's retaining wall. Joe did not like having mud against the retaining wall while other people at the lake had blue, clear water against their walls, and he tried to dig away the mud to allow the clean, God-given precious water to flow up against his wall. All that usually happened was that more and more mud flowed against the wall, no matter how much digging Joe did. And, as the mud had to be piled within reach of the backhoe's arm, Joe ended up with mud on both land and lagoon. This aggravated Joe greatly. He was a trained Army civil engineer and ex-captain who had spent his career at the desert Depot at Pueblo, Colorado, and this disorder when he wanted order did not sit well at all.

Joe was always wishing that the big yellow backhoe had a longer reach, and he'd run the backhoe over to the very edge of the retaining wall, even to the point of putting the treads on the top of the retaining wall itself, to reach into the lagoon further to dig out more mud. One unfortunate day, when the treads of the backhoe were on the wall, and Joe had the backhoe's arm fully extended out into the lagoon, Joe got onto the wrong control while trying to eat a donut from Viking while operating the yellow machine, and the end of the backhoe's treads toppled into the lagoon mud, burying the arm deep into mud as well. As the backhoe was of a large size, it was not hard to activate the treads and climb out, but the climbing destroyed a large chunk of the concrete wall. Word got around the lake quickly, and many men came to see the flaked and broken wall, and to hear the story about the bad, bad backhoe that Joe told all afternoon while eating chicken and donuts with pop drooling out of the corners of his mouth.

Joe's favorite social activity was to go to other people's houses for a little bite of something, preferably a house that had a woman doing the cooking, but anything would do. These social invitations were likely to occur on birthdays, which meant that Joe could pitch horseshoes, or around the holidays, which meant even better than average food. Joe's favorite place to locate at a holiday gathering was an easy chair, in which he would spend the afternoon or evening happily eating all the nice, delicate food he could. Between bags of potato chips at home and occasional invitations to eat out, he was not in danger of getting too thin, and life was quite pleasant. Joe had found one of the great truths of life: namely, feed people fried chicken, and they will feel morally compelled to invite you over to their house for better food. The second thing Joe had learned in life was that even people who do not like you will come to your house for free food, and so one need never feel lonely again. Companionship, according to Joe, was based on giving people something – typically food – while apparently expecting nothing in return.

In the evenings, Joe would invite all the men over to see action movies on his big-screen television. He was the only one of the Colorado men who could afford the money to buy a big television, which he had set up in the living room so he could lay in his bed and watch it. On guest nights, he'd surround his bed with wooden chairs, and he'd lay on his bed with everyone sitting around him, watching a war movie with Army captains in it on the big television. Joe always allowed everyone who came to movie nights to help themselves from the fridge to all of the pop they wanted, and he bought many one-pound bags of chips and passed them around as little snacks. He liked the rippled chips the best, although he also liked to eat the spicy pepper chips, as they reminded him of southern Colorado.

Joe thought that George had been right when he had written that the lake was a fine place to live, and Joe, in his annual Christmas cards, began to write the praises of the lake to his bitter family who now lived in apartments in the Springs, instead of on the 14 pine-filled acres with a beautiful view of Garden of the Gods. In due time, his grandson came to New Jersey for a visit, caused a considerable amount of damage to the property, and had such a fine time killing geese and ducks that he moved into Joe's house permanently. As Joe was not poor, the grandson didn't have to work. In fact, he had the luxury of goofing off all day at the lake and running wild all night in town.

Joe liked to walk across the road to the group boat landing, place a chair on the dock, and use his binoculars to spy on the couples over at Picnic Island. The best viewing was with the ex-Ranger night glasses he had stolen from the salvage area at the Pueblo Depot. With a little moonlight, the goggles, which could be strapped to one's head, provided quite the view. Joe would sit on the dock sucking down potato chips, his head and the night goggles combining to look like the head of a giant ant, and revel in living as he wanted, without any wife.

He died of a heart attack in his bed in June 1993 at 3 a.m., after consuming nine one-pound bags of chips a week for 48 years, and averaging eight cans of pop a day for 52 years. His grandson had him cremated, dumped his ashes out by the yellow backhoe, and inherited Joe's money, mud, and other stuff. He especially likes the night goggles.

Iris and John

Iris and John had retired to Kansas City when their old friends Earl and Emabel sent them some pictures of the lake and their flower garden, and wrote about the fine fishing to be found up on the north end. The information about the fishing piqued the interest of John, who liked to smoke and fish. Iris smoked also, so she didn't mind John's habit. Both John and Iris were rail-fence thin, tall, and well-tanned from working in their garden and from sitting on their front porch during the late afternoons, watching the sun set over Kansas.

In any case, having nothing to do except fish and garden, they figured they could do that as well in New Jersey as in Kansas, so they moved to the lake. They bought a one-story, white frame house with a steel stovepipe chimney and an open deck porch on the north end, where John would not have to row far to find bass. John's rowing was done in a small aluminum rowboat with three seats. In the evenings, Iris would sit out on the deck overlooking the lake, and watch John sitting in the boat by the floating island, with a gentle wreath of smoke above his head. As John was basically lazy, he never kept anything he caught and didn't try too hard to catch anything. His tackle box was an old cloth sack in which he kept a few lures. He didn't use a net since it didn't matter whether the fish ever made it into his boat or not. His pole was an old Garcia spin-cast model with an old 10-pound test line on it. John was a man who liked to be retired and did not feel any particular urge to do anything. Fishing was a good pretense at doing something approved by society, and so he put up a good show.

Sometimes, he would attend the monthly Fishing Club meetings, where he met many World War I vets and sometimes got some fried chicken to eat. John would always sit in the rear of these meetings and smoke, his tan lined face turned towards whoever was speaking of lures and lines. At social time, his stooped shoulders were lost below the taller men in the club, but he could put away a few beers with the best of the fishy drinkers. He liked to tell fish jokes, especially bad ones that played on the words "tail" and "tale." Since Iris was always out and about in the car with her friends from the Senior Center, John always walked to the club meetings and later, after all the beer was gone, walked slowly back up the long hill toward the north end of the lake to home, settling in the chair by the dock for a nap.

Iris liked flea markets and flowers and being a Senior Citizen, which allowed her to get the New Jersey Seniors Shopping Discount. Her day was made if she were off to some little yard sale over in Boonton, followed by lunch at the Shack out on Route 46 near Indian Lake. The Shack had the best seafood – especially fried clams – between the Gap and Manhattan, on all of Route 46. While it was not possible to get a seat on a weekend night when the teens were out and wild, lunchtime was not so crowded. Iris and her lady friends, all in sunglasses, would settle in for baskets of clams and mugs of brown beer. The greasy clams were piled on red and white checkered cloths in plastic red baskets, and the beer mugs were fake dented tin.

The lunch conversation was always about upcoming sales and hospital volunteer work, especially the big St. Francis Fall Festival. Iris and her lady friends all volunteered to work at the beer booth each year, serving out luke-cool beer in paper cups, their plastic red dime store earrings jingling while they filled the cups. This Fall Festival was always regarded as a good place to flirt with the men from the City, as not only did the beer flow, but there was an evening dance held in the hospital cafeteria from 8 p.m. to midnight on Saturday of the Festival. The band for the dance came from the high school and was led by the high school music director, Mr. Baark, who also directed the bands who played at the lake clubhouse. Unlike the teen dances sponsored by the JayCees, the Festival dances were more sedate, with lots of slow music, which allowed close dancing and good feels. As John was not interested in dancing, nor very much else of a social nature, Iris was free to attend the Festival dances with her widowed friends and make the most of the evening. She did, usually coming home with a Cheshire smile on her face at 2 a.m. after the dance, telling John she helped to clean up afterwards, which was pretty much true.

The house of John and Iris was comfortable, with rocking chairs, beat-up tables, worn pink rugs and old oil paintings on the walls making a pleasant and relaxing mix. Iris liked to putter in the old tile kitchen while John read the latest copy of *Fishing Times* so he could speak about lures at the Fishing Club meetings. Iris liked cats, and had two black ones which howled when they wanted food, and who picked on Mildred's little white dog whenever Mildred was visiting the area. At night, the cats slept on John and Iris' ankles with their paws crossed, preventing either John or Iris from turning over at night. Iris talked to the cats, who made themselves comfortable by clawing all the furniture. She'd learned to remove any china which was in the way of their movements. When John wasn't fishing, he would sit in his comfortable chair, smoking, while Iris sat in a rocker with both cats on her lap. The cats, John, and Iris were content and had a good view of Dave chasing the geese from his lawn.

John and Iris died of lung cancer seven years after coming to the lake, and were buried by Route 46. The cats went to live with Dale, and made themselves at home by clawing his furniture, too.

Maureen

Maureen's father was a retired electronics schoolteacher and her mother was a nurse. Maureen was successful at completing her MBA at New York University in 1991. She was thin and flighty, into walking like an Egyptian and MTV, with a thin face, thin legs, and a thin wallet. She watched her income, dated everyone, and had trouble deciding what her life's work would be. She rented an old house one row up the mountain from the lakefront homes on the side of Bald Hill, and was thereby forced to use the west beach to swim.

She always invited her friends from the City to come to the lake for a swim on the holidays. She issued each guest the proper colored beach tag to be pinned to the swimsuit so the beach guard could see it, and gave each guest a bright beach towel. Her fridge was stocked with imported beer and lite snacks. At 5'7", she had the figure of a model with deep blue eyes, and a slangy way of speaking that was always in the current style. She read *Self* and *Cosmo* magazines, liked to attend concerts in Central Park, and regarded New Jersey as a backwards and dull country.

She was a commuter, catching the 6:10 electric train to Hoboken, and then the PATH tube into Manhattan. Each evening, after a drink at a New York bar, she'd make the return trip, change from her suit into cutoffs and a tank top, and head for the beach with a cooler full of beer. She had learned early in life that people who received presents would be nice in return, and she gave the beach guard a beer in a Coke can in return for not being asked too closely about what she was drinking. At sunset, it was off to the house for a microwave dinner, a few more beers, and several hours of watching MTV and practicing new dance moves for Saturday night at the dance clubs on 34th Street. Life was pretty much a set routine for Maureen.

She had no goals in life except to be young and when she turned 30, she was devastated to learn that her routines had not made life pass any slower. She worked in a financial firm located on 52nd Street near Fifth Avenue, and ate lunch at La Crepe when she could afford it. When she could not afford it, she ate lunch on the street corner by the vendor's cart, which supplied fine hot dogs and mustard. On the train, she used her player with headphones; at home, she had her CD player, and in an emergency, she hummed to herself. Life was full of weekends, parties, swimming, and beer. She saved 5% of her pay, never bought anything not in style, and was always interested in anything new, as long as it was fun. She and her dog were both bouncy and cool, and she hopes that 40 will never come to be part of her life. This hope will not pan out.

Roy

Roy was fat and 58. He liked holiday cookouts and red meat, and lots of red strawberry pie. He lived with his large wife and large children in a blue house built in 1937, just to the south of the one-lane bridge. His hair was thinning and he was well organized. His family had lived at the lake since 1944, after his mother collected on his father's GI life insurance when Roy was three years old. Roy grew up to be a mediocre lawyer in town, with an office in a white concrete two-story building with cracked windows near the railroad station. His specialty was family law, and he spent his days in court arguing about custody and visitation rights.

With three children, the house was pretty beat up. The fireplace had loose bricks in it from the children throwing large hunks of wood into it with vigor, and the porch screens were full of holes from jousting tournaments which the eldest child always won. Roy didn't care about the house. By the time he came home from the office, he was too tired to do anything but eat and take an after-dinner nap. He did not nap on the porch, as flies got in through the holes in the screens, but instead retired to the bedroom with its pink, flowery wallpaper, for a little snooze after dinner.

Roy's diet was typical of the about-to-retire-and-die generation at the lake. He liked potatoes and steak, lots of gravy made from New York Gravy Mix which came in a little aluminum packet and was easily made with water, some corn or beans on the side, and a couple slices of pie. In Roy's case, this was strawberry pie. The pie was served best with ice cream and whipped cream swirled together, and heaped on top of the pie. If Roy should be in need of a snack, a couple of boxes of microwave French fries killed any lingering hunger.

On hot days, Roy sweated while he walked from the lake house to the car, which was always parked along the street, and from the car to his office. He never sweated in the big black Oldsmobile since he always had the air conditioning on full, the roar of the circulating blowers covering the sound of the stereo. He had to sweat again if he walked from the office to the car in order to drive the four blocks to the municipal court, and of course, sweated walking from the car into the court building. What with several cases a day in court some weeks, Roy was able to get plenty of sweaty exercise which relieved the suspicion that he was not getting enough of a weekly workout. Roy did not swim or row, but as his weight leveled off at 250 pounds, he felt that he was doing okay. His wife and kids regarded him as a leader in the community. He was shot and killed by an unhappy client in a divorce case outside of his office on May 5, 1986, and buried off Route 53 near Morristown. His wife and kids collected the insurance and still live at the lake.

Jeff

Jeff came to the lake from prison, after getting busted for cocaine use in 1972, and being sent to the Illinois State Prison at Joliet for 10 years. Jeff had been a lawyer, but was disbarred due to this incident. In 1982, he rented an old cabin on the top of the hill, and went to work at the diner in town as a night cook. He was especially good at making omelets. He could make ham omelets, bacon and sausage omelets, cheese omelets, turkey omelets, chicken omelets, beef omelets, and shrimp omelets. He could also make a wicked chocolate malt, and many people would drop by the diner for an omelet and a malt after watching a movie at the mall off Route 80.

Had Jeff thought life worth living, he would've made a fine trial lawyer. As it was, his law career paralleled that of Roy's in that he worked in family law and mostly did easy divorces for poor people who could never pay much. Jeff had a sort of social unconsciousness that came from the Vietnam War days when he was not in favor of the war, and when he was in favor of drugs. The lack of being a veteran harmed his career in numerous ways, as did being one of the jolly boys who used drugs and abused prescription pills. Obtaining prescriptions from several doctors at the same time did not particularly help his career. After he was caught using drugs that were illegal, he found out that being jolly was not nearly so career enhancing as being morose, and that there was an inverse relationship at work in the legal world which he'd never grasped too well. The more morose one was, the better the legal career, whereas the more jolly, the more likely it was their career would run off the tracks. Jeff fit right in with the other people living on the top of Bald Hill, for all of their careers had derailed off the tracks and wrecked along the way, which meant most of the people on top of the mountain were now morose.

Yet, in some ways, Jeff was happier making eggs than in trying to put egg on the face of his opponent in the courtroom. There was a basic simplicity of egg-making that appealed to the artist in Jeff. There was none of the doubt about the outcome of a messy divorce when one created a meal. Either the meal tasted good, or it didn't. There were no halfway measures as often happened when the judge handed down a decision. For Jeff, the fact that life was not black and white meant that life was full of unanswerable choices and decisions which he couldn't deal with.

Jeff had grown up in Chicago in a rundown middle-class neighborhood in which everyone sat out on the stoop in the summer, and talked and talked without ever saying anything of importance. Jeff learned early that talking without saying anything was not productive, so he learned to spend his time reading classical works. He learned to read in German and Latin, and though he had no friends in school, he did gain a career and thus a way out of the old neighborhood. He left without regrets, taking one suitcase on the New York Central to Syracuse University, having never met his father. His mother, at that point, was an alcoholic who went to Mass every day while living on Social Security and wine.

After he obtained his law degree from Case, he went back one time for his mother's funeral. The whole neighborhood seemed more run down and poor than he remembered, the priests older and the funeral Mass short. The paint in the church was cracked and the gold of the wine cup dull. There was only him and a few of his mother's old friends at the funeral Mass. The old ladies were all Slavic, hardly understanding a word of English. They patted Jeff on the head and hugged him, and he felt no connection with them at all. After communion and the burial in a weedy cemetery, he went over to the old house where he was raised. There were immigrants living there now, the big oak tree next door cut down, and no coal smoke from the chimney. He remembered his room upstairs to the right, with the faded bear wallpaper that an aunt had paid for, where he slept alone, waking when his mother came in from work at 4 a.m., bent and broken from night work. She'd lay out his breakfast of cereal and a banana so he could eat before school, and then go to sleep until it was time to go to her other job at noon. An accident at work finished her, giving her disability payments and the urge to drink. She had worked to put her son into a good life but never had time to get to know him, and so he had been known only by the nuns at school as a smart and gifted student who took to logic and language in a manner not usually found in the city. He was a thinker among workers, and felt increasingly out of place outside of school. The obtaining of his BA in Classical Languages was easy, as was Law School. He was an editor for the *Law Review* and a member of the Moot Court, and graduated with honors into a boring world that had no challenges left. Indeed, the only thing which made life tolerable was the application of various drugs that Jeff had been introduced to at Syracuse University. Indeed, his marriage to someone he didn't love at all was the final admission that he, like the people sitting at Mass in his old neighborhood, had no expectations except escape.

In his practice, he was competent if bored, and spent his weekends out in a big garden with a pool in the middle of the backyard at the ranch house. The encountering of endless people who hated their marriages impacted Jeff in a very negative manner, showing him the world as full of unhappy people who'd made a hash out of their lives. He found that the only thing of value in his own life was the growing of vegetables in the backyard. After a day in court, Jeff would go home, ignore his wife, and after changing clothes, go out to the metal shed and get out the hoe and attack weeds in the garden.

If Jeff's life were mostly adrift, in the garden he had order. The neat rows produced huge heads of cabbage and tall corn without worms. He planted potatoes and carrots, started tomatoes from seeds, and lovingly repotted them in the spring until they were ready for the soil, then dug a hole for each plant, added bone meal, and protected the plants with individual aluminum cages. He planted onion sets and pepper plants, planted sugar pod peas and tied them gently to wire mesh to aid their growth. The beets were eight inches in diameter by fall, and the bean plants heavy with produce. If anything in Jeff's life ever produced, it was his garden. The pumpkins and gourds were legends and in late September, he would harvest all the root crops. He dug the potatoes and carrots and beets, picked the pumpkins and gourds, and hung the tomato vines in the garage with the green tomatoes on them to ripen over the winter. The onions were dug and hung to dry for Thanksgiving in mesh, and the garlic was picked and placed in glass jars for storage. Seeds were gathered from the sunflowers and the marigolds and stored for spring. In the gathering dusk of fall, Jeff would set out in the garden in a chair, and feel the cool winds of October. He could never bring himself to clean out the garden in the fall, preferring to try to save a few plants into November by covering them with boxes at night when the temperature was cold, and uncovering them during the day when the sun shone. At night, he would sometimes rise from his bed and walk out into the garden in late October when the frost was falling, and touch each plant he wanted to save for a few more weeks under its box, praying that it would live until dawn. After a freeze killed all of Jeff's beloved plants in November, he would sit by the bay window on a Saturday, looking at the blackened plants he had tried to save, and do nothing all afternoon except wait for the seed catalogs of spring.

He'd go to the doctor and obtain some pills to help get him through the winter darkness, and if he hadn't been turned in to the police by his unloved wife for using illegal herbs to get him through winter, life might have been pretty settled. As it was, he finally came to the lake, lived on the mountain, and cooked eggs for a living at the diner in town.

It turned out that not just the locals liked his eggs – so did New Yorkers. He ended up as Second Chef at the Plaza, commuted on the 3:30 a.m. train to Manhattan each day, returned to the lake each afternoon, accumulated a very nice nest egg, and at least had a career that he liked: making eggs into classical works of art that were just as transient as his life.

Becky 2

Becky 2 was the mother of a little boy who liked to paint. She was a pharmacist who worked in the drug store in town two stores away from the Grand Union at the shopping center, and drove a rusty red Chevette. She thought that life was centered on her son, and she wanted the best for the little fellow. She was beautiful, with eyes of deep brown, long legs, and the best smile ever seen west of Hoboken.

Becky was a night owl type, and many nights she'd take the canoe out to the float in the middle of the lake and swim alone, looking up at the big jets headed into Newark, and listen to someone playing a flute in the dark of the night up on the north end of the lake. She rented a frame ranch style house painted red along the row of houses across the middle of the hill with an electric heater fireplace. Becky had been married, and after the divorce had moved to the lake from California to be near her cousin, Becky 1, so they could travel together. In reality, they never did.

Like her cousin, Becky liked to fly, finding something mystical in being 40,000 feet above the fish mating in the lake water, and whenever she had saved enough money from her job at the pharmacy in town, she would go to Hill Travel Agency on Route 53 and book a flight to nowhere. Well, the flight went somewhere, but she never cared where as long as it was a food flight, was cheap, and she got back in time for work. Of all of the qualities that Becky had, the greatest was thriftiness. She saved for her son's future, bought her clothes at Kmart on Route 46 at Parsippany, bought day-old food, shopped at the bakery outlet at the Dollar Store, and grew tomatoes in the poor soil of the mountain. Becky did a lot of her holiday shopping at garage sales, and was always happy to find a little something at the All for One store, in which everything that could be wrapped for someone's birthday cost just a dollar. The odd thing about Becky's thrifty habits was that she never really saved much, for whatever she saved was spent later on airline trips to anywhere.

Whenever she could fly, she would dress like a tourist, wearing shorts and a flowery top, carrying her camera and her travel book on board the airplane, while asking everybody about the sights at her destination. Between travel and working all the time, she never had time for either her son or other acquaintances. Becky went through life on the surface, working and traveling over and over, while her son sat with a sitter. Her surface life ended on US Air Flight 1016 at Charlotte in July 1994. Her son went to a foster home at Union, and grew up to be a musician after attending Julliard in the City. He didn't ever remember much about his mother or father.

Ruth Anne and Dave

Ruth Anne and her husband, Dave, were typical of the good, solid American workers who had vanished during the 1960's. They thought it important to get to work on time and to help their neighbors, they thought it important to stay together through life, and to save money. Ruth Anne worked as a legal secretary in town for Roy's competitor. She had a brown wooden desk facing the brown wooden door with a little silver bell on the back which dinged whenever anyone opened the door to come in. Her highest education was secretarial school, which suited her just fine. There, she had learned to type and to file and to organize an office. She liked to own American cars, thought that American products were just fine, and she owned a Caprice Classic. She did not cook with a microwave, but instead cooked real fried chicken and fried vegetables for her family's enjoyment.

Ruth Anne's view of food was a tribute to the American work ethic. At every meal, she ate a diet of meat and potatoes and gravy. The meat was fried: fried chicken steak, fried Chinese beef, fried chicken, fried pork ribs and chops. She liked donuts in the morning filled with jelly, and she liked a little snack during the afternoon of a white cake with icing on the top. These little cakes could be bought at the A&P in town in the bakery section, and came underneath a plastic snap-down cover to keep the dust from the streets off the cake. The cakes were only about inches inches in diameter, which was just the right size for an afternoon treat. The surprising thing was that Ruth Anne, who also smoked a pack of Camels a day, blowing the smoke into the computer keyboard, was a thin woman with no health troubles. Her cholesterol was fine, she could walk upstairs without panting, and she worked hard and ate hearty. She liked to attend the pork festivals held down in South Jersey, where she could get pork chops, pork rib, pork steaks, and pork loin burgers covered in kraut and mustard. When she went into a diner, she ordered whatever she wanted without worry. Her dad had lived to be 83, and Ruth Anne knew that she would do just as well.

Her hobby was watching NASCAR auto racing over in Kentucky, Tennessee, and Michigan. She always said of Indy Car races that they were not fun because the cars were too far apart. She liked to see the cars going 150 miles an hour and only an inch apart. She and Dave would leave the lake on Friday for Kentucky, taking the Pennsylvania Turnpike out to I-79 south to Charleston, then I-64 to I-65 south to whatever race was on for the weekend. In the race stands, she would wave at the cameras to all of her friends back in New Jersey, eat popcorn and drink pop, and jump up at every crash. If a driver were killed at the race, she would weep as if a family member had been lost, and if a driver won whom she didn't like, she would boo as his car crossed the finish line. Life at the races was a fine counterbalance to life in the legal office, where people were always doing wills and house sales closings and suing over an auto accident. At the races, accidents were not met with lawsuits, but with high interest and cheers for the brave drivers who survived a crash. With her 9 to 5 job, the races, and her family, Ruth Anne's life was full, and she was content.

She had three children: Betty, Barney, and Bob. None of them lived at the lake. Betty lived in Kentucky, Barney lived in Michigan, and Bob lived in Ohio. They had all remarried numerous times and had numerous children, so at Christmas, Ruth Anne shopped for all the kids at the Dollar Store in town, and sent large packages off to them the week after Thanksgiving. She had all of the grandkids' pictures hung on the wall by her desk, and marked all of their birthdays on her desk planner.

She came to work every day at 9 a.m. and went home at 5 p.m. She took an hour for lunch and never cheated on her timecard. Life was best when it followed a pattern, and she followed the pattern of her life without question. Whereas Becky 1 spent unhappy nights flying across the country, and Dallas went fishing rather than be at home, Ruth Anne always went right home after work, made dinner, watched racing on cable TV, went to sleep, and did the same thing the next day without the slightest feeling of discontentment. People who met her were amazed that she was always cheerful at her job, happy to come to work, and satisfied with her life. She always said that education just made a person unhappy, and there was much truth to that statement. Ruth Anne was living proof that a little education was just fine in life.

Her husband, Dave, liked racing also. He and Ruth Anne had decided in 1981 that when all the kids could manage on their own as best as they ever would, the two of them would go and see something of the country. This came to pass in the form of renting a car from Hertz and driving around aimlessly. Neither had been away from the Midwest much in their lives, and so having gotten on I-80, they eventually arrived purely by chance at the little town by the lake for Texaco gas and some lunch. Dave, who always carried his pole along, asked about the local fishing, and after lunch they drove over to the lake for a look around. The day was rainy and the hill was hidden in the afternoon fog that often drifted about after a shower. The whole lake was like glass, reflecting the trees in the calm water. The fishing boats were all tied up at their docks, and Dave saw four swans come down from the north end of the lake and slowly fly the length of the lake, their huge wings waving slowly a few feet above the water. Dave knew that this was a lake to fish. The trees promised a cool summer unlike the summers in Ohio, and the quiet was a pleasant change from all the grandchildren who came to visit with no notice. Dave felt this was the place for him to retire while Ruth Anne worked a few more years if she wished, as she liked working. Dave had been a firefighter in Ohio, and he could already see a place for himself at the volunteer fire department in town, where he could tilt his chair back along the white concrete wall, and watch the cars go by. He saw himself out in one of those boats, doing nothing except fishing and waiting for life to end. Of all the things that Dave wanted, he had always sought a little peace and quiet, and now he had found it in New Jersey.

He was happy to have met Ruth Anne when they were both in high school, and to have said to her one day, "Want to settle down?" and she had said, "Yes." And that was that. There was not a whole lot of romance in their relationship, but the taxes got paid, the cars ran, and life didn't have any difficulties in it. Dave liked auto racing and beer and an occasional smoke in the afternoon after a job was done well. Dave always thought, as did Ruth Anne, that there was no point in putting on airs. He was a down-to-earth person who wished the grandkids were quieter, and he found it hard to keep all of them straight, especially with the kids always marrying and getting divorced and moving all around the country.

They bought a two-story red house on the second row of houses on the hill, and Dave bought a wooden rowboat that once belonged to Wally a long time ago, and that Milt once bumped his head into while swimming over to visit Billie and Wally one night after dark. The two oars in the boat belonged to Ralph once, until they blew off the dock in a big wind one night and floated away southward, and were found out by Picnic Island. Dave would stoke the fireplace full of maple wood in the winter and sit, drinking coffee and staring at the flames while the ground was covered with snow, and Ruth Anne would sit and write long letters to the kids about the virtues of life at the lake, telling all of them they should move on down to New Jersey and learn to relax. Dave hoped none of them would ever show up so he could fish in peace. They never did, although visits were often discussed.

In time, Dave came to meet John and Iris, so while Iris and Ruth Anne went shopping out on Route 46, John and Dave would go fishing, sitting quietly out on the lake in the late evening, when the geese were flying in for the night and the bats flew by the ends of their fishing poles. They never said much, just sitting out there with the shadows stretching out from the floating island, listening to someone up west of the island playing the flute at the base of the mountain. Out on the float, they could see someone lying face down, reaching into the water, apparently feeding the fish that hung out under the float, waiting for a little snack. Sometimes, someone would play taps at sunset, just as people said it had been played at the lake in the 1950s by an old fellow. Dave and John thought it was a nice gesture that showed respect for people who had died so that they could fish and live in freedom.

In the boat, they never felt they had to say much. If one of them got a fish on the line, the other would calmly pick up the long-handled net and wait until the fish arrived by the boat, flipping all about, and then net it and see what had been caught. There was nothing to get excited about, for they always threw the fish back, and often caught what appeared to be the same fish the next day. While Dave went to the firehouse in the morning and John went over to watch Joe try to start the big yellow backhoe, the evenings were always reserved for fishing. One day a month, they met at the Fishing Club meeting and sat together silently in the back of the room, waiting for the free lunch, which was the best part of the meeting.

Some nights, all of the friends – John and Iris, Ruth Anne and Dave, Libby and Dale, George, and Earl and Emabel – would have a little cookout by the lake. Earl would sit in his rocking chair, surrounded by the other men outdoors, and the ladies would retire to the kitchen after dinner to talk about the sales coming up the next week in town.

The men would sit out under the stars shining on the water, and talk about being young and foolish. If life ever taught anything to anyone, it was that it was better to be young and a fool than be old and still a fool. And so they wished to be young, and in the dark, when they could not see the age lines and the stooped shoulders, they *felt* young, and told stories of living out west. There were stories of big trout in the Colorado rivers, along with stories about cars their fathers had owned, with names like Studebaker and Nash and Peerless. Sometimes, Earl felt that he wanted these nights to last forever, when he could stay up without falling asleep during the conversation, as he often did now. Dave and the others wondered what it was going to feel like if they lived to be as old as Earl, but they never talked about it, preferring to talk about fish and rivers and cars and their childhood homes and the smell of bread in the oven on a December day, when the windows were covered with real frost that would hold a sketch scratched with a key. All of them could remember threshing wheat with a steam-driven threshing machine, the local hometown parades on the Fourth, and the homemade Christmas gifts. They tried to capture that time long passed by sitting next to the water – the one symbol that men have always regarded as lasting as long as the earth. All of them could remember a boyhood swimming hole, a river their fathers had taken them to, or a pond where they'd picnicked once. In their hearts, they all wished they could go back, and walking home later in the dark, they were quiet, and hoped to live to see the sunrise.

Meg

Meg came to the lake in 1991 at the insistence of her sister, Maureen, who had found a nice waterfront Cape Code style brick house with a central chimney on the northeast side, south of Grace's old red house, for rent. Meg did not feel like a stranger when she arrived driving a red BMW convertible, for she had been friends out in the Midwest with several of the other people who were on the lake. Meg had known Jeff in Illinois before his little detour to state prison, when they were both members of the American Bar Association and partied all night long at the American Bar Association conventions they attended in order to discuss law, but ended up pretty well wasted instead. She had, through contacts in the same association, known Roy, and Ruth Anne and Dave. Her dad was a retired teacher and her mother a nurse who worked over at St. Francis Hospital. So, arriving at the lake was equivalent to going to a reunion of friends, rather than moving from Cincinnati, where she had been a public defender.

She was sick of defending poor people who had committed crimes, but said they had not. Every morning in Cincinnati, her brown eyes looked over the coming court cases and despaired of either having the time to really defend a client who was innocent, or getting true justice for those whom she knew to be guilty. Almost every case was plea bargained over lunch at the Omni Hotel's dining room with the prosecutor, followed by a short trip to Carew Tower Mall next door for a little shopping, or a trip to the beauty salon to get her blonde hair washed and set. Her days were full of paper, while the interesting cases were delegated to part-time defenders just out of law school, who had no idea at all of what they were doing. Whatever glory the law had held while Meg was in law school at Cleveland State had come down to just trying to get the paperwork done so it wouldn't have to be redone. Meg had worked in legal aid in Wooster and Eaton, Ohio, before going to the public defender's office, and had come to see that the poor really did live differently than she did. They were always in trouble, yet Meg valued their lives and families, and wished she could do more to help them.

This sense of class identification led her to dress well. She always wore good clothes to work, including gold jewelry and high heels, and she did her hair every day, put on eye shadow, and carried an expensive purse. She wore diamonds around her neck and a little handkerchief in her suit pocket. In every way, she looked classy in court and in the office, while her clients looked like hell. This often had the unfortunate results of getting her clients sent to jail, since jurors could recognize the vast difference in culture between Meg, who of course, had a J.D. degree and fashion sense, and the client who had little education and no sense of any law, and was thus in court in the first place.

Often, Meg stood away from them in court when standing before the judge. This unconscious distancing from the client sent a subtle message to the judges and jury that the client was not worth getting close to, and so in toss-up cases, the client usually went to jail. Sometimes, an appeal could be filed that would release the client, but usually the client Meg represented would have some time away from society to learn a sense of fashion and law.

Meg had been invited by Roy to enter into a partnership with him, but instead decided to run a small private practice in family law. She leased a small office on South Main Street, went to the local bar association lunches, got to know everyone who was anyone over at the social security office and the welfare office, and after a couple of months, had a decent practice going with private paying clients and referrals from legal aid. Her cases consisted of divorces and wills and child custody rights. Every time there was a holiday or a full moon, business would boom. Meg hired Ruth Anne away from Roy's competitor to work for her, and they had a nice social office, with Meg all dressed up every day, watching her weight and eating right, while Ruth Anne ate what she wanted and drove her big American car to work every day. While the shopping at the lake was not up to the standards of Cincinnati, there were lots of good bookstores available in the city, as well as good theater and music, and so Meg spent most weekends going to culture away from New Jersey.

Meg's desk was always orderly. She liked the feeling of being in control of life and work and religion, and so she started every morning with a list of cases which needed attention, and as the day progressed, she would check off each case as it was dealt with. The case folders would be piled by Ruth Anne on the left side of Meg's desk, and after they were acted upon, the folders would be placed on the right side of the desk for return to the file cabinets. She listened to classical music on her CD player, which was one of five which she owned, while working on cases of the poor. Her upscale umbrella always stood in its brass umbrella stand in the corner of the wood-paneled office, and her impeccable coat – spot free – hung neatly behind the office door, covering a large mirror. Each day, before going to lunch at the New York Deli, the Corner Place, or the Hub, she would remove the coat from over the mirror, and check her makeup and lipstick to make sure she projected a professional image. She would always make sure she carried her business cards and appointment calendar, and looked professional in every manner.

At the lake, Meg liked to sit out on the long dock constructed of steel I-beams protruding from the retaining walls with a wooden deck above the beams. She would be coated with sun protector, and would read *Longevity* magazine. She was concerned with such topics as fat in the diet, exercise, and how to eat out all of the time while not eating fat or calories. She also liked to read *Traveler* magazine, and planned her twice-yearly vacation trips to Florida, the Caribbean, or the national parks out west. Each vacation trip was well planned, just as her job was.

When a trip was approaching, she would start a list of things to pack (often derived from *Traveler*), a list of things to be done around the house before leaving, and a list of errands. The trip itself also involved a list, in this case a list of things to do on the trip by day and time. A trip was no fun unless there was a plan, and even short weekend trips required a plan in order to ensure full enjoyment. She had heard a slogan somewhere around the lake that people who plan eat bass, and she had modified this saying to people who plan were efficient and successful. At night, she would plan out her clothes for the next day at work, laying out her jewelry, her dress, and her shoes so she would not have to think about dressing in the morning and could watch the world news instead.

Meg found Ruth Anne to be interesting. How could it be that someone could eat whatever she wanted, and still be slim? At lunch, Meg would order a salad, while Ruth Anne ordered fried potatoes, fried chicken, and ice cream, yet Ruth Anne remained looking like a pole, while Meg was constantly on some sort of diet or whatever, trying to get thin. Ruth Anne understood nothing about nutrition, fat, sugar, or calories, and yet she never gained weight. Meg believed there was something wrong with this state of things, but could not figure out what was wrong. She just knew that it was not fair that Ruth Anne was skinny and never exercised, while Meg jumped about in an up and down motion three times a week to her Jane Fonda videotape.

Meg also found that she was surrounded by uncaring lawyers in New Jersey. She had been used to working with professionals in Ohio, and to find that lawyers were generally corrupt on the East Coast was something of a surprise. She met Roy at a bar association party shortly after she arrived at the lake, and was shocked to hear him tell of how he overbilled hours to clients who could afford it. Her suspicions that corrupt lawyers migrated to the East Coast were confirmed. She learned that judges were taking kickbacks in municipal courts and that one judge was sending men to prison so he could sleep with their wives in return for later getting them out of prison early. She also found that no one in the Bar Association ever bothered to dress like a professional. Lawyers went to court wearing ties splattered with lunch and blue jeans on occasion, while the judges sat in their robes wearing shorts and tennis shoes underneath. Even worse, at the quarterly tax seminars that were actually drinking parties attended by all the county lawyers, she found that everyone was on the same side. The lawyers wanted to make money and the judges wanted to speed up the court process. At the bars in town, lawyers and judges and prosecutors all gathered together to gab about their clients and their troubles, so that most civil cases were settled in a bar, and most criminal cases were plea bargained in the same bar, which was called the Red Mule.

The Red Mule was full of crappy antiques, dirty leaning tables, and pool tables in the rear. While the local workers thought of it as a good place to drink oneself into oblivion, the lawyers who hung out there thought of the place as a good location to get to view the people, and to feel like real working people. What usually happened was when the lawyers rolled in after their offices closed, and often well before, the locals would leave, and go outside to watch the trains, and would return later after the lawyers had gone home. If it were raining, the locals would congregate in the rear by the pool tables, while the lawyers sat up front and talked about their clients, some of whom were probably hanging around the rear of the bar. The surprising thing was that after a few beers, there was not much apparent difference between the locals and the lawyers. Sometimes, the local township cops would drop by for a few beers also, and about 7 p.m., the cops and lawyers would all leave together, weaving slightly, in a feeling of camaraderie and love. If they were lucky, they would be able to back their cars out of the rather tight parking spaces without too much mishap, and find their way home or back to work safely.

When Meg didn't have to associate with other lawyers, she liked to do cross-stitch work from kits. She did little lighthouses and castles and Tudor houses, had them framed at the expensive frame shop in town, and hung them around her house in locations where visitors would be sure to see them, and offer praise. These visitors were few, as Meg preferred her own company to the company of fools. She thought herself as one of few people on the lake with any education or sense, and she was often proven to be correct. She liked to sit on the dock with her binoculars, looking at the people over on the west side, muttering to herself, "Don't put that flower pot there," or "Don't let that fat man get into that canoe," or "Don't let that dog jump on that small child." Often, she could see that people were not too smart, and she wished she could run their lives for them, since she could surely do a better job than they were doing. With her books, job, vacations, and binoculars, she was satisfied, and lived long.

Gail and June

Gail and June learned about the lake when they were eating lunch at the 76 truck stop at Kansas City East, and happened to strike up a conversation with John and Iris, who showed them photos of the lake when they were preparing to move there. Gail and June had lived in Kansas City most of their lives, having met and married in high school. They continued to write to John and Iris, and finally decided that after Gail retired from the printing business, they'd move to the lake. So they packed up the old station wagon, called United Van Lines, and headed east. They bought a brick house up on the second tier of hill houses, north of Marilyn's place. The house had no porch, but came with a fake gas log fireplace and an open deck on which they could sit with their binoculars to watch the cove people at play and at rest.

Gail was a tall, pale man with thinning sandy hair and a long, sharp nose, but a pleasant imbecilic smile for everyone. He believed that all people could be friends and that the world was full of goodness. In his goodness, he fathered four boys, none of whom liked New Jersey or wanted to live there. Gail had no hobbies except looking around the lake with his binoculars. He was quite shocked to discover that many of the lake people were doing exactly the same thing. The lady who sat on the dock across from him, doing needlepoint, often looked right at him, making him go inside for a little sandwich. He found that some of the cove people often were looking at him also, and he discovered on a moonlit night someone sitting on a dock at the south end, wearing what appeared to be night vision goggles. This was very disturbing for Gail, who had been in ROTC at the University of Kansas and therefore knew that real night vision goggles worked far better than plain binoculars. Gail was forced to scuttle back inside his house again when he saw the man at the south end looking towards him. Eventually, Gail bought a large telescope, mounted a tripod on the deck, and greatly increased his viewing capability to the point that he could look into people's rooms across the lake without much trouble. At the Friday night clubhouse get-togethers, he could surprise people to no end by commenting about their new living room décor, or that pesky toaster that wouldn't work, or the cat that clawed the furniture when the owner wasn't home. Gail's spying was only of the fun sort, and never intrusive with regard to bedroom scenes. But it sure was fun to watch the family arguments and know what all the across-the-way people were watching on TV.

June always loved to watch 1960's television on Nick at Nite, and always thought of herself as a modern June Cleaver, raising four Beavers. While Gail had gone on to college and gotten his B.A. degree in Humanities, June had always known that the intellectual life was not for her. She just wanted a husband and children, a house to clean, and a kitchen to cook in. She did not regard high school as the highlight of her life, as did most of her friends, but she did regard having babies as the best thing she'd ever done. She was tall with a thin face, and curly, short brown hair, and she was happy when Gail took her over to the clubhouse, with poison ivy nearby in the forest, for the Friday night get-together of lake people.

At these get-togethers, she chatted with the other housewives about raising children, cooking meals, and decorating for birthday parties. Although her kids were grown and gone, she felt as if her life as a young mother would never go away. She pretended when she was out for an evening at the clubhouse that life was the same as it had been 30 years ago, and that the children were still in their four beds at home with the sitter. She was never interested in business or politics or women's issues; just in being a good mother.

To her credit, the boys, who rarely visited New Jersey, had turned out okay, with all four of them graduating from college on scholarships. They all lived in the Midwest, with one a teacher, one a preacher, one a farmer, and the other a dance performer. Of all of the families at the lake, perhaps Gail and June were the most American.

When they got together with John and Iris, they played cards or cooked beef on the grill, or watched a rented movie on television. Not for them was the nightclub scene out on Route 46 or the big parties over at the clubhouse. They liked the suburban retired life of not having to accomplish anything at all. Sometimes, Gail would take June for a rowboat ride, she wearing a big straw hat that made it hard for Gail to see behind the boat, and they would row slowly around the shoreline after dinner, observing their neighbors' lawns and visiting with the other retired couples. These were pleasant times in their lives, when all the stress of life was gone and the summer breeze belied the winter that was only 120 days away. If Gail and June ever talked about anything important, they never remembered it in all of their life together. Through raising children, they'd never encountered a problem they couldn't solve, nor an issue they could avoid discussing. Their life together had been productive and good, and they had sampled and enjoyed life to satisfaction. They wanted only the peace that sometimes comes with retirement. When June was diagnosed with advanced breast cancer, she went to a friendly doctor for some pills. On June 7th of their last summer, Gail and June ate dinner, mixed some vodka cocktails, sat on the porch together, and took their pills just like in the movie *On the Beach* with Gregory Peck. The boys inherited and sold the house, dividing the profits four ways. Gail and June were missed by their friends.

Val and Marty

Val was Myrtle's daughter's ex-husband's sister. When Myrtle corresponded with Mary and Charles, Val's parents, in 1959, she sent Mary and Charles lots of photos of the lake and suggested they might want to retire there and be friends with everyone. Myrtle had no animosity toward Mary and Charles, even though their son and Myrtle's daughter did not get along well (though they got along well enough to have a son). Myrtle felt she had to show Mary and Charles the right things to do in life, as they had come to America in 1922 from the Slovak region of Europe. Their English was heavy with a foreign accent which they never lost. Much of Myrtle's attempts to improve the life of Mary and Charles were wasted, as they were perfectly happy being caterers in Newark, and even owned a two-story brown duplex and rented out the bottom floor to a family from Ireland who did not fit in the Slovak neighborhood at all. Mary and Charles are pictured below at their wedding in Newark, New Jersey.

Mary's Mother, Marija Mulicka, 78 (Taken in Slovokia, 1936):

Mary at 103 Years Old:

Mary and Charles decorated their house with eastern European décor which included a number of caved Catholic statues. They ate light Slovak pastries covered in white sugar powder and thin noodle soup. Charles was squat with a head shaped like a blacksmith's anvil, while Mary was short with a round cabbage head. They both had huge consuming smiles with big teeth, and if people smiled back, those people were likely to have a light pastry inserted into their mouths, as Mary liked giving pastries to her friends and relatives. Their backyard contained a poor little garden which did not do well in the Newark air, but did provide a few tomatoes and potatoes a week during the summer. They worked at being good caterers, and in due course had a son, Bill, and a daughter, Val. Bill got divorced and remarried, and had another son. Val married Marty and had two daughters, Valerie and Tabitha, who eventually grew up to live in Louisville and Tampa. Valerie became a kindergarten teacher and had three daughters of her own; and Tabitha became a drug dealer in the lucrative Florida environment.

Val and Marty settled down to live in Hillside, New Jersey, while Marty worked in the shoe industry, making shoes out of scarce leather, and in due time, Marty retired. They moved to Palm Coast, Florida, after Charles died. Mary went with them, prolonging her life and living with them until she was 103 years old. After Mary was gone (she was buried next to Charles in the Catholic cemetery back by Route 10 in New Jersey), there was nothing to do around the house; Val and Marty were soon bored with afternoon croquet and the annual Caribbean cruise. Val had been Lois' sister-in-law and, every Christmas, Lois would have her Christmas card custom designed by Kmart on Route 46, with a photo of the lake during the winter on the front of the card. She'd write a happy little poem about the holiday at the lake, and sent it off to Val.

Now, Val had never been too enamored of Florida, and when the violence and robberies against older people in Florida accelerated during the late 1980's, she thought it might well be time for a change. Of all things, she missed the northern winters. There was something very boring about the Florida winters which were all alike, with the flowers still in bloom and the temperature in the 70's. Val had lived in the north all her life, and she believed that there was nothing like snow on the ground during the holiday season, with a temperature that would nip at one's nose. Val's nose was particularly long and susceptible to being nipped at, as was Marty's, and they were both tall, though later in life, Marty became quite stooped and lost some of his height. Marty, too, thought Florida had grown boring. In fact, he was finding that the best part about Florida was that the beer was cheap, and he was always fond of beers after work in New Jersey. He continued the tradition of afternoon beers in Florida, followed by a light dinner. As they grew older, they both felt the pull of their home state and knew they were really New Jerseyites at heart. In spite of the traffic, poor air, icy roads, and deep snows, they recognized a growing sense of homesickness which could no longer be alleviated by summer trips back to Newark and Hillside, then over to Route 10 to visit the family graves.

So, Val wrote to Lois that they were coming home to New Jersey, and in 1987, both they and their two cats came, with all their stuff hauled in an Allied moving van. They rented a single family dark blue frame house near the west beach at the southwest corner of the lake, and made friends with all the folks who went to the clubhouse with the leaking sewage pipe on a Friday night for drinks. There, they found people younger than they, who liked to drink and party and who were not boring. Marty eventually found beer lovers in the form of Iris' husband John, and Beth from the west side. Also at the Friday night gatherings were Jeff from the top of the hill and Roy from the legal profession. Ruth Anne and Dave were interested in drinking good old American beer, too, and so Marty found that life on the lake, especially Friday nights, was pretty satisfying. He'd sit at the bar looking out at the Florida sun setting over the lake mountain, and knew at last the sense of contentment without being bored. Val found friends to shop and gossip with, and generally enjoyed taking the bus to the City with her new friends. They'd shop a little, eat a little, go to an afternoon play off Broadway, and take the evening Lakeland bus back to the country. All in all, Val knew it was good to be back home again, to the world she knew and had grown up with. They bought burial plots at the cemetery on Route 10 by her parents' plots, and preplanned their funerals. Walking home from the clubhouse, hand in hand, they couldn't think of anything they hadn't done that they wished to, or that they weren't content to reflect back upon. Life had been, and was, good for them.

Connie

Connie hated New Jersey and everything about it. She didn't like the eastward traffic rush in the morning, nor the westward traffic crawl in the late afternoon. It was her life's goal to get out of New Jersey and live anywhere else. The only problem was that she had a good job in New Jersey. She'd come to New Jersey to study at Rutgers, and after graduating, stayed on to get her MS degree. A contact in her professional society offered her a job at the Parsippany-Troy Hills Acute Care Center at a salary she couldn't turn down. In an attempt to get away from any sense of New Jersey, she bought a small log house up on top of Bald Hill. It was heated with propane gas logs instead of a real fireplace, and had no porch. In fact, it had a living room, kitchen, bathroom, and two bedrooms with a half basement cut out of the granite underneath, but no porch. Her view of the lake was obscured by the pine trees, which dropped their needles into the gutters, clogging them up. The surrounding ground was rocky and not hospitable to growing flowers or tomatoes. In fact, there were rocks everywhere, poking up in the dirt driveway and around the house so that an unwary person – or even a wary one – could trip over them.

Her house was one of the highest around the lake, making it an excellent location for lightning strikes and poor water pressure. The water sometimes was only a dribble out of the faucet if the township pumps were off line for a few minutes for maintenance work. The log house had been one of the first built on the lake, built in 1910, with running water added afterwards. The kitchen contained old wooden glass-doored cabinets for the dishes, and not enough room for the propane stove and the small green refrigerator. The door to the outside, which was in the kitchen, always stuck in the rain and had to be kicked open. The bedrooms were wood paneled, and the living room was dark and smelled vaguely of mildew. Connie did her best with lace curtains, and putting flowers around that were bought at Flowers-by-Candlelight out on Route 53 in Mt. Tabor by the railroad tracks. This made things smell better, but did little to brighten up the old place. It was sort of like living in a big shoe, with everything tied up and stuffy. Connie always told herself that the living location was only temporary, and that she'd be gone in a few months. She didn't go, and didn't associate with anyone at the lake.

She was the classic case of work 'til one drops, and after putting in 60-hour weeks for 10 years, she died of a stroke due to stress. Her parents, who had been proud of her accomplishments, had her buried back in the family plot in Norton, West Virginia, up where the air was good and there was no mildew. She never learned that life at the lake was much better at the bottom of the mountain than at the top.

Church at Norton, West Virginia

Bill

Bill visited the lake as the father of the boy who won the three boat race trophies in 1961. They hardly knew each other even then, for Bill had gone his own way back in 1953 before the boy had moved to the lake with his grandparents and mother. But in accordance with social norms, Bill came to do his duty as a parent, and so took the express Lakeland bus from Port Authority to the lake twice a year for a parental visit. There was not the slightest emotion involved in these visits to the lake. Bill had worked for the State Department in classified jobs ever since World War II, spending much time in Vienna and Paris. He was tall with Val's nose, and spoke Slovak, Russian, German, French, English, and Spanish, all of them well. He had no emotions and always made the correct decisions. He's pictured below as a young boy in Newark.

When he arrived at the bus stop by the Grand Union, he always carried a leather briefcase and wore a sport jacket, tie, and slacks that looked expensive. While other people in town wore boat shoes or sneakers, Bill wore expensive leather shoes that befitted a business man in New York City more than rural New Jersey. His work for the UN as an economist provided him with a sense of diplomacy that served him well, allowing him to float along through life doing damage everywhere while appearing to do his duty. He never left behind any sense of having visited at all, but rather of having passed through a given location. He effectively insulated himself from everyone, and so was able to look at the world logically. If he ever felt any pride in his son or any affection for him, it was never shown other than the dutiful birthday and Christmas cards, which always included a money order from a Manhattan bank for $50.

His visits to the lake were punctual and routine. After arriving, he would eat pastries from Viking and drink coffee from Peers on the porch of Myrtle and Ralph's old house. He would take off his tie to indicate he was now in the country, and put on a sweater or causal shirt in place of his jacket to confirm he was no longer in the city. He never arrived dressed for the country, and when he did change into his country attire, it always projected a sense that he was used to a richer country life than he was apt to get in New Jersey, more like a Long Island Sound lifestyle. Like the New York bankers of old, he was happiest in the city with all of its vitality, and felt lost when away from it. He was happy when he could put on his tie and jacket again, and climb on the 3 p.m. bus back to Port Authority. He never fished on the lake in 40 years of visits, never watched the sun set or listened to the geese in the morning. His world was Paris and Austria and Washington. When he flew out of Kennedy airport over the lake, he never once looked out the window or wondered what was happening below, where people were sitting on their docks looking at the sailboats on the water. He lived to be 96.

Louise and Clifford came from West Virginia after their daughter died, and moved into the cabin she'd lived in, up on a hill. This was the cabin surrounded by rocks which people were always falling over. The fact that the water pressure was bad and the cabin dark and depressing did not bother Clifford and Louise at all. They had lived in far worse places in West Virginia up in Tucker County before moving to a more modern house over at Norton in Randolph County. Clifford had dropped out of school in the sixth grade to go work in the mines owned by Pinkerton Coal Company, which produced good Pocahontas coal. This was back when all the mining was done by hand.

Clifford, who was called "Tuck" for no known reason, had worked in mines only 30 inches high, digging coal by hand, placing the coal on low hoppers that were skidded out of the mine. In the process of this work, he had broken both arms and gotten black lung disease. He often rotated shifts, going to work on the hoot owl shift when everyone else was in bed asleep, carrying his black lunch bucket and thermos of coffee in a poke down from the company house to his green pickup truck, and off to the mine, sometimes driving in snow so heavy that the headlights would hardly penetrate it. Tuck was thin as a rail, chewed tobacco all the time except when he was eating, and liked to eat beans and potatoes. His garden in West Virginia was an acre large, in which he grew everything that the family would need for the year. He picked berries and walnuts, hunted squirrels for food, and dreamed of killing a wild turkey over the ridge for Thanksgiving. He never did, but he served in Italy during the Second World War, and actually met Patton (whom he always said was a real bastard and not good to his men). Tuck was content with his life. He bought a new truck every year, had a rototiller and three guns, and spent the summer evenings talking with the neighbors. Tuck's brother, who was thin also, lived next door to the west with his wife, had a green cap, and a 16-inch chain saw. Behind Tuck's house on the south side lived Johnny and his wife. Johnny fixed cars in his front yard. No one lived on the east, and across the hard road, Route 33, to the north, there was only forest extending up towards Belington, West Virginia.

This forest was a wonderful place to roam, full of deer trails and squirrels. Early in the mornings when he was off work, Tuck would take his rifle and wander through this forest. In the fall, the forest was full of reds and golds, and the leaves would pad the trails. Sometimes Tuck would just go out and sit in the forest, watching for deer but never shooting anything. He'd just spend the morning sitting near to a trail, taking in the scenery. At night, instead of watching deer, he'd watch all the ballgames on cable TV. He liked baseball and football and basketball. He was one of those millions of people who were damaged when the players would go on strike, for he wouldn't watch anything on television except sports.

Tuck could repair and fix anything. What he lacked in book learning he had made up for in learning about life. If a shovel handle was bad, he could fix it. If a tractor wouldn't run, he could work on it for 30 minutes and it would run as if it were new. If the weather were poor for a good garden, it never bothered Tuck. His garden always grew plenty of beans, tomatoes, cabbage, corn, and potatoes. He grew his own pole bean seed and kept it from year to year, giving the excess away to the neighbors, so that in Randolph County just about everybody ended up growing beans from the seed that had come originally from Tuck's pole beans several years ago. He was one of those Americans who are almost all gone now, who had no credit cards, never went to a mall, and who gave his paycheck to his wife each week to manage the bills. All Tuck ever wanted was a little Red Man each day and a good sports show. He didn't crave anything else at all, and so lived his life feeling content.

Louise was part of that contentment. They had been married 35 years when Tuck retired from mining and took his pension. Louise knew how to can and freeze the produce that Tuck raised, and so she spent her summers pulling up food for the winter. The kitchen was always steamed up with quart jars of beets and beans and corn sitting on the counter cooling after being sealed. She, too, traded for a new car each year. In her spare time, she cut the grass, riding along on the green John Deere tractor, did all of the sewing, and kept Tuck in line. She saw to it that they went to Sunday school and church each week at the little church at Norton, and listened to the sermon preached by the circuit minister. She helped with the garage sales and bake sales that raised a few hundred dollars for the little church with the steeple on top.

Their house in West Virginia had been a company house, like all the others in their area. The front porch was 20 feet from the dirt road that had been the main road until the hardtop two-lane went through behind them. They had a living room, a dining room, two bedrooms downstairs, a bathroom, and a kitchen which overlooked a small back porch and the hardtop. A two-car garage out by the new road housed their truck and car, and there was a little workshop tacked on behind the garage. Next to the garage was the big woodshed in which Tuck stacked all his firewood for winter. It held 10 cords (a typical winter would require about eight cords).

They moved to the lake for one big reason: it had better hospitals than did Elkins. In fact, Elkins only had one hospital by 1994, the old Davis Memorial Hospital that had been built about 1900 and was in terrible shape. Anyone who was seriously ill was sent 60 miles over to the University Hospital at Morgantown. As this was a teaching hospital, it had lots of neat equipment for patients, and lots of young inexperienced doctors who learned on the patients.

The move to the lake was easy since their daughter's cabin was vacant. They left the cabin in West Virginia to their son, and loaded up the pickup truck and the car, and moved to New Jersey. Tuck was afraid he wouldn't like the traffic, which he didn't, and Louise was afraid no one would like them due to their mountain accents, and that she'd have no friends. That turned out not to be the case. The first thing they set about doing at the New Jersey cabin was to hook Tuck's four-wheel drive Ford by chain to the rocks in the driveway and around the house, and pull them out. This action brought out the men in the area, Jeff among them, who knew when someone was living in their midst who had a hold on life instead of life having a hold on him. Each day Tuck went after the rocks with his chain and truck, men from the hilltop would appear to watch. Louise knew the way to gain friends was to feed them, so she'd bake pies using berries picked from the wild, west side of the hill, over on the Pennsylvania side. In the fall, she'd bake a turkey breast and corn, and offer people who dropped by some lunch. Pretty soon, Tuck and Louise had made friends with the lonely people who lived up on the hill.

Tuck turned over a terraced garden plot by hand, went out to west Jersey in the truck and got some cow manure out on Route 23, and put it in the garden. Louise, using the materials that Tuck bought at the 36 Lumber Co, took out the old cabin windows and built new, larger windows that let in the light. She and Tuck installed them together, and the cabin was brightened. They built a deck on the back of the house overlooking the lake, and Tuck cut trees and brush to let in the light and improve the view. Much like the old couple in *Foxfire*, they would sit out on the deck in the evening, watching the fireflies. Tuck would talk about life back in West Virginia, while remarking about how good the doctors were in Jersey, and how many stores were close by. Louise found that she could buy fresh produce at the truck farms over behind St. Clare's Hospital in town, and that even though their garden wasn't as big as it had been in West-by-God-Virginia, it was big enough for the two of them with what she bought at the truck farms. Their basement was full of canned beans and canned corn, and bins of potatoes for the winter. Tuck found there were more sports television shows in Jersey, along with more truck dealers, and that life in Jersey wasn't really so much different from life in the mountains of West Virginia. Their obvious success at living inspired many other people up on the hill whose lives had been derailed, and many of their neighbors began to do better at the task of living. In the winter, Tuck and Louise sat by their Franklin stove and drank coffee, and listened to the pit-pat of sleet on the new windows, and watched for deer moving through the trees. They knew that when they died, they'd be going home to the real mountains, but for now they were content to complete their daughter's life in the cabin.

Lisa and Elsa

Lisa and Elsa were thought of as twins, but they were not. They were the grandchildren of Anne and Milt. Elsa was the elder by two years. They came over from Scranton to spend the summer splashing in the shallows and looking for aquatic wildlife.

They went everywhere together and did every activity together. Their favorite occupation as children was to fill those diner red and yellow plastic ketchup and mustard bottles with lake water and have a spray battle. They caught minnows in small-mesh nets and fed the ducks stale bread. Lisa got nipped once when trying to feed the Canadian geese by holding the bread between her fingers rather than using a flat hand. Lisa let forth a howl that accompanied Eddie's playing of taps one evening in a very satisfying, harmonic manner.

They learned how to fish while young by throwing their bait straight down into the water off the end of a dock rather than outwards. Their favorite bait was bread balls, and each time a bluegill grabbed the bread and yanked the pole tip downward, they screamed in unison. They had little plastic red children's fishing tackle boxes for their red bobbers and hooks with their names painted in each box. They came to the lake chaperoned by a large red setter who played with Billie and Wally's black lab at herding the geese off the shore and into the water.

Lisa and Elsa's rented house 20 yards from the water was built all of round stones rather than square rock. Even the chimney was built of fist-sized round rock. Next door were two boathouses. The one closest to the house was made of the same round stones, while the one farther away was made from solid concrete, two shuttered windows, a yard door, and double doors opening to the dock. This boathouse stored handy items such as oars, boat cushions, oar locks, ropes, nets, and poles. It had two concrete steps to the water that were the width of the

154

boathouse, and it could store two rowboats on the gravel-filled interior. Those boats had to be brought in out of the water through the white wooden double doors facing the lake.

The big attraction was the other boathouse made from the round rocks. Like the rock house, this must have been one of the very early structures on the lake. Not only was it made of hand-laid round rocks, but two boats could be floated inside through large-hinged white wooden doors that opened outward, just higher than the water. Their friends, the sisters Mary and June, loved to play in the spooky boathouse that looked like a haunted mansion. It was taller than most of the other lake boathouses and had been unused for decades. By 1957, the boat doors had rotted off the hinges and fallen into the lake, and the door from the yard with tall wild grasses was missing. There were no windows. Inside, around the U-shaped water, a concrete walkway enabled people to walk around the boats.

By 1957, there were never any boats in either boathouse. That being said, in the one with water inside, there was plenty of aquatic wildlife: snakes, lizards, peeper frogs, bullfrogs, and muskrats all came up out of the dark, still water and onto the low walkway. With only the reflection from the water illuminating the interior, it was as scary as the fright house at the Morris County Fair on Route 10, across from Alderney Dairy. Many afternoons the girls crept in through the land doorway into the concrete walk-around and stared into the yellow-colored water (from the accumulated leaves). There was often a loud plop as a bullfrog jumped back into the water, or the sound of a water snake leaving. Occasionally a painted turtle could be seen in the water beneath reflections.

The four of them are remembered always as children, when play was the main occupation. Mostly, they are remembered in bathing suits, spraying each other with lake water from red plastic ketchup bottles. Lisa and Elsa stopped coming to the lake when their grandmother died, and no one at the lake ever saw them again. The stone boathouse and house were bulldozed in 1961 and a new modern electric house with a flat roof and wrap-around second story deck was built. The concrete boathouse was improved, a new floor poured, and a modern deck built, and it's now used for evening suppers and a place to read on rainy days. June grew up to live alone in her parents' cabin. Mary bought Margaret's former house by Bloody Gulch (the one with mice in the basement) and raised twins there.

Chipmunk

She came to the lake in 1973, after graduating from college in Randolph County, West Virginia. Many times in her life, she had driven past Tuck and Louise's house, but never met them either in West Virginia or at the lake. She had green eyes and freckles, and grew up as an adopted child in Greensburg, Pennsylvania. Her father worked for the Pittsburg-based electric company, and her mother worked as a secretary. She was educated to teach little kids how to

155

grow up. Like Jeff, all of her college friends had been involved in drugs during the last days of the Vietnam War. She came to the lake because she was offered a job teaching over at Mountain Lakes, and after earning her New Jersey teaching certificate, she settled into the routine of the lake. Like many young people, she had no real likes or dislikes, but drifted through weekends lying in the sun out on the float or going shopping at the mall on Route 80. She liked country music and rock 'n roll, fudge and trains, and eating out a lot. She didn't know how to cook well, but liked to watch television while eating.

Her house was a small brick Cape Cod up on the northwest corner, near to where in later years the lake road would finally go all around the lake, instead of dead ending up at the north end. Her house was heated by propane, with a screened-in porch located near the water, and an old granite fireplace which she never used at all. She liked to watch *The Mod Squad* reruns and was happy being alone in life. To her, college had never been important at all, just something to be completed so that one could get a job in life. She drove a Chevrolet because her father had said it was a good, solid type of car and that she couldn't go wrong driving one. She bought a Maytag washer and dryer and had them hooked up at one end of the kitchen because her mother said she could never go wrong with a Maytag. Commercials ruled her life, and she believed what everyone told her about various products.

Life was always insecure because down inside somewhere, she missed her real mother and the father she had never known. She had only seen her real mother once, when she was walking down the aisle toward the stage at her high school graduation, and had seen gray eyes looking right at her. In that second, she had known who the brown-haired mousy lady was, and it had shocked her into doing nothing but walking on down the aisle. When she went back after the ceremony, her mother was gone, but in the mail the next day was a money order for $1,000 as a graduation gift. She always wondered how much her adopted parents told her real mother over the years, for they must have been in touch. Her new parents would not discuss it, and Chipmunk was never allowed to openly mourn her lost parents. This loss trailed her though life, making joyous events plain, and plain events boring. She never really understood her craving to know her mother, or the sense on every holiday that no one wanted her. She went to work, went home, went swimming, went to the float, and went through life without ever meeting anyone she was able to love as much as they loved her. Yet, for all of her distancing, she was loved not only by her adopted parents, but also by many of the lake men. Whether they were professionals, technicians, or laborers, Chipmunk impressed all men with a sense of always being somehow lost in the world and in need of male protection. As Mae West had once said, every man she met wanted to protect her, but she never knew from what. That was Chipmunk's view of life. She didn't need protection, and really didn't need men. This disdain for men who were enamored of her and her freckles simply kept more and more invitations coming.

She received invitations for dinners at the country clubs, invitations to dances at the lake clubhouse, invitations to card parties and the opera, and invitations to picnics and swim parties. She rejected almost all of them, preferring to go out to the float and lie in the sun, or sit in her living room and watch old reruns on Nick at Nite. Life simply was better when spent alone, rather than being surrounded by unreliable people. Somewhere along the way through college, all of the warmth that her adoptive parents had given her as a child had been erased through involvement with drugs that left her empty inside.

At work, she was punctual and proper, doing her teaching job without innovation. She believed in the omniscience of the writers of the school texts, in the guidelines of the school board, and in the infallibility of the principal. As the product of the 1960s, all of the people she had known had been out of step with society; yet, when she grew up, she was no longer a rebel trying for change, nor was she a leader in an adult society. Rather, she had simply drifted out of the mainstream of vitality until there was no fight left in her at all. She had come to accept the rightness of society and its rules, and as a teacher, she had come to accept the ruling of authority completely, and to communicate that acceptance to her students. It was highly unlikely that any of her students would achieve greatness in any field, preferring the safety of being average. Nor would any of her students ever challenge authority with any form of revolt. Her little charges would fit into the world well, doing their jobs by devoting just enough energy to do okay; no more, but no less, either. The students she taught would not fail at life, but would be nicely average. Most would finish high school, and some would go to college and graduate. Most would marry, live in ticky-tacky houses in housing developments, have two to three children, a dog and a cat as pets, and 50% would divorce.

Chipmunk fit the mold of the suitable teacher, doing the job expected without flair or turbulence. She led a safe, dull, quiet life full of dull values, and she taught those values well. She still lives at the lake.

George 2

George 2 came to the lake as a friend of Lois in 1965. He was a widower, and brought his daughter Nancy with him. He had met Lois at a medical convention in Philadelphia in 1963, and they became friends. He owned an Aero Coupe airplane and liked to spend the weekend flying over the North Jersey lake country, and taking all of Lois' friends up for rides in the two-seater underwing plane that he housed over at Basking Ridge Airport. He was tall, bald, and dead looking, with a pasty white face that never got tan, no matter how long he sat on the dock of his east shore waterfront house (located five houses north of Linda's place).

His house was old – one of the earliest on the east shore, according to some – and built of granite blocks like the ones in Grace's fireplace. This fireplace sent up a huge haze of gray smoke all throughout the two-bedroom house, and in the summer the house had ants, as Margaret's house did. There was red linoleum in the living room and kitchen, wooden floors in the bedrooms, pink and black tiles in the floor of the bath, and a screened-in sleeping porch, complete with two single beds that were used as couches during the day. This sleeping porch was on the front of the house towards the water, but was smaller than most porches, it being designed just for sleeping. There was a card table and four chairs in the middle of the porch, as George liked to play bridge in the evenings.

George had been in the pharmaceutical industry, working for Merck Company in Union as a researcher, until retirement. He lived comfortably and could afford good shoes, which he was careful to never get in the water. His dock was a short one, jutting out towards some rocks in the water. It was made like Fred and Ethyl's, being six feet of two-by-fours held up by two steel I-beams that came out from the shore. The locals suspected that the dock had not been original, and they believed that an ornate fishing dock with a little viewing tower on the top had been on the site in the 1930s.

Nevertheless, George liked the feeling of being in an original lake home, even if the dock was new. He spent hours at the local library and at the historic society looking at photos of the lake houses, and he had several good black and white copies made of photos which he thought were of the house he had bought. Besides research work, George liked to use his telescope to watch the skies and the people over on the west side of the lake. Having bought a very powerful scope, he liked to sit on the little patio outside of the sleeping porch, where the yard dropped away down to the water, and scan along the west shore on a Sunday afternoon when there was

nothing else to do. Just as Majorie studied the lake people close up, George studied them, too –
but at a distance, as if researching some sort of large virus for publication in a journal.

When he wasn't at the lake, he was over at the airport. There, he met Linda's dad, the
FAA inspector, Majorie, and Dave (who was always flying below minimum altitude, doing
simulated bombing runs), and joined them in technical talk. Dave was just the sort of pilot
George regarded with disapproval, for George was a very careful pilot who never took chances.
He believed in authority, much the same as Chipmunk later did, and followed the rules. He
believed that rules were written for a reason, and he didn't need to know what the reason was.
He never flew below minimums, always filed a flight plan, and always flew IFR if Flight Service
said that the conditions required IFR flying. He did not fly using Esso maps, as Majorie did, but
used approved FAA maps for all flights. He had compiled 8,000 hours in the air over the years,
which wasn't bad for a weekend pilot. George had always wanted to be a military pilot, racing
through the skies in an F-86, but had been unable to pass the vision test for pilots. When he flew
in the winter, he wore a leather jacket and white scarf and sunglasses, and really looked quite
impressive with his bald head.

His 6'2" would be crammed into a little Air Coupe, and he liked to rev up the single
engine while holding at the end of the runway to just below the red line, then release the brakes
and start off with a lurch forward. One time, he overdid this method of starting, and gouged a
large hole into the asphalt when the propeller dipped down a little during the starting lurch.
While other pilots out of Basking Ridge airport talked informally to the tower, George used
precise military language, calling for weather, traffic, and altimeter for "Xray-2-7-9er-Foxtrot"
on each and every touch, and go pass on a windless Sunday afternoon at the one runway airport
that had no night lights. The tower was a two-story wooden box with an open platform on top,
where the radio operator and controller sat with red patio umbrellas open over their tables. The
tower operated weekends only, from 9 a.m. to 8 p.m., closing off the air earlier if the weather
were bad, or during the winter if no one was flying.

After a snowstorm, Hank, the manager at the airport, would plow off the taxiway and the
runway, since he knew if the weather weren't too bad, George would appear with the wind chill
at minus-20 degrees on Saturday, expecting to fly. With a lone controller shivering up on the
platform, George would march out to his plane, drain gas out of the wing tanks to see that there
was no water in the gas, check the propeller and oil, the flaps and wings, and do all the other
preflight checks as his leather jacket stiffened in the cold and his breath froze to his glasses. He
would slide open the glass canopy above the seats, climb in and start the motor, and allow
everything, including himself, to warm up, then call the controller sitting on the platform in a
parka, without the red umbrella up, and taxi to the end of the east-west runway. Usually, takeoff
was westward, and George would take his red and silver plane up, blasting snow behind him,
climbing up towards the hazy winter sun. He always flew north, keeping below Newark traffic,

with one radio set to the Bernardsville platform, and the other radio set to Newark area control. Sometimes, he would fly several thousand feet below the big jets up at 11,000 feet heading into Newark, flipping the nose of the little airplane up in mock missile attacks on the big planes while he imagined them to be Russian transports. Of course, the jets outran George's little airplane in a few seconds, but as they pulled away, George would look up at them through his binoculars bought at Sears, and imagine himself in their cockpit, headed for a landing on the long Newark runways. He could imagine passing over the outer markers, the flaps down, the airspeed at 140, and the feel of the wheels as he landed to cheers from the controllers for having the smoothest landing of the day. Flying around the lakes of Jersey never seemed boring or tame to George, because he was always imagining that he was somewhere else flying another type of aircraft, engaged in military activities.

This ability to imagine was George's salvation. The research work which he had been involved in required infinite patience and attention to details, so while he researched drugs, George learned to while away the day through the use of imagination. His father had called it daydreaming and his mother had called it the gift of whimsy, but George just thought of it as thinking about other things. It was useful, for he could spend his flight time off in a world of adventure. He could do the same thing when using his telescope, imagining everything about the lives of the people over on the west docks, and imagining all sorts of stories about the stars and planets he observed through the lenses. He was essentially a bookworm, who, though widely read, was not widely traveled at all. One trip that he had taken, however, was down to Epcot Center, where he had seen the Imagination Pavilion and been impressed with the power to imagine anything. He got better and better at it. He bought several of the Figment stuffed animals at Epcot, and placed them on his mantle as souvenirs. He found that if he read a book about a place, he could sit afterwards on his dock and daydream all sorts of plots and characters. George would've been a fine fiction writer and storyteller, but his daydreams took no practical form of application. They were just to make his retirement fun. To George, daydreaming was better than a hobby.

One of the books he liked best was *Walden*, and he often tried to examine the lake from the point of view of being isolated from society, while searching for meaning of life. Well, this was not real successful, for there simply was too much noise at the lake at times, especially Friday and Saturday nights, and too many people. George inevitably felt the crushing presence of lots of people hidden in the trees around the water. When the leaves fell in November and he could see all the houses stacked up on the mountain, and even more people through his telescope, he despaired of reaching the peace that Thoreau had found at his pond. George found that the only way to have peace was to imagine that everything was different from the way it really was. For example, when the rock bands at the clubhouse blasted apart any quiet which may have existed at the lake on Saturday evening, George tried to think of the music as an opera in Paris, and himself as a struggling composer modeling his music after Mozart. When the children next door were screaming at volleyball, George tried to imagine Hawaiian dancers doing ritualistic dances.

George did not have a lot of interaction with other people at the lake. He was reserved by nature, and the fact he was set in his ways and picky about the details left him out of social circles. He liked to watch the 10 p.m. news on Channel 5 and was not a night owl or partier. He always left parties promptly at 9 p.m., so as to be able to get home and be ready for bed before the news came on. He drove an older Oldsmobile which always started in cold weather because George always had the proper maintenance performed at the correct intervals. He wore galoshes in rainy weather, and carried an umbrella in case rain was forecast.

One of George's great concerns was the weather, for that affected his flying days. He owned a little Radio Shack weather radio which was tuned to the National Weather Service band at Newark Airport. In addition, he always watched the weather forecasts on the 7 a.m. and 10 p.m. newscasts. He often thought he would've made a fine military weather officer, and imagined himself giving the forecasts for all the great invasions and battles of this century. His favorite scenario was giving the forecast to Eisenhower for the D-Day Invasion of Normandy. He could picture the discussion in detail, himself scholarly and wise and doubtful, with Eisenhower asking his advice, pleading for a good forecast which George refused to grant outright, but finally giving a positive outlook so the general could order the invasion to proceed, while George went back to his maps and weather charts in London.

Nancy thought her father was brilliant, and she ignored him as irrelevant to her growing up. The only time she ever thought of him was when she took him to Father-Daughter Night at Morris Knolls High School, and on Father's Day. She didn't miss her mother, long dead, and didn't miss her father, either, when she was away from the lake. She never learned to daydream as George did, which was just as well. George died on the Bernardsville Runway when he imagined himself landing a 707 at Newark, and stalled the Aero Coupe 20 feet above the runway when he flared out. Nancy sold the old house and moved to Fullerton, California, where she drove past Becky I before Becky moved to the lake.

Edgar and Bonnie

Edgar and Bonnie came to the lake after the Korean War ended, and moved into a stucco house built in 1927 in the northwest corner of the lake, up where the farmers had hidden their pigs in the glen during the Revolutionary War to save them from being eaten by the soldiers. Edgar had a Ph.D. in philosophy and was a high school dropout. He was tall, with a red beard, sandy thinning hair, and no feelings. Bonnie had an M.S. in structural engineering, brown curly hair and glasses, and no feelings. She started work on her Ph.D. in foreign cultures after she arrived at the lake, driving to Princeton each day for classes. She had a daughter from a previous marriage who was of a serious nature and knew four languages, including British English, Italian, Greek, and Latin. This daughter had dreams of working for the UN in the city as an interpreter, but her parents had more accomplishments in store for her, including a real European education.

Edgar liked guns and followed his father's beliefs since his father was a member of the NRA. Edgar owned a rather impressive arsenal of automatic pistols and rifles. His prize possession was a World War II German machine gun which he had made unsafe so that it really operated. Some nights during the 1950s, he would fire short bursts up into the glen that he owned. This practice had to stop after the lake became fully populated, so Edgar built an underground shooting range, doing the digging and blasting himself so the neighbors would not know what he was building under the house. This 20-yard shooting range was equipped with targets that could be sent down along wires to the desired distance from the shooter, and retrieved after being shot at without Edgar having to walk down range. It also had lighting which could be dimmed to emulate different times of day or night. Edgar's favorite type of shooting was done in near dark. He would have Bonnie set up different silhouettes of bad guys and good guys on the range, dim the lights to near dark, and then run across the shooter's end of the range, firing at the dim targets, trying not to shoot a good guy. He usually did well, shooting the good guy only rarely.

Another favorite type of shooting was rapid fire. Edgar would line up tin pans at 30 yards, and use an old-fashioned western six shooter to play a little tune on the pans in just a few seconds. Sometimes, he would figure out the notes that each pan would make when hit with a rubber bullet (so as not to damage the pans), and he would play tunes on the pans with his bullets, while Bonnie tried to guess the tune in the fastest time possible.

Edgar's shooting was not limited to the indoor range. Up in the glen he owned, he set up a combat range for Bonnie and him to play in. This range had trails dug into the sides of the two hills that framed the glen, which ran due north from the lake. Their games included shooting at water-filled balloons, watermelons (these exploded nicely when hit with 12 gauge shotgun deer slugs), and trap shooting clay targets hidden in bushes and trees. These clay targets were handy for use in the timed combat run. This involved Edgar hiding clay targets along the trail and Bonnie running along the trail with her sawed-off shotgun, firing at the clay targets, reloading, and firing at more for a timed score. Each target had to be destroyed before running on to the next one. Bonnie enjoyed this very much; it was one of her favorite shooting games.

Bonnie liked guns as much as Edgar did. In fact, it was one of the things which kept their marriage together so well. At birthdays and Christmas, they usually gave each other a new gun or two, or some new type of deadly ammunition to play with. Her favorite gift she received from Edgar was a laser sighted rifle, which was accurate to 400 yards. Unfortunately, there was no place at the lake to test its full range, so one weekend they flew out to Kansas in a charter jet and tried out the range on the I-70 signs west of Hutchinson. They found it worked quite well, and bagged their limit of interstate signs while blazing away at 3 a.m.

Like Edgar, Bonnie was not at all social. She had her books and her studies, and found most people to be dull, if not stupid. She did not ever go near the water, since some neighbor might see her and want to chat. She allowed their property to be overgrown to the point that it looked abandoned. But among the weeds and trees, she strung barbed wire and rigged up little explosive smoke grenades and traps to upset the unwary who wandered over the property line.

Edgar agreed with these measures to keep the neighbors at bay. Edgar wanted no socialization at all with anyone at the lake. He had been in the Korean War and had been awarded the Purple Heart as the only one of his platoon to survive a firefight. As an Army agent in Eastern Europe right after the war, he'd learned to bury his feelings in order to do well at the job of spying. This Army job had come with a lot of fringe pay benefits, so Edgar found that within a few years after the end of the Korean War that he could invest his savings, rather than work. This he preferred to do, and so he took to reading, moved to the lake, finished his education, and eventually stayed home, educating Bonnie's child while Bonnie went to Princeton daily.

Edgar and Bonnie's move to the lake had been driven by an odd reason. Edgar had heard there were wild turkey on the mountain – the last wild turkeys in New Jersey. His father had always told Edgar that the wild turkey was the most difficult of American game to shoot, and Edgar believed this to be true. He wanted to settle down near a large city which had culture for Bonnie's daughter, and at the same time be near to a good university for Bonnie to attend to finish her education. It turned out Edgar's uncle was a friend of Ralph's. They'd hunted wild turkey together in Westfield before it was paved over for shopping centers and roads. This uncle had written to Edgar's father regarding the turkey hunting in New Jersey in the 1940s, and Edgar's father had passed this family knowledge on to Edgar, who never forgot anything. Thus, after Edgar finished his stint in the Army, he and Bonnie moved to the lake to kill turkeys. It turned out there were still wild turkeys up on the hill, for the road up there was so poor and the water pressure so lacking that the mountaintop was not very populated.

Often, in the 1950's, Edgar and Bonnie would go up on the mountain to their turkey blind which they had built at the base of a tree out of canvas and netting, place turkey decoys about, and wait for hours for a shot. These shots did not miss, and for several years they were able to eat the last wild turkeys alive in New Jersey. By 1960, they had killed the last of the wild turkeys on the hill, and went looking for other things to shoot. As the mountain became increasingly populated, they were driven back to hunt only in their own glen, where they were able to shoot birds, mice, and water rats to their heart's content. After a few years, there was no wildlife in their little glen, only clay targets. Edgar did not mind this, as long as there was something – anything – to shoot at.

Around the house, they dressed in a style that George II would have approved of. Edgar wore military camouflage shirts and pants, and wore twin pistols in holsters without the pearl handles, and sunglasses. The porch rail around the house deck was provided with brackets for resting a rifle in to shoot at game, catch boxes for empty casings, and reloading tables. Edgar spent much time out on the deck dressed in his camouflage outfit looking for movement that would signal dinner. But after 1962, all of the game around the house was eaten and gone over the years. To assuage Edgar's disappointment at having nothing to shoot at, Bonnie would get up early and tie little plastic targets to the tree trunks, and hide water balloons in the ground plants, so that when Edgar walked out onto the deck at 8 a.m., his face would light up with joy when he saw targets willing to be shot. With a big grim grin on his face, he would draw both pistols and start shooting while Bonnie cooked breakfast in the kitchen opening to the deck. The pistols he wore were Australian-made, modified to hold 23 shots each, which usually was enough ammo to kill all the targets Bonnie had lovingly put out earlier around the house. At any time of day, the roar of gunfire would echo out of their little glen, as one or the other found something to shoot at. At night, under the gibbous moon, they would sit lovingly side by side on the deck, wearing night Army goggles, their M-16s with infrared sights poised, waiting for nature to appear in their sights. They still hold hands and live at the lake.

Majorie

Majorie arrived at the lake in 1947, just after the war. She had been working as a nurse in Manhattan, while during the war she had flown transport airplanes for the Army Air Corp. Her love of flying carried her into private ownership of a two-seater airplane, and she was one of the early members of the Ninety-Niners, the women's flying association. Not only was Majorie one of the early proponents of women's flying activities, she was a very good friend of Amelia Earhart, and followed her friend's career with interest. After Amelia disappeared, Majorie gradually retired from active flying to pursue an academic career in the 1950s.

In this area, she succeeded in fields that were again mostly managed by males. She earned a Ph.D. in both English and Anthropology by 1958, and came to know Margaret Meade well. Majorie's dissertation in anthropology was about the cultural similarities between the Alaskan Indians and the Indians of Brazil with regard to the use of sewing tools. Her efforts in researching this little-studied topic earned her the attention of the Pratt Institute in Manhattan, which offered her a teaching position she held for 32 years.

Since commuting to Manhattan five days a week from her little unpainted wood frame house on the east side of the lake, six houses south of the cove, wasn't very practical in her view, she leased a small apartment in Greenwich Village on McDougal Street. The apartment had the benefit of coming with numerous door locks, a small balcony which overlooked the abandoned and locked inner sunken courtyard, a fireplace that didn't work, and a large amount of living area for a very reasonable price. It was only a short walk to the Square, where unlike now, people could pass a quiet evening outdoors listening to the various musicians, visit with the people of the neighborhood, work at crafts, play chess, or write poetry. In Majorie's time, the Square was a community gathering point for the people of the Village rather than a place to be avoided. Today, the Square is abandoned at night, the street lights shot out. No one goes into the Square at night now, not even the down-and-out people looking for a safe park bench on which to spend the night. Buildings surrounding the Square once had their windows open at night to the sound of the community. Now, barbed wire rings all apartment buildings facing the Square and people do not come out after the sun sets. Majorie would hardly recognize the places where she walked at night during the 1960s without fear. Today, no one walks in the Village alone at night.

One of her favorite pieces of decoration in the apartment was a wooden airplane propeller from one of her planes that she had flown in the 1940s. The center of the propeller had an electric clock in it in the popular fashion at the time, and this clock sat on the fireplace mantle for all of the years that she taught. When she retired, she moved the propeller to the mantle at the lake cabin, along with all her furniture and costume jewelry and scrapbook photos of her flying days. Like her flying and academic achievements, she took after retirement with a vengeance, determined to do her best at it.

She was so soft-spoken and little, that people at the lake who were used to more boisterous women were often set back many notches by Majorie's intelligence and wit. She saw through people with an uncluttered eye trained in years of anthropological studies, and her logical analysis of comments which people made to her without thought defeated conversational arguments before they were well developed by their proponents. She had a nice way of stopping the Friday cocktail hour conversation at the clubhouse by asking small, soft questions that her conversation partner could not answer. She was thus left pretty much alone by the men at the clubhouse on Friday nights, but was increasingly surrounded by younger women who came to admire her intellect. Much as Margaret Meade had collected a group of young female intellects around her for the purpose of developing knowledge, Majorie later became the elder leader of the smart women of the lake who were so logical that everyone left them alone. Majorie's women were not cowed by the threat of exclusion, since they did not wish to belong to anything except their own little group.

For fun, however, they made a point of appearing en masse at open lake meetings such as the property owners meetings, and, whenever debate lagged about a certain question, they would ask the chairman of the meeting a devastatingly simple question, such as, "Is there a quorum present?" which often ended the meeting. The result was that lake business came to be conducted with a careful precision borne of past embarrassments. She liked to sit calmly with her group of lady fans around her while the men argued through the evening, and then, during a pause, note that the men were discussing a symptom rather than a problem. Whenever Majorie scored an intellectual victory at a lake meeting, the corners of her eyes would crinkle in pleasure behind her bifocals, and she would twist her necklace in simulation of how she was twisting her opponents, and smile a cherubic smile at the disturbed men.

She saw the people of the lake as a sort of anthropological study. In addition to watching people at meetings, she could be found early in the mornings watching the ladies of the Flower Club snipping away at the natural foliage and flowers. She would wait near the lush flower growths by the boat landings, leaning on her oak cane that she had been presented with in England, the glass in her bifocals reflecting the morning sun. When the early morning ladies from the club appeared with their steel scissors in hand, Majorie would watch intently as if she were taking notes while they wiped out fine growths of wild roses and tiger lilies for display on their dining room tables. She would appear at the west beach dressed in a sort of muumuu tent falling around her thin frame, with a little straw hat on her head with the word "Bermuda" woven into the straw, set up a firm, folding rocking chair painted white and yellow, and proceed to stare at everyone on the beach for hours. Some of the teens found this so uncomfortable that they would leave and go over to the east beach, where Majorie was likely to appear after lunch, carrying the same folding rocker. She never read or swam, but just sat in her chair watching, as if she were in a duck blind watching for targets. It never bothered her if people looked back; indeed, she was likely to wave them over and start a deep discussion. If the participant were female, Majorie was likely to take the newcomer under protection and begin to really educate her about logical thought and the great philosophers.

When Majorie tired of playing intellectual bowling with the men of the lake at meetings, or in watching the lake people at play, she would seek the company of other women of her same age and class. Among her friends were Margaret, who, after Dallas was gone, would work as a housemother at the University of Akron during the winters for a while, and Myrtle, who had attended Milliken University in Illinois. Grace and Lois were also members of this group, as was Mildred. All of the members had to have had some college, be interested in intellectual pursuits, hold their sherry well, and be interested in readings that were better than romance novels. This group of women, many of whom were members of the Association of American University Women (AAUW), met informally whenever one of them invited the others over for an afternoon or evening discussion. The topic for discussion would be passed out along with the invitation, and the group would gather, discuss, eat imported finger foods, and have a little sherry. The topics were diverse, ranging from the military mind, to the impact of literature on students, to a discussion of the current economic impact on grade school students. As these women were among the few at the lake who read good newspapers such as the *New York Times* Sunday edition, their discussions actually were most interesting. Sometimes, in more modern times, they would gather to watch a PBS show together or listen to the Saturday afternoon opera on the radio, broadcast from the Met and sponsored by Texaco as part of its public relations efforts.

Majorie died of Parkinson's disease in the 1970s. She had no family, and was cremated. Her ashes are buried by the pine tree at the center front of Myrtle's lower patio. Her clock was sold on commission at The Hangar Shop on Broad Street in Fairburn, Ohio. Its current location is unknown.

Myrtle

Myrtle was Margaret's best friend. She was tall and thin, and her glasses hung from her neck by a black twined cord with gold fastenings. Myrtle and Margaret loved all things of culture, and were prim and moral. Myrtle was born in 1890 in Blue Mound, Illinois, married, and moved to Washington, D.C. in 1915. Then, she and her husband and daughter moved to East Orange, New Jersey, where she met Margaret at an American Association of University Women meeting. Myrtle and family then moved to Elizabeth where she lived for 40 years. Margaret, who also had lived in East Orange, told her about the lake. Myrtle and her husband, who worked for RCA and had been in France during the war in 1918, moved to the lake in 1954 when they bought a summer fishing cabin for $8,000 cash. Myrtle helped to buy the cabin by using her degree from Milliken University in Domestic Economy to teach Home Management at the Girls' Vocational School in Elizabeth. In 1937, she transferred to the Thomas A. Edison Vocational and Technical High School where she taught Science until she retired in 1954. She was a member of the Westminster Presbyterian Church on North Avenue in Elizabeth, the Meta Shirrefs Garden Club, the International Retired Educators Association, and the AAUW.

Myrtle and Baby Lois, 1918

Myrtle operated everything in her life in a seasonal cycle. To her, the cabin was mostly for summer use. In the spring at the Elizabeth house, it was time to take up the winter rugs and put down the lightweight summer rugs, and to hang the summer curtains and window screens. The coal dust was shaken out of the heavy curtains and they were stored with moth balls in the attic until September. The big Westinghouse fan that stood on two metal feet was positioned to force a breeze through the house. There was no air conditioning. There was another identical Westinghouse fan at the cabin. In May at the lake, the water was turned on by turning a valve in a pit beneath a metal cover by the one-lane road. The cabin was opened, inspected for varmint damage, then aired out. The furniture was moved from the living room out onto the screened porch, and the floors of green or brown linoleum or gray painted wood were scrubbed. The first meal of the warm season was cooked on a green propane stove. This usually consisted of fried tongue, slaw, boiled whole Idaho potatoes, carrots, and bread. The yard was checked for storm debris and bedding unpacked from moth balls.

Myrtle owned a yellow, metal, high-backed rocking chair. This was placed on the flagstone patio near where the tulips were showing. After she finished her work, she sat in the bouncy rocker and rocked with her fingers touching her left cheek. Her favorite place at the lake was the sagging green hide-a-bed on the east end of the gray porch. All afternoon, she would stretch out on that bed, looking up at the trees through the screens. She especially liked doing this in October, when the leaves on the huge oak tree 10 feet from the house turned color.

Her great fear in life was cats, which may have been why her friend Margaret's house was encumbered by mice. Though she had no memory of it, something traumatic involving a cat had happened to Myrtle when she was very young. As she was an orphan with a younger sister, there were no family members to remember her childhood. She was always kind to cats but could not tolerate the feel of their fur. If a cat rubbed against her leg, she would let out a shriek that could be heard across the lake. The neighbors attributed the shrieks to marital bliss, but they were the way in which she acknowledged cat affection. She was too kind-hearted to turn away a stray, hungry cat, so she often had one or two living with her. The cats, especially a large calico named Apache for some unknown reason, soon learned to purr but not rub. Any forgetfulness on their part would result in a terrifying shriek usually at dinnertime when Eddie was playing taps. The cats would be shooed outside for the night, where they encountered skunks and raccoons. The cats fought heroic battles against the wildlife in what remained of the neighbors' flower beds after Billie's big black lab had dug through them all day.

Myrtle had been in her 40s during the Depression and she remembered hundreds of terrible-looking dark shacks between Newark and New York City in an area derogatorily called "The Meadows," a wet area along the Pennsylvania Railroad tracks to New York. It was a place of mud with no trees where the noise of passing trains was enough to wake the comatose. She always had her pantry stocked with food, especially turnips, beets, beans, and potatoes. Her daughter survived scarlet fever. Myrtle lived through the 1918 flu pandemic. She had a round scar from a TB shot on her upper left arm, and a scar on the left side of her throat where throat cancer had developed and been removed.

She like to sit in the rear seat of a rowboat to tour the lake, visiting with the other ladies who were sitting on their docks in the evening. She took her last boat ride in 1970 on a crisp September afternoon when the first fires were lit in fireplaces, and the neighbors were raking leaves with broad wooden rakes.

She cooked for everyone's birthday: roasts, turkeys, geese, pheasants, and ducks. She made jams and preserves, stocked the old chest freezer in Elizabeth full of meat, and baked bread every other day. Vegetables that she bought were first displayed in a wicker basket and delivered to the door every other day by Henry, a short, bald man who would stand outside the door and yell, "Vegetables!" several times. He never knocked. These vegetables were grown at the farms along a branch of the Rockaway River behind St. Clare's Hospital close to town, and were picked by seasonal workers. Her two quarts of milk from Alderney Dairy on Route 10 were delivered at 5:50 a.m. every other day.

Coal for the colder weather came from Young's Coal Yard in town on Esterling Road or the Blue Flame Coal Yard. A ton of cannel coal was enough. Since the cabin had no central heating, Halloween was usually the limit to staying at the cabin, and only if the water were dripping at night so as not to freeze.

If cold weather arrived early, Myrtle would declare it was just too cold in the cabin away from the fireplace to stand it any longer, especially if ice were forming around the lake along the shore. The furniture would be moved inside, the long porch wooden storm blinds taken down, the sulfur candle lit, mothballs thrown everywhere, beds stripped, and the water heater lever set to "off." The fridge would be propped open, the propane tanks shut off outside, and the house water shut off at the road pit. All of the taps were opened and gasoline poured in the toilet bowl.

Then, it was off in the Buick to the winter house in Elizabeth. The trip took one hour and 15 minutes via Route 10 east, then local streets down to North Avenue to 845 Kilsyth Road. Today, with I-280 and I-80 built, it's 39 minutes. The Elizabeth two-story house in a generally Italian neighborhood was heated by a coal furnace in the basement that burned five tons each winter. Coal was carried to the coal bin after going down the basement steps by workers carrying open-top cloth bags on their backs. The steam radiators always clanked when the heat came up, and on top of each radiator there was a deep 36-inch long water evaporation pan to add moisture to the air. Myrtle was content to face the snows in Elizabeth rather than at the cabin.

She kept her house well, fed her family, and after her husband died in 1973, sold the Elizabeth house, wintered over in Trenton and spent the summers at the lake. She dressed every day of her life for meals, said grace, cooked food (often tongue), cleaned the dishes, managed the finances, and fixed every holiday meal. She never cheated on her husband, and they had 55 years together. The only thing she ever asked was not to cook on Christmas Day. So her husband, who loved her, took her to Radio City Music Hall in the 1951 Buick to see the Christmas show and movie every December 25th for 34 years with dinner afterwards at the red-carpeted Lynne Restaurant where sales girls with the strap behind their necks came around with trays of cigarettes for sale. The best sellers were British and Algerian cigarettes.

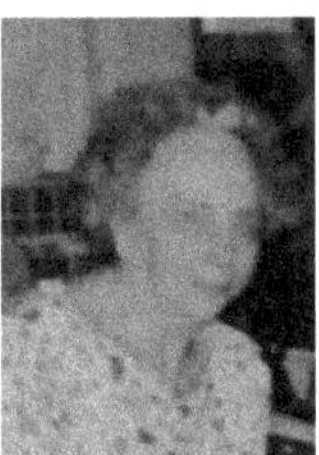

She died of heart failure on March 14, 1975, at Mercer Hospital in Trenton, with her daughter holding her hand. She died with dignity. Her wedding ring and pin-on watch went to her grandson. She was cremated and buried in the Smith family plot near Dalton City, Illinois. On her tombstone is carved the following, as written by Grace Barber at Humboldt, Kansas, on August 26, 1891:

May you live a life that when you die,

You may laugh while those around you cry.

In the late 1960s, Susan lived in her parents' house on the north side of the house that Edna and George would later buy. It was brick on the first story and white frame on the second, containing a brick fireplace with glass doors trimmed in brass. Like Edna and George's house, the kitchen was away from the lake and provided the entrance from the blacktop road, while the living room and bedroom overlooked the lake. Susan attended Morris Knolls High School, graduated in 1967, and attended college in Massachusetts. Her favorite way to spend time was to drive her little two-seater white Triumph around the lake at high speed, winding up through the gears on the rare straight stretches, and downshifting with a fearful whine at the curves or the little one-lane iron bridge on the east side. She was one of those people who always felt that her life was whatever God willed it to be, and she was content. She always knew she would go to college, live on the lake forever, and be popular.

She was right about two out of three of those assumptions. She did go to college and was popular, being elected Lake Queen, and riding in the leading boat at the Labor Day Regatta, with her blonde hair spilling over the cheap white royal sheet. She was loved by everyone at the lake for her Madonna-like smile and goodness to all of her friends. She wore that glassy-eyed peaceful stare that people wear when they have somehow come to believe that their lives are controlled by some higher power other than themselves or their parents. She believed that she was destined to be content, and therefore was. In due time, she met a college boy majoring in physics, they married, and he took her away from the lake to live in Cranford. So she was wrong about her third assumption. She was wrong about being content, also, for her husband liked to play the New Jersey lottery. In 1979, he gave her lottery tickets for Christmas. One of the tickets was worth $2,000,000. Ever afterwards, she was neither content nor happy.

All she had wanted was to be married and have children and help the church. She found that life was now full of decisions about investments, travel, styles, and giving the proper gifts. She was invited to the best New York parties, met the best men, wore the best clothes, and saw the world in splendid isolation. Her husband, lucky at gambling, was also lucky at investments, and so her $2,000,000 became worth over $12,000,000 within five years. The tax-exempt money rolled in so fast that it could not be spent faster than it was earned. She lived in a mansion in Basking Ridge with servants, her children attended Baird and Pingry schools, and her husband dressed in debonair fashion and was good to her in his own way. She was diagnosed with breast cancer in 1969, and started treatments that put her on a slow road of decline. Much as the characters in *On Golden Pond* returned to their lake every year, she saw that her life might be ending, and she wished to find again that simplicity of destiny she had felt growing up at the lake. She had her attorney rent a cabin for her two houses south of the single lane bridge from which she could look across the lake to her old house. As the treatment continued, her hair fell out, and she took to going out on the lake at night, when she would not have to wear a kerchief on her head to stop people from staring at her. She would take the old red canoe that was kept by the cabin (it had belonged to a friend of Dallas' in the 1950s), and paddle out to the middle of the lake, under the stars. Out there, she could sit down on the bottom of the canoe, look up at the mountain, and see the lights of the houses. In her mind, she pictured what all the people in all the houses were doing, what they were wearing, and what they were saying to each other.

She could feel her life receding slowly, minute by minute. She knew that life was terminal, not in a theoretical way, but in the way of knowing in her gut. She knew that one day she would not ever paddle out on the lake again, or listen to the cry of the loons from her bed at the cabin. She had no need of the upscale lifestyle that the lottery had brought her, nor any need to visit with her family, for in those last months, she learned they did not have the soul of the lake in them.

They wanted her to go to the best doctors in the city and get the best treatments. They wanted her to die like a socialite, to assume her rightful station in society as the poor, distraught, dying rich wife. She wasn't interested, and remained at the lake at the cabin, while the family stayed at the mansion in Basking Ridge. She finally told them not to visit her anymore, had the phone disconnected, and spent her time by the water. For company, she acquired a little white dog, descended from Mildred's little dog. Two months before her death, she called her attorney and had him buy her a little white Triumph, and she drove it around the lake roads at night, feeling the wind where her hair had been, remembering the time she had driven it to the Beatles' concert at Shea Stadium in 1966. She thought more about her years on the lake than she ever thought about life after the lottery. The priests came from town to give her communion each week, and she read her Bible at night when the bats were flying over the dark waters. Sometimes, over the water, she'd hear the voices of people on their docks, sitting out in the dark, reviewing the day. Or sometimes, she'd hear the sound of a flute from the north end of the lake, or see the moonlight glint off the backs of the swans while they rested. She knew that nothing had changed on the lake in over 60 years, and she wanted nothing more from life than to hear the honking of the geese wafting in over the water at dusk.

She died in October 1990, when the leaves were red and yellow in the sunlight. The cabin she rented with the red shutters, which could be closed during storms, is still there. The red canoe she paddled is also still there, on the eastern shore, just south of the one-lane bridge. You can go see it tomorrow, should you wish. The geese will be glad to have your company.

Susan at Graduation, 1967

Beth

There are hundreds of additional people who have been on the lake since 1954. But, one has to stop somewhere, or else this book would be 2,000 pages. There's a well-known saying that novels stop not from being finished, but rather from the exhaustion of the writer and typist. The typist for this book was Hady Wolf, owner of Hady Wolfe Transcription and Typing of Redlands, California. Thank you! Due to technical difficulties, in 2020, Hady had to retype this entire book which was first drafted on a MAC 512 in 1994. By 2020, all that we had of the original effort was one faint dot matrix printer copy with the printer holes along the side along with bundles of loose pages in the wrong order. But let this book be a lesson to new writers: don't throw anything away! After 26 years of this draft waiting in the closet, this writer came back to it. So, here's the final person on the lake whom you'll meet. Refresh your coffee and savor a buttered muffin with cinnamon sprinkles, and meet Beth – someone very, very special.

Beth was the prettiest lady at the lake in her time, and also the smartest. Her page boy brown hair, freckles, tan, svelte figure, and husky voice could have made her an Atlantic City stage star. The daughter of an Air Force volunteer, she became a poet who was awarded a grant of $50,000 from the Kettering Foundation to develop a national education plan of teaching grade school children the importance of poetry. This grant led to her being well-known in Washington, D.C., and thus one of the most widely known members of the national artistic community. An accomplished poet who had published several books of poetry, including such titles as *Memories of a Cat in Twilight, What I Saw in the Sky*, and *Understanding Homer's Claws*, the planning of part of a national educational program allowed her to use her Master's degree in management in designing a curriculum. Every grade school child in America would come to know the works of American poets.

She attributed her success in life to her early teachers who made her memorize grammar rules. Since she didn't have to think about using correct grammar, she could think about poetry and feelings. A confirmed introvert (confirmed by the Briggs-Myers Personality Test), she'd sit out on the float in the middle of the lake at night, working on rhymes, dictating her poems into a small tape recorder, which her secretary would later type for publication in such magazines as *The New Yorker* and *The Atlantic Monthly*. She came to the attention of the Washington establishment, who saw her as a possible political candidate, and was appointed to the position of Under Secretary of Education two years after receiving the big grant. Like many people at the lake, she commuted, taking the Lackawanna train to Newark, a cab to Newark Airport, and the morning Eastern Airlines shuttle to Washington.

She bought a bright, modern condo in Washington for entertaining, even though she hated it. She much preferred to sit on the float in the middle of the lake and think about poetry and life. Whereas John always thought he should be teaching life instead of grammar, Beth had actually achieved this bliss in that she didn't worry about communication rules but instead freely communicated her feelings. She never felt that she was part of the fun crowd, as Maureen would be, but she felt very much in touch with the forces of this world. She wondered how the geese felt when the weather was cold, disapproved of people who liked to eradicate free-spirited birds while they were in the air, and wondered if fish felt fanciful.

When Beth was a child at the lake, she lived in the small wooden family cabin that her grandparents had bought in 1951. During the winter, she used to sit three feet from the granite fireplace. When the bitter winds slid down the Pocono Mountains and across the Delaware River, she would carry in Pennsylvania cannel coal from the shed behind the cabin using a hod. In February, the lake was a sheet of blank frozen ice thistles. She would sweep the ash from the hearth, fill the box grate, and shiver in her childhood bed listening to the sleet slapping the defenseless window glass a few feet from her wide-open golden eyes, and she'd wish that she were loved.

She learned that to avoid the conflicts of growing up, it was best to sit on the wooden deck of the swim float in the middle of the lake. Nine sealed 50-gallon barrels kept the swim float from sinking. While the teens were at the clubhouse dances, she would sit in the middle of the lake, wondering if geese were happy when rains came in from Sparta and whether blue herons got their kicks up on one leg over on the floating island.

A Blue Heron at the Cove, 2020

Like many of the lake people, Beth liked to feed bread to fish that congregated under the float directly from her hand. She'd only go to the float if no one else were there, but early on a Saturday or Sunday, she'd paddle out from the west boat landing to the float, lie with her head hanging over the side of the float, the ends of her brown hair in the water, and hold out bread in her hand underwater for the fish. Soon, the bluegills and sunfish would come, slowly approach her hand, and take the bread with their little fish lips. She felt like a god, thinking that the fish would not eat if she were not holding out the bread to them in her hand in the sunbeams which slanted under the edges of the float to stroke the rusty barrels underneath. In the sunlight, even the little motes of floating matter could be seen drifting about: little specks of protein that may or may not ever be eaten by something larger. Each time she stretched out her arm to the fish, she recognized in herself the arm of God reaching out on the ceiling of the Sistine Chapel to give life. Beth had a sense of relative size as being related to power: she felt power over all things of lesser size, and felt herself not as competent when surrounded by larger people as she did when alone. This feeling was not so much an inferiority complex as it was a recognition that all too often in the world, size was an indication of relative power. It made her feel powerful to feed fish, and gave her a sense of control that could never be found on the Eastern shuttle, which flung her out of the yellow, stinking Newark murk to Washington, D.C., at 8:10 in the morning several times a week.

Each time she settled into her blue and red cloth seat, with the little paper and wax air sickness bag tucked neatly into the pocket in front of her, she wondered if she were going to die in a flaming ball of metal and aviation fuel in the next 15 minutes. She would always set her watch to count down the minutes and seconds until takeoff, and lay in the seat with her eyes closed, imagining how she would spend those final minutes as if they really were her final minutes. She always chose the same daydream, that of riding on the back of a sailfish, jumping through the wild waters of Diamond Shoals, out by the graveyard of the Atlantic, the blue waters running through the light blonde hairs of her arm, with everyone on shore waving to her.

On the shore were all of the people from her past, all of the ones who had seemed to love her. From the back of the sailfish, she could see each face on the shore. She remembered each person's name and all that that person had ever said to her. Like the man who sat on his dock in the middle of the night, she never forgot anything that anyone had ever said. She remembered each farewell and every broken promise. She remembered each kiss on her neck, remembered every Christmas present that she'd ever received, and how each one was wrapped. She remembered each pet she had lived with and how it had died. She remembered the cat who died on her lap in the vet's office of old age, the dog that was hit by a car and then died in her arms, while she crouched in a ball by the curb, crying into its bloody white fur, and her goldfish floating dead in its bowl on the day she graduated from high school.

Life was intolerable simply because there was so much of it running through her mind in an endless cycle of memories that sometimes made her cry in her old four-poster, sagging, wooden bed at 2 a.m., when she knew this cycle of memories could only be broken by death or complete absorption in meaningless tasks. Life was full of waiting for something to happen. Sometimes on takeoff, she would wish for something exciting to happen, but as the nose of the MD-80 rose above runway 22R, she was thankful nothing too exciting *did* happen as the New Jersey Turnpike passed under the silver and blue wing. In the air, she wished she were back on the lake, stretching her arm out to feed the little fish who came to her in their need, and took life from her fingers. They asked only that she be there for them, and care for them. When she stayed over in Washington in her condo, she felt a sense of worry that the little fish at the lake were all alone, and she missed them. As soon as she could escape on Friday afternoon, she was back on the shuttle home, running in her black high heels, hose, and pleated tan skirt from the taxi down to the water at the boat landing. She took the canoe up to the island on the north end, or out to the float if she had beaten the work crowd and teens home, without even bothering to change out of her office clothes. Sometimes, even all dressed up, she'd lie on the float in the afternoon after flying up from Washington, just to say hi to her blue and yellow fish.

If she were patient, which she was, and lay quietly for a while on the float looking into the water, the lake fish would come and stay without being fed right away. She knew these were the fish that truly loved her, for they came to her without any reward. If she held bread out in the water, then more would come, until the water was full of little nibbling fish that were feeding from her. In the sunlight, their orange tummies sparkled and their dark blue eyes looked up at her in praise and adoration. Sometimes, she tried to pet them, her red nails gently brushing their blue and silver sides and tails for a few seconds as they came in search of bread. They would dart away a few inches, then turn back, looking for nourishment. Sometimes, she would close her hand slowly around a minnow, only to feel it wiggling, and then release it to swim off into the sunlight. The minnows that she held never swam far away after she let them go, but kept coming back for more. This ritual with the bluegills and sunnies often went on for several hours, ending when people started coming out to the float with their blankets and radios.

When people came, Beth left, paddling up to the north end of the lake where there were never any swimmers. She'd allow the canoe to drift into the channel which went into the middle of the floating island, and once inside the island, she'd sit and listen to the red-winged blackbirds which nested on the island, the sun shining on her freckles, while she thought of couplets and rhythms. She felt that all of living could be expressed in a poem, and couplets were the universal synthesis of all communication.

As twilight brought the fireflies, she'd paddle out from the channel into the wide lake and follow the shore south. She'd go back to the house with the granite fireplace built in 1926. She'd sit on the screened-in porch in a cast iron chair with a white cushion, making small holiday decorations which would later go on the mantle. At Christmas, along with her hand-made decorations on the mantle was a little village set in plastic snow, with all the little people standing around a frozen pond by the village square, happily singing carols. She often stared at this mirrored pond on the mantle, wondering what lived beneath the surface. At Easter, she'd place small china bunnies in a dance line, while at Halloween the decor was plastic pumpkins. She was proud of her decorations and kept their images in her heart.

Beth believed that meaning was found in details that suggested couplets, rhythms, and cycles in time. The feel of a wet fish, the sound of the goose on the 20th of October when the first appearance of Jack Frost was only days away, the smell of popcorn in the big iron skillet with the aluminum lid – all of this gave meaning to her world. Her golden eyes saw clearly the passing of life. She was the last of her family to sit in her grandmother's oak rocker in the upstairs bedroom with photographs of old people in gold metal frames sitting on the oak dressers.

On warm June days when the rains sometimes gurgled in the gutters, and the geese honked over on Goose Island, Beth would take the canoe out onto the flat lake and drift through the surface mist and drizzle. She wore an old, dark green raincoat with plastic buttons, tight cut-off jean shorts, boat sneakers with no laces and no socks, her string of real pearls, and gold hoop earrings. Her uncovered brown hair dripped water onto her cheeks and ears as she listened to the patter of drops, knowing she would never leave this lake or her grandmother's rocking chair.

Through the lowering clouds, she could hear the whine of jets approaching Newark towards the 10,000-feet runway 22L, and she could imagine the passengers in their little enclosed world peering out the windows for that first reassuring look at the ground.

The rain came in harder from Budd Lake, Mount Arlington, and Rockaway, silencing the geese, and dampening the various sounds into silence except for the rain drops hitting the wooden canoe bottom.

In the warm June rain, she'd kick off her boat sneakers, stretch out on the bottom of the canoe, her parted bare legs hooked up over each side, toes with red nail polish rising into the rain, her arms and hands stretching on the wood decking past her head and wet hair. The shadows of the jetliners just above the clouds looked like sailfish in the waves, while the rain covered her mouth, freckled nose, and half-closed eyes.

The canoe drifted toward the floating island to the north, rocking back and forth as little gusts of wind pushed rhythmically against her stretched out form. Smoke wafted down from the cook stove chimneys of cabins on Bald Hill and from the pipes of the fishermen sitting on their screened porches with their loved ones close by. She closed her eyes all the way, feeling herself becoming one with the rocking motion.

Out under the misty surface of the lake, below the last goose of the evening landing for the night, there were pairs of dark-lustered eyes, wide open, staring up into her world. Wet, soft lips. Backs rising above the surface of the water, then lowering in unison. From all over the lake they came to her.

Hundreds of fish.

Their tail fins surged from side to side, their dorsal fins extended above the surface. All of them were moving around her canoe in a counter-clockwise circle, trying to tell her that, out of all the people on the little lake, she was loved.

About the Author

John Stibravy has made his home in northern New Jersey for years and years. He obtained a Ph.D. from the University of Denver, and an M.A. from Wichita State University, where he studied with Ben Santos of the Philippines. His undergraduate studies were at Davis and Elkins College in West Virginia, where he was a radio deejay. He taught technical writing at Edison Community College in Piqua, Ohio, and commuted by car to his lake in New Jersey on weekends. His final active job was at the West Point Prep School, where he taught English and coached fencing. He is a 20-year USAF Cold War veteran.

He's the author of *Aortic Heart Valve Replacement: Through the Dark Curtain*; *I Was DEAD! Cardiac Arrest and My Journey Back to the Living*; *World War I (56th Engineers) and Great Depression Letters of Ralph W. Green*; *Cardiac Arrest: Facts for Every American*; and *Dayton Steam: 1983 – 1992*.

Tony Smith is a communication professor at St. Petersburg College in Florida. In April 2012, he was recognized as the third-highest rated professor in America on RateMyProfessors.com, and included in *The Best 300 Professors in America*, published by The Princeton Review.

He's the author of *Finish Your Damn Speech!* and *Strength on Wheels: What My '96 Cavalier Taught Me About Life* (available at Amazon). He's the narrator of *Aortic Heart Valve Replacement: Through the Dark Curtain* and *Finish Your Damn Speech!* (available at Amazon, Audible, and iTunes).

He lives in Dunedin, Florida, and enjoys music, movies, hiking, photography, and playing basketball.

Dr. Becky Gingras earned her Bachelor's and Master's degrees in English Literature from California State University (Long Beach, CA). She earned her Doctor of Public Administration degree from the University of La Verne (La Verne, CA) in 2001. She surveyed police record management systems in the Los Angeles County Sheriff's Department as part of her post-graduate work.

Dr. Gingras started her career as a technical writer at Hughes Aircraft Company in Long Beach, then joined McDonnell Douglas (now Boeing) as a Senior Systems Analyst. She worked on projects such as optical disk-based systems for retrieving engineering drawings, computer-aided graphics, and computer systems for training writers of aircraft maintenance manuals. She coordinated an international group of documentation experts seeking to develop a limited vocabulary for aircraft maintenance manuals (Simplified English).

Dr. Gingras taught technical writing at the University of Southern California, California State University (Fullerton), West Coast University (Los Angeles), and Orange Coast College (Costa Mesa).